John Cross Publications

CW01668503

The Holistic Spine - Reflections and Associations

Acupressure and Reflexology in Action

John R. Cross FCSP Dr.Ac.

BOOK TWO

Part One: Practical Considerations of each Vertebra

The following associations and reflections are discussed – Spinal Nerve, Autonomic Nerve, Venous/Arterial, Muscular Tendinous, Linked Vertebra, Linked Organ, Acupuncture influence – Governor and Bladder meridians, Major Chakra with Minor Chakra link, Reflections on Arm, Leg, Ear, Foot, Hand, Skull, TS line, Mental and Personality.

Chapters

1. Coccyx and Sacrum
2. Lumbar Spine
3. Thoracic Spine
4. Cervical Spine
5. Occiput and Sphenoid

Part Two: Treatment of Spinal Conditions

This section discusses how to treat pain, acute and chronic spinal conditions using various subtle bodywork techniques, acupressure and reflexology.

Chapters

6. Assessment and Analysis
7. Acupressure and Reflexology in Acute Pain
8. Acupressure and Reflexology in Spinal Conditions
9. Sacro-Occipital Therapy - Original and New Versions

Part One
Practical Considerations of each Vertebra

This section will 'fine tune' what was discussed in Book One and make referencing much easier for the reader. Each of the segments of the vertebral column (with the addition of the Occiput and Sphenoid) are associated with many different aspects - anatomical and subtle energy. They are: -

- Spinal Nerve and Dermatome
- Autonomic Nerve (Sympathetic/Parasympathetic) and subsequent linked internal organ(s)
- Muscular/Tendinous insertions and supply
- Effects of Spinal Misalignment
- Spinal Couple and Harmonic
- Linked internal organ via the energetic system
- Posterior Major Chakra influence
- Reflections on the Arm, Leg, Foot, Hand, Skull and Ear
- Emotional and Personality Link

Chapter One – Coccyx and Sacrum

Coccyx

The coccyx is a small vestigial bone and has very little anatomical influence although it is very important in energy medicine and can have profound implications to the remainder of the body when there is imbalance in the region.

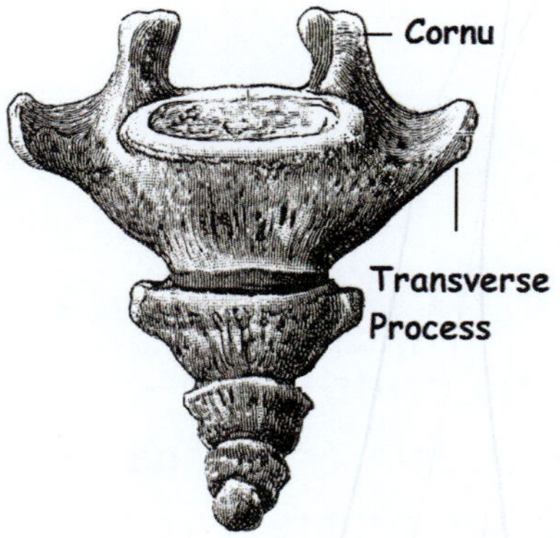

Figure 1.1 The Coccyx (anterior aspect)

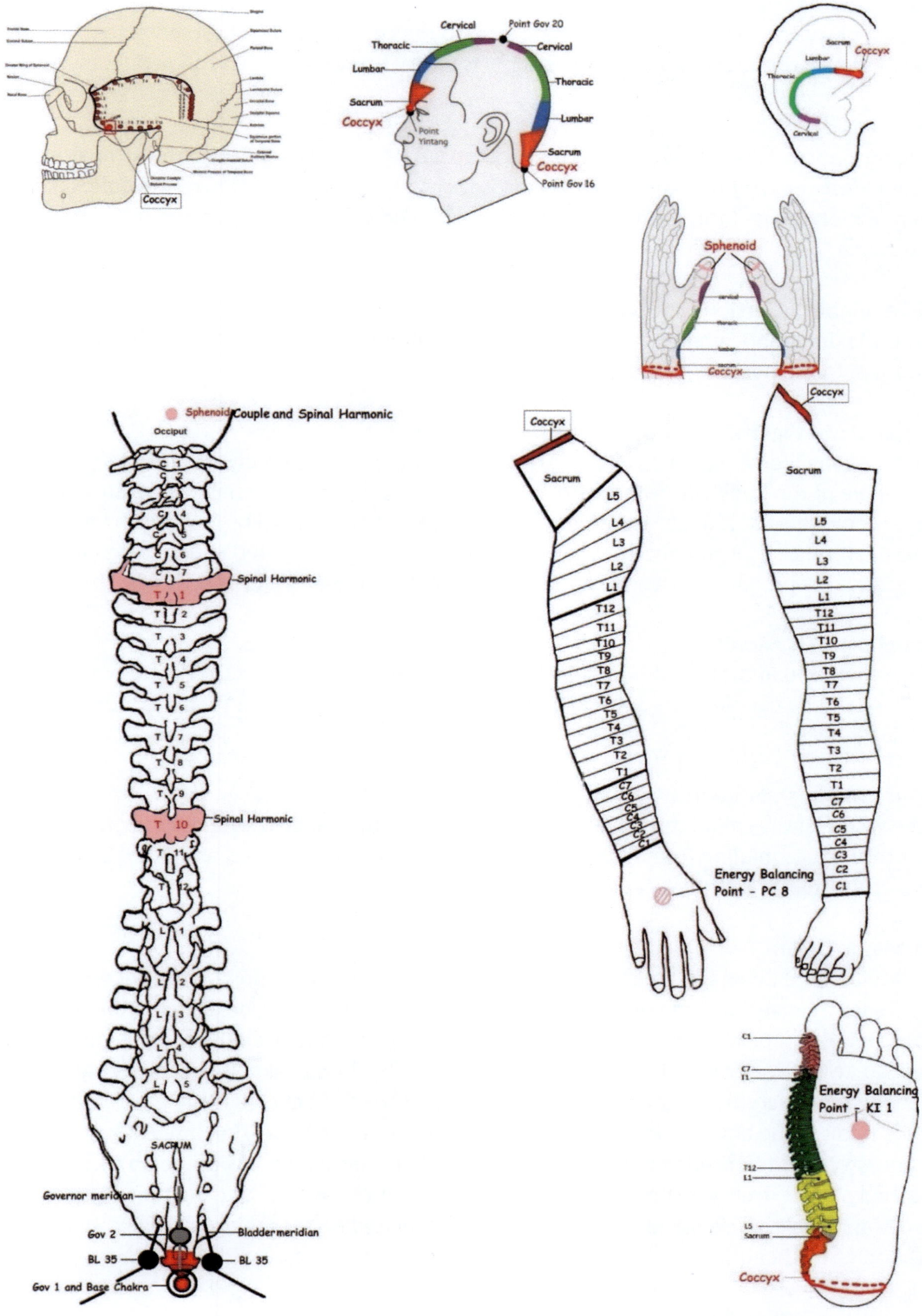

Reflections and Associations of the Coccyx

Spinal Nerve and Dermatome
The coccygeal plexus of nerves supplies the skin local to the coccyx and the anal sphincter, pudendum and part of the rectum. The dermatome is a very tiny area around the perineum.

Autonomic Nerve
There is no autonomic supply from the sacro-coccyx space (S4/Coccyx), although the sympathetic nerve system descends as far as the front of the coccyx in a small ganglion named the *ganglion impar*. Gentle mobilising of this ligament can have a profound effect on the parasympathetic nervous system.

Musculo-Tendinous Insertions and Supply
The Gluteus Maximus and Sphincter Ani Externus attach to the anterior surface and the Coccygeus and Levator ani to the posterior surface.

Effect of Spinal Misalignment
A subluxed, or even worse – a fractured, or dislocated coccyx is an extremely painful injury and can affect the whole of the body with altered posture over a period. When bruising occurs around the area, there is nowhere for it to go. Treatment of this painful condition will be covered in Part Two. In the case of chronic misalignment, that has not been adequately corrected in the acute phase, may give rise to chronic coccydinia and cause local congestion as well as haemorrhoids.

Spinal Couple and Harmonic
The coccyx is involved in the only 4-way spinal harmonic that also includes T10, T1 and the Sphenoid. Its genuine couple is the Sphenoid bone. This may be utilised on the spine or on the various reflex areas.

Acupuncture Meridian influence
As with the whole of the spine, the Governor meridian (Sushumna nadi in Ayurvedic terms) affects the coccyx through its midline. The Bladder meridian lies to the lateral aspect and BL 35 is situated just lateral of the middle of the vertebra.

Posterior Major Chakra
The Base (Muladhara) Chakra is situated at the perineum between Governor 1 and Conception 1, but there is such a powerful range of energy influence that it is often considered to be on the same acupoint as Gov 1, just distal to the coccyx bone. As readers of my books on the chakra energy system will be aware, for practical purposes in acupressure the Base chakra is usually treated from Gov 2 (between the sacrum and coccyx). It may be said that the Base chakra is the most powerful point on the body as the analysis and treatment potentials are enormous. The Base chakra deals with our ancestry and inherited imbalance as well as most chronic conditions of the physical and emotional body. It is extremely important when treating most chronic spinal conditions. The associated Minor chakras are the Knee and Elbow and its related Major chakra is the Crown chakra at Gov 20 (top of the head).

Reflections on the Arm and Leg
The reflected regions of the coccyx on the limbs are to be found above the shoulder and hip, as shown in the diagram. There is often a Focal point within this area that becomes tender when the coccyx is in a state of acute or chronic imbalance – this happens to be a moveable feast so isn't

indicated in the diagram – feel for it. Leg and arm reflections can be very useful in treatment when it is difficult to touch or massage the affected region. Once the Focal point is found, this may be energy balanced with KI 1 in the foot or PC 8 in the hand.

Reflections on the Foot and Hand

These are positioned as in the standard foot and hand reflexology charts on the medial aspect at the base of the spine. The foot reflex is especially useful in the treatment of acute coccydinia. I have long believed as well as there being specific reflected points on the hand and foot, there is also an area of influence that girdles the foot or hand on the same vertical level as the recognized reflex. So, we have a 'girdle' reflex of the spinal vertebra on the leg, foot, arm and hand. All this adds up to very powerful treatment possibilities and extends the scope for the reflexologist.

Temporo-Sphenoidal Line (TSL)

Although the skull reflex per se isn't very useful (as it is usually the same point as the Brow chakra), the TSL point can be very useful in the treatment of acute coccyx pain.

Emotional and Personality

As discussed in Book One, the coccyx, as it is the foundation of the building that we call the spinal column, is linked to our ability to move freely without constraint. Family worries and general security are also linked with the coccyx. So, when family worries and security become long term, they can be transposed in giving symptoms in the coccyx region. This may give rise to stiffness, pain, bladder irritation, haemorrhoids, pelvic floor weakness, scrotal pain and skin lesions in the area. Pain and stiffness in the coccyx region that become long term and chronic may then start to cause issues further up the spine

Sacrum

The Sacrum consists of 5 fused bones and is the largest of all the bones in the vertebral column. Although the coccyx is the bottom vertebra, it is the sacrum that is the powerhouse, fulcrum and foundation of the spine – therefore making it very important regarding its anatomy, physiology as well as its subtle anatomy and connections.

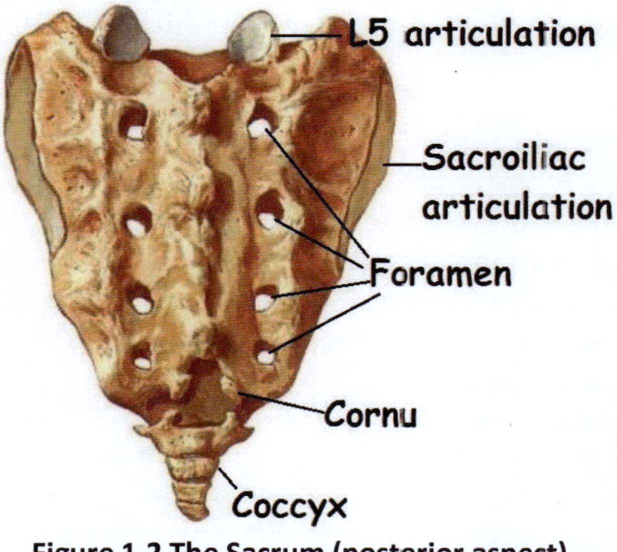

Figure 1.2 The Sacrum (posterior aspect)

Spinal Nerves and Dermatome

The sacral plexus, described earlier, gives nerves that supply muscles of the leg and perineum. Nerve complexes include the sciatic (common peroneal and tibial) and pudendal nerves. The dermatome is shown in Figure 1.3 The sacral dermatome is colour coded for each segment.

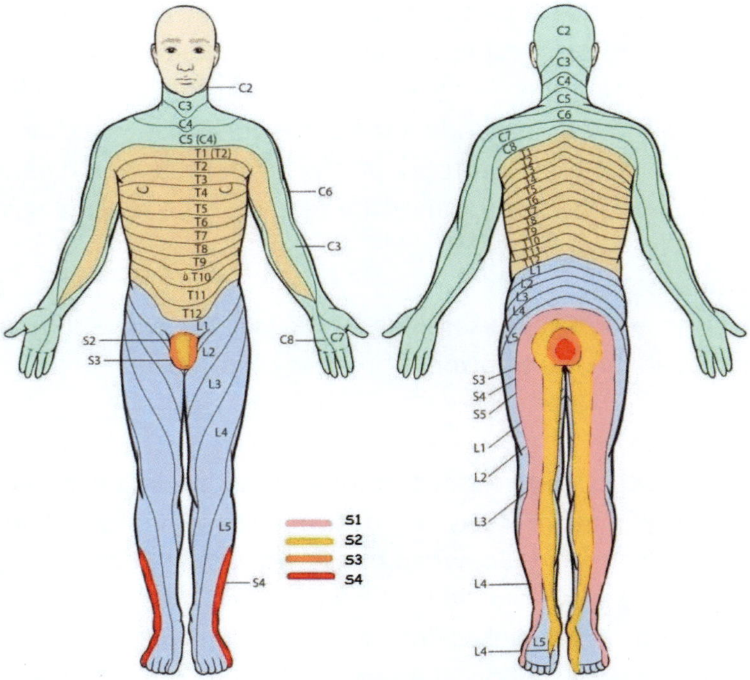

Figure 1.3 The Sacral Dermatome (colour coded)

Autonomic Nerves and Supplied Organs

The sacrum is unique in the spine in that both sympathetic and parasympathetic nerves emanate from the central nervous system complex. Most anatomical authorities insist that only parasympathetic nerves emerge from the sacrum to supply lower internal organs. However, Gray's Anatomy clearly states that 'the pelvic part of the sympathetic trunk is situated in front of the sacrum medial to the sacral foramina'.

The **sympathetic** nerves supply the Small Intestine, Large Intestine, Rectum, Bladder and Testes/Uterus via neural links from L5-S1 and S1-2. The **parasympathetic** nerves (from S2-3, S3-4 and S4-5) form the pelvic splanchnic nerves to then supply the Large Intestine, Rectum, Bladder and Testes/Uterus.

Musculo-Tendinous Insertions and Supply

The sacrum has many strong ligaments attached to it that protect and strengthen the lower spine and pelvic diaphragm. The main muscles that insert on the sacrum are the Piriformis and Gluteus Maximus. The sacral plexus (see Book One) supplies the following muscles: -

L5-S1 – Tibialis Posterior; Tensor Fascia Latae; Gluteus Medius and Minimus; Semimembranosus; Semitendinosus; Extensor Hallucis Longus; Extensor Digitorum Longus; peroneus Tertius; Peroneus Brevis; Peroneus Longus; Gastrocnemius

S1-S2 – Some of the above plus Soleus; Plantaris; Biceps Femoris; Gluteus Maximus; Flexor Hallucis

S2-S3 – Some of the above plus Flexor Digitorum Longus and Brevis

S3-S4 – Some of the above plus Foot Intrinsic muscles

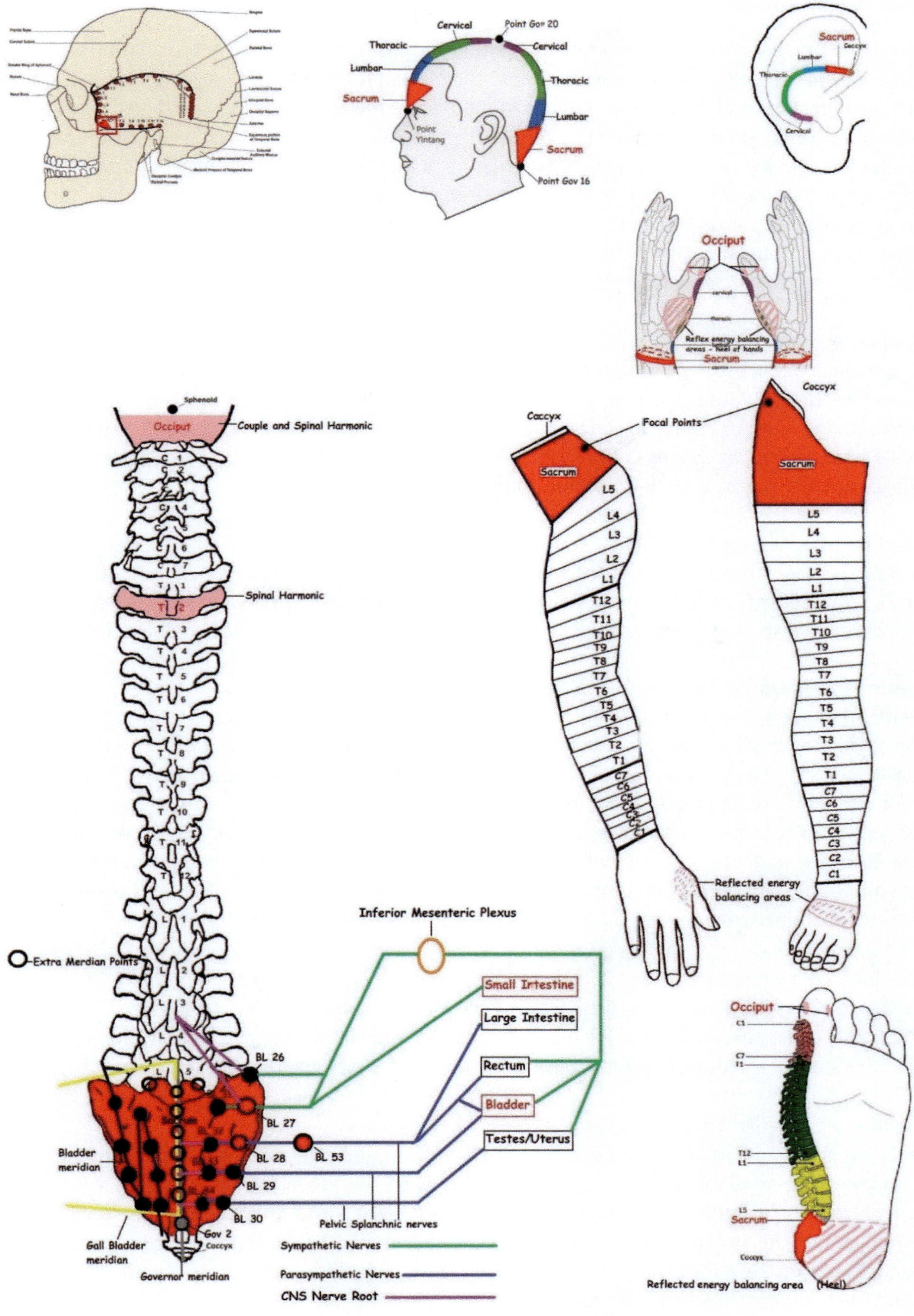

Reflections and Associations of the Sacrum

Effects of Spinal Misalignment

The sacrum may be affected in several ways, either by injury or posture. The articulation with Lumbar 5 is particularly strained posturally and the human frame has the most acute lordotic angle (concavity) at that level, especially in women who have borne children. The sacro-iliac joints are just as vulnerable, but, at least this joint is a very strong, non-synovial one. Chronic lesions of the sacrum can, and do, affect the various internal organs that the autonomic nerves supply. When in practice, I lost count of the number of cases of uterine and bladder imbalance that were 'cured' with an adjustment or other treatment on the sacrum. The main anatomical function of the sacrum, though, is to support the rest of the spine. It is the foundation of the building. So, when the sacrum is in a state of imbalance it affects the remainder of the body.

Spinal Couple and Harmonic

The spinal harmonics that go with the sacrum are T2 and the occiput. It is a powerful triad in treatment. The link with the occiput is profound in that it has spawned several ways of spinal analysis and treatment. These include Sacro-Occipital Technique, Cranio-Sacral Reflexology, Cranio-Sacral Reflextherapy as well as Cranio-Sacral Therapy. This is such a huge topic in our therapies of acupressure and reflexology that a whole chapter is dedicated to it in Part Two.

Linked Internal Organs

The Back-Transporting Points of BL 28 (level with S2) gives energy to the Bladder and BL 27 (level with S1) supplies the Small Intestine. Treatment to conditions of both organs may be via these excellent acupoints. The Back-Transporting points are indicated in RED inside a black circle.

Acupuncture Meridian Influence

As with all the vertebra, the Governor and Bladder meridians affects the sacrum energetically. Several Bladder acupoints are found on the posterior surface as well as non-meridian points along the midline. The acupoints on the sacrum are very useful in treating local pain as well as sciatica. A deep channel of the Gall Bladder meridian is also to be found in the sacrum. It is midline from L4-5 to S5. From these two points it joins its main channel around the hip joint at GB 30 and GB 31. There is therefore a strong link between the sacrum and hips. The main diagram shows the links via the sympathetic and parasympathetic nervous systems to various internal organs. I believe that these two systems are affected by the outer sacral bladder points (BL 26-BL 30).

Posterior Major Chakra

No major chakras are situated on the sacrum, but there is profound influence from the Base at Gov 1 and Sacral chakra at L4-L5. Because of this 'sacred' influence, the Sacral chakra is often linked with imbalance of the uterus/ovaries with its link with the ovaries and testes endocrine system.

Reflections on the Arm and Leg

The size of the reflected area is indicated by the size of the sacrum i.e. large! As you can see from the diagram, the reflected areas are above a line between the top of the shoulder and axilla on the arm and from the groin to the hip on the leg. Remember that these reflected regions circumvent the limb, and in the case of the leg is very close to the sacrum. The Focal points within these reflected areas are at ST 30 and BL 50, but you will have to feel around the area to affect the most tender 'ouch' point. These are then energy balanced with the heel of the foot and 'heel' (thenar eminence) of the hand, as these are the reflected areas of the occiput (the sacrum's couple)

Reflections on the Foot and Hand

These are positioned in the classical lower spinal areas on both. As stated before, I believe that the foot and hand reflexes girdle around at the reflected level – the classical ones are merely the Focal areas. Don't, however, forget that the sacrum can be treated with reflexology circumventing the heels.

Skull reflection and TS Line

The skull has two large areas (depicting the size of the sacrum) just superior to the Brow chakra at Yintang and Gov 16. This can be useful as an adjunct treatment whilst working practically on the occiput – sacral link. The TS Line is useful in acute pain around the sacrum. Whilst on the topic of reflexes in the skull and head – I have found that sacro-iliac pain may be treated with reflexology by the temporo-mandibular joint.

Emotional and Personality

The sacrum deals with communication and relationships. If these two are in good order, then the sacrum should be fine, except for, say, a road traffic accident affecting the stability of the pelvis. It is when these two traits are problematic that symptoms may ensue. These would include pelvic stiffness, osteo-arthritis, sciatica, heel pain, and symptoms with the uterus/testes, bladder and intestines.

Chapter Two – The Lumbar Spine

The lumbar spine consists of five vertebrae with L5 the lowest and just proximal to the sacrum and L1 inferior to the 12th thoracic. The intervertebral discs are much larger than in other parts of the spine. The lumbar spine should have a natural concavity known as the lumbar lordosis

Lumbar 5

The lowest lumbar vertebra articulates with the fourth lumbar and the sacrum. It is the largest of the lumbar spine and takes the strain of the rest of the spine.

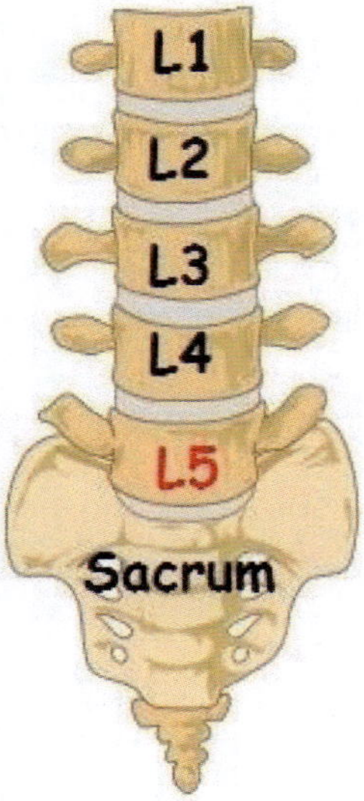

Figure 2.1 Anterior aspect of Lumbar 5

Spinal Nerves and Dermatome

The nerve root that emerges from L5-S1 forms part of the Sacral plexus and between L4-5 is the lower part of the lumbar plexus. The dermatome is shown in Figure 11.2. It innervates the lower back, the extreme lateral aspect of the upper leg and lower leg, plus the medial four fifths of the sole of the foot.

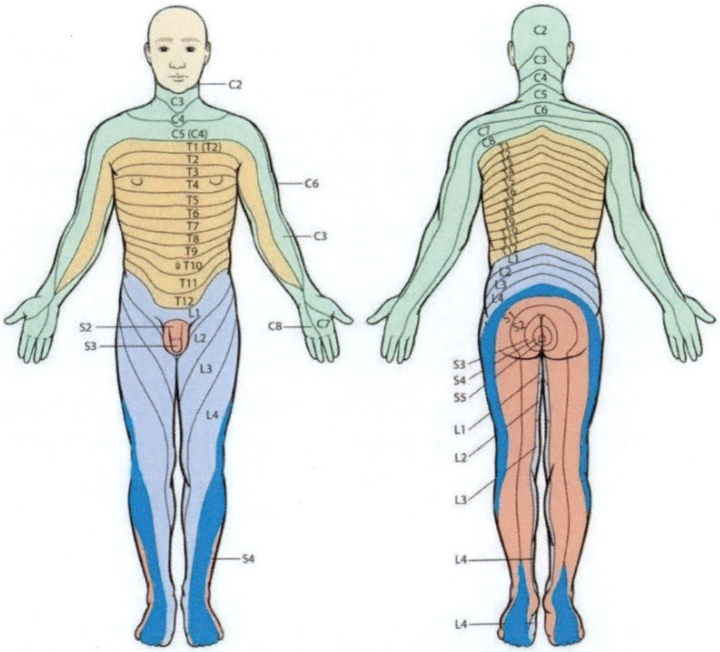

Figure 2.2 Lumbar 5 dermatome (in blue)

Autonomic Nerves and Supplied Organs

The autonomic nerve outflow from L4-5 is sympathetic, leading to the inferior mesenteric plexus and the internal organs of the rectum, bladder, testes/uterus and lower section of the large intestine.

Muscles Supplied

The following muscles are innervated from L5 nerve root - either total or partial innervation: - Tibialis Anterior, Tibialis Posterior, Tensor Fascia Lata, Gluteus Medius and Minimus, Hamstring group, Peroneal group, Extensor Digitorum, Extensor Hallucis Longus.

Effects of Spinal Misalignment

These include sciatica, paraesthesia, foot drop, bladder irritation, prostate irritation, cold loins, ankle oedema, weak ankles and irritable bowel.

Spinal Couple and Harmonic

The coupled vertebra is C1 (atlas) and the spinal harmonic is T3. When you are faced with an L5 lesion that has not been adequately treated, in time there will always be an atlas misalignment as well as 'pressure' on T3.

Linked internal organs via the energetic system

The Back-Transporting point BL 25 (level with the spinous process of L4) can affect the energetic supply of the Large Intestine

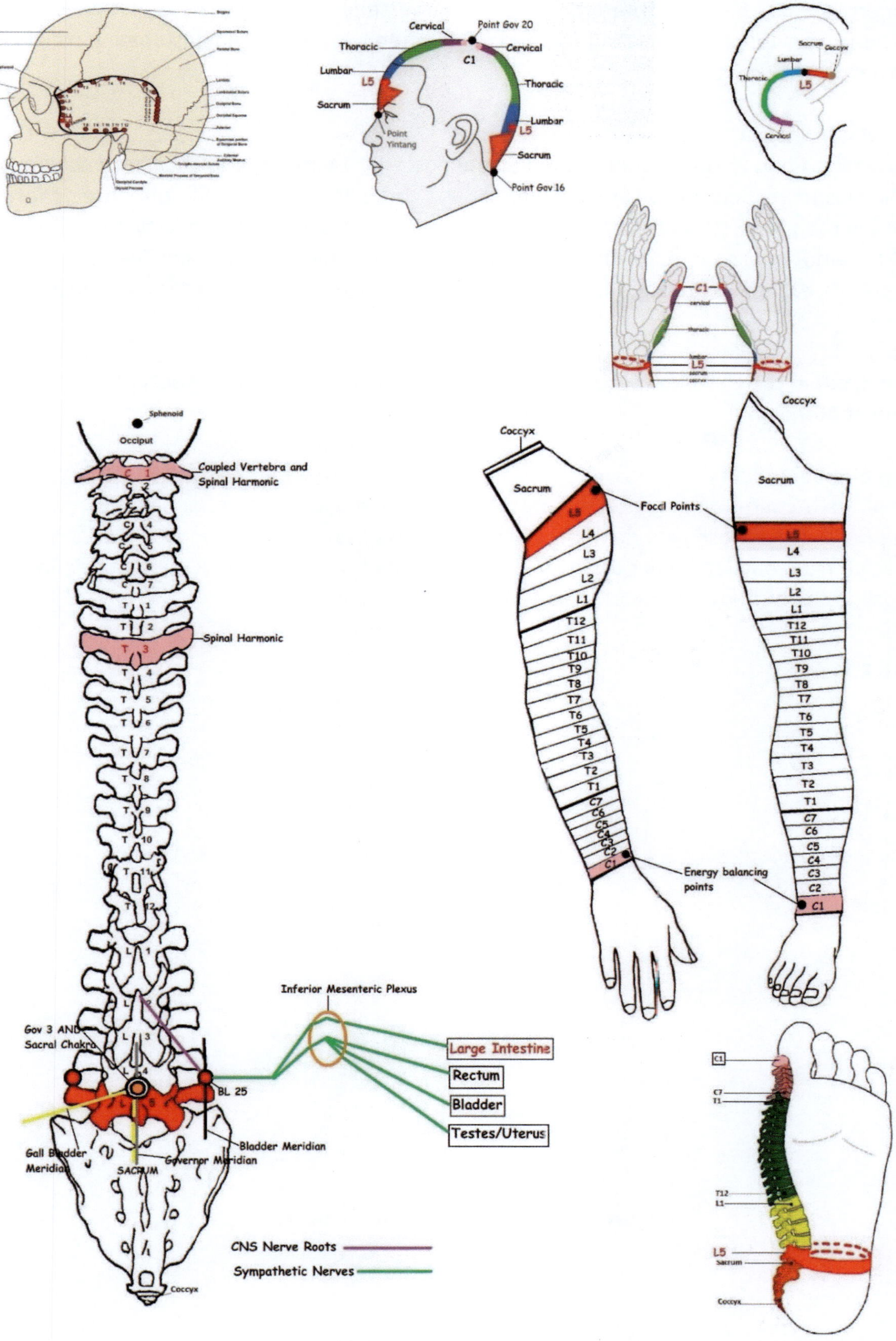

Reflections and Associations of Lumbar 5

Acupuncture Meridian influence

The Governor meridian is midline with its acupoint Gov 3 distal to L4. The previously mentioned Bladder meridian passes over the vertebra at the transverse process and there is also an influence from the deep channel of the Gall Bladder meridian – often explaining troublesome hip pain referral from an L4-5 lesion.

Posterior Major Chakra

Gov 3 between L4 and L5 on the mid line is also the posterior Sacral chakra. The Sacral chakra influences the sacrum and the lower three lumbar vertebrae. It is also a major influence on internal organs within the pelvis, with affinity to the ovaries/testes and the reproductive system. See later in the list for emotional conditions that mostly originate from chakra imbalance. The relate major chakra is the Throat chakra at Gov 14 (C7-T1) and the associated minor chakra is the Spleen chakra.

Reflections

As per the diagram the L5 reflex is around the upper arm and upper leg with Focal points at the lateral aspect of the area.

Emotional and Personality

L5 is part of the 'Action-Doing' region of the spine both in the overall and regional aspects. Anomalies here affect those who do not move and exercise as they should and emotionally are stuck 'in a rut' from outside influences such as a dull occupation of lifestyle. Other emotional traits are jealousy, envy, lust, low self-worth, pleasure and enjoyment

Lumbar 4

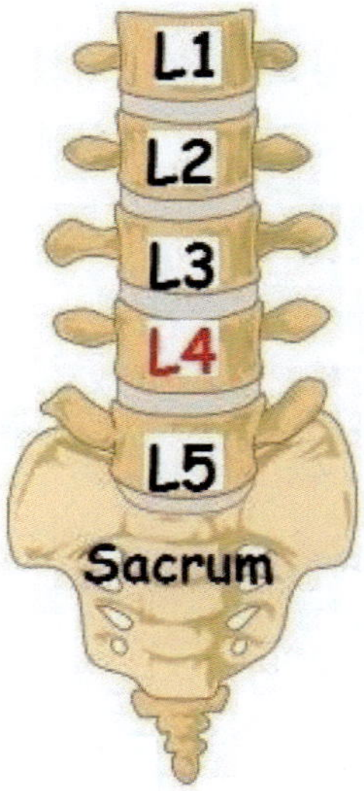

Figure 2.3 Lumbar 4 (anterior aspect)

Spinal Nerve and Dermatome

The nerve root from L3-4 forms part of the Femoral Plexus and forms part of both the Obturator and the Femoral nerves. The Dermatome from L4 is shown in Figure 11.4 – supplying the lower spine, the anterior aspect of the thigh, medial aspect of the lower leg and great toe.

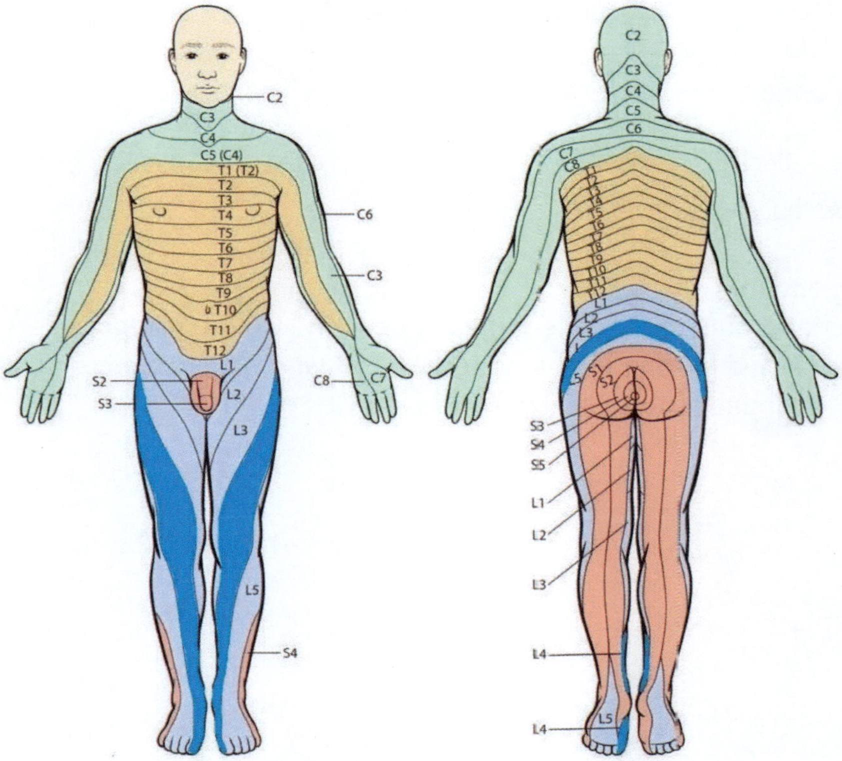

Figure 2.4 Lumbar 4 dermatome (in blue)

Autonomic Nerves and Supplied Organs

The sympathetic outflow from the paravertebral sympathetic chain goes to the Inferior mesenteric Plexus to supply the Kidney, Bladder, lower portion of the Large Intestine, Testes/Ovaries and Rectum

Muscles Supplied

The following muscles are totally or partially innervated from the L3-4 nerve root : - Adductors Longus, Brevis and Magnus), Quadriceps, Tibialis Anterior, Tibialis Posterior, Tensor Fascia Latae, Gluteus Medius and Minimus.

Effects of Spinal Misalignment

These include femoral and obturator nerve pain, quadriceps and adductor muscles weakness/spasm, lumbar fibrositis, frequent urination, dismennorhia, impotence.

Spinal Couple and Harmonic

The Coupled vertebra is C2 (axis) and the other harmonic vertebra is T4

Acupuncture Meridian influence

As with all the vertebrae, the main influences are the Governor and Bladder channels. BL 24 and BL 25 sit either side of the transverse processes and Gov 3 is iimediately inferior to the spinous process

of L4. Between the spinous processes of L3 and L4 is a non-meridian acupoint, even though it lies on the Governor meridian (one of the anomolies of traditional Chinese medicine!) Please note that the so called
Ah-shi points (paravertebral points) are not drawn in any diagram as it would make them look too busy.

Posterior Chakra
As previously mentioned the posterior Sacral Chakra lies between L4-L5

Reflections
These are as per the diagram above.

Emotional and Personality
L4 is part of the 'Action-Doing' part of the spine but as an individual vertebra relates to feelings. Many L4 lesions are caused by long term emotional upset when the person cannot fight back or cope with the overwhelming anguish of their predicament.

Lumbar 3

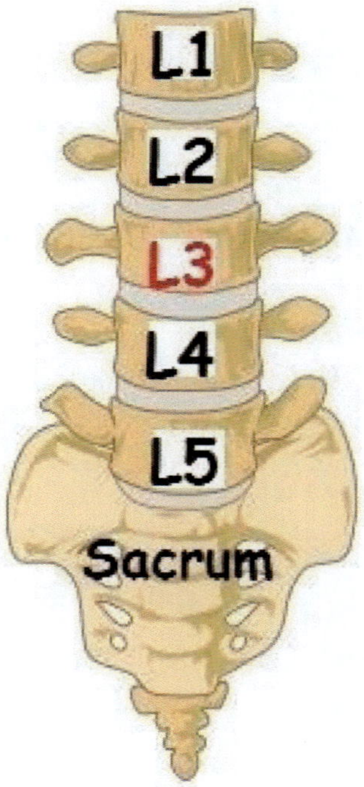

Figure 2.5 Lumbar 3 vertebral position (anterior aspect)

Spinal Nerve and Dermatome

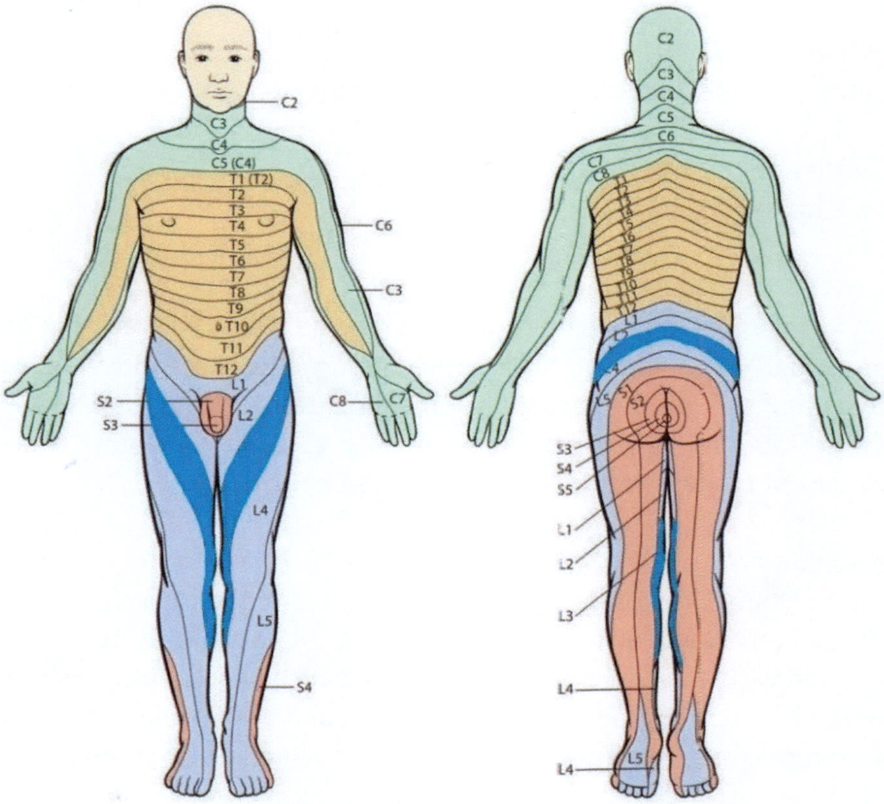

Figure 2.6 Dermatome of L3 (in blue)

The nerve root leading from L2-3 forms part of the Lumbar Plexus that becomes the Femoral nerve, Obturator nerve and Lateral Cutaneous nerve. The Dermatome (see Figure 2.6) covers the lower back, antro-medial aspect of the thigh and medial part of the lower leg to just below the knee.

Autonomic Nerve and Internal Organs

The sympathetic outflow from the paravertebral chain goes to the Inferior Mesenteric plexus and on to supply the Bladder, Testes/Uterus, Rectum, Large Intestine and Kidney

Muscles Supplied

The following muscles are totally or partially innervated by the L2-3 nerve root – Iliopsoas; Sartorius; Gracilis; Adductors, Quadriceps; Obturator Externus

Effects of Spinal Misalignment

Cystitis and Bladder stricture; Urinary Frequency; Painful Periods; Impotency; Menopausal symptoms; Irritable Bowel Syndrome; Quadriceps/Adductor pain and spasm; Nephritis

Spinal Couple and Harmonic

The Coupled Vertebra is C3 and the Spinal Harmonic is T5

Linked Internal Organ via the Energetic System

BL 23 and BL 52 (Inner and Outer Bladder meridian) are linked energetically to the Kidney. This is a powerful reflective link in both acupuncture and acupressure.

Acupuncture Meridian Influence
As with other vertebrae, the Bladder and Governor meridians exert influence on L3

Posterior Chakra Influence
The posterior Sacral Chakra influences L3

Reflections
These all sit halfway along the lumbar spine reflections (as you would expect). The best focal points are LI 14 on the arm and ST 32 on the leg. As discussed before, these are movable feasts. You must locate the girdle reflected area and feel around for the most tender or 'ouch' point – there will always be one if the vertebra is in a state of imbalance. The L3-C3 link is a particularly powerful couple in the treatment of many emotional conditions (see below)

Emotional and Personality
L3 falls into the 'Action-Doing' area of the spine and is also one of the individual vertebra that is linked with Thought and Intuition. Each vertebra that lies in the 'middle' of its spinal region i.e. L3; T6/7 and C3/4 are linked with indecision and not knowing which way to turn. Lesions at this level tend to occur with folk who are 'trapped' and stuck in a rut and are unable to move forward in their lives. This may sometimes create psychosomatic disorders such as schizophrenia.

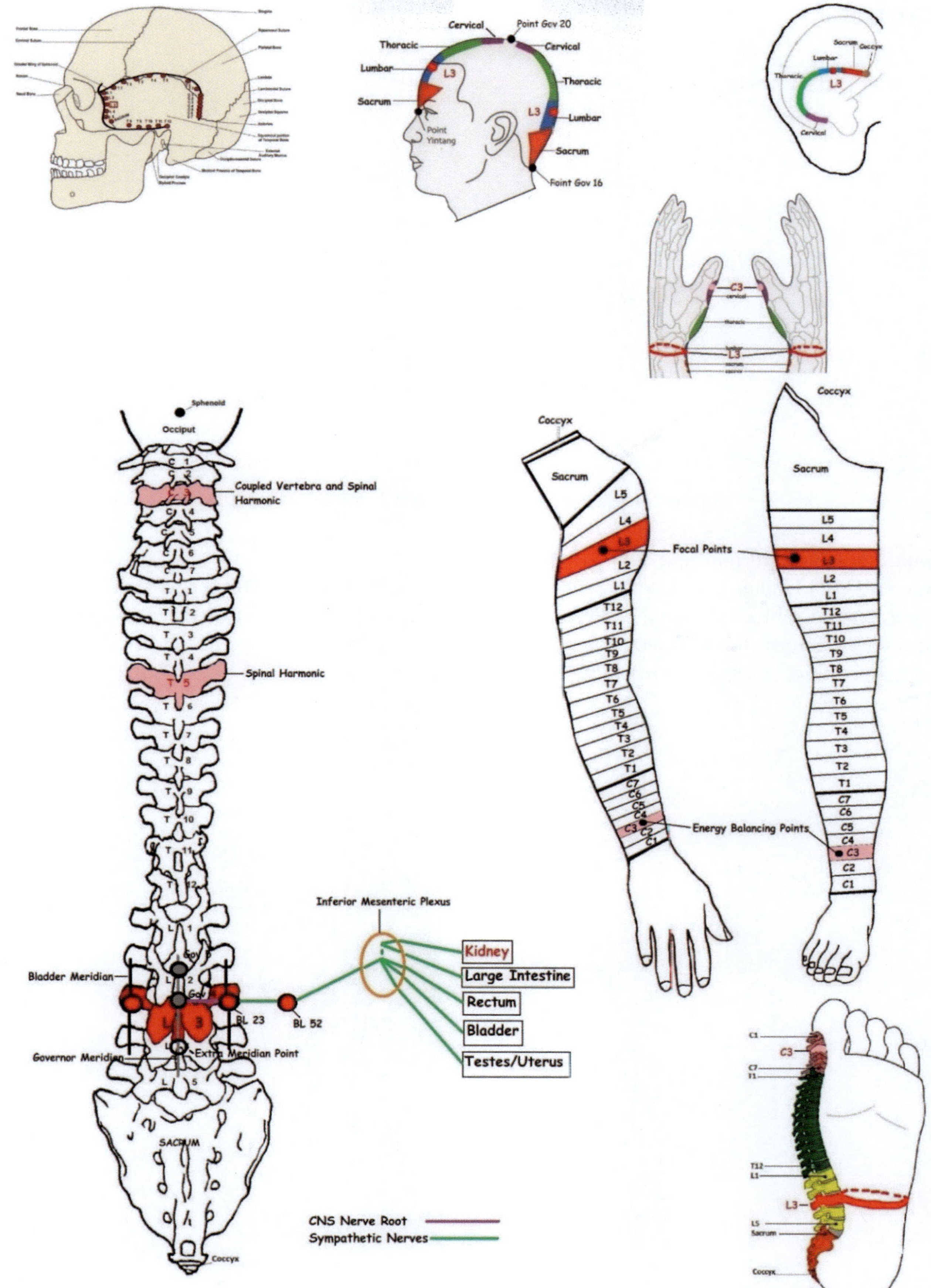

Reflections and Associations of Lumbar 3

Lumbar 2

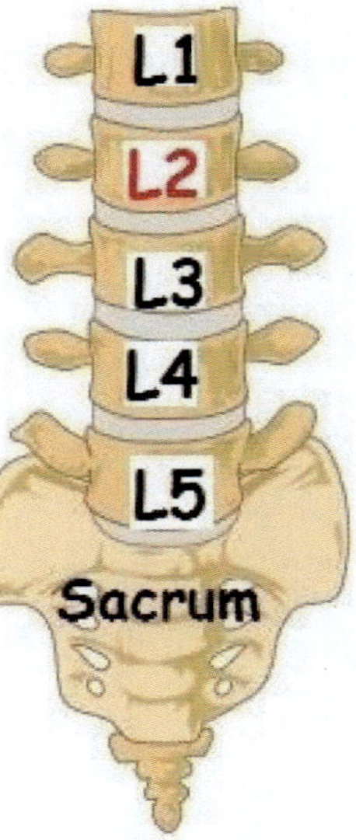

Figure 2.7 Anatomical Position of L2 (anterior aspect)

Spinal Nerve and Dermatome

The nerve root leading L1-2 forms part of the upper part of the Lumbar Plexus and forms part of the Femoral nerve, Obturator nerve and Lateral Cutaneous nerve. There is also a smaller branch called the Genito-Femoral nerve. The Dermatome covers the lower back, the inguinal and groin regions and the very medial aspect of the thigh to mid upper leg.

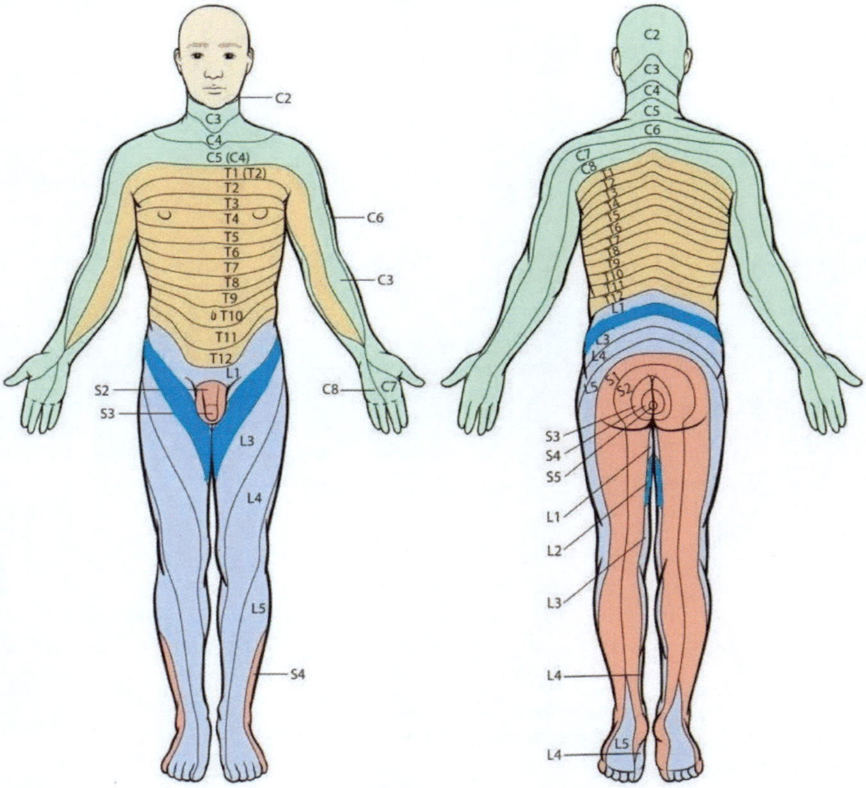

Figure 2.8 Dermatome of L2 (in blue)

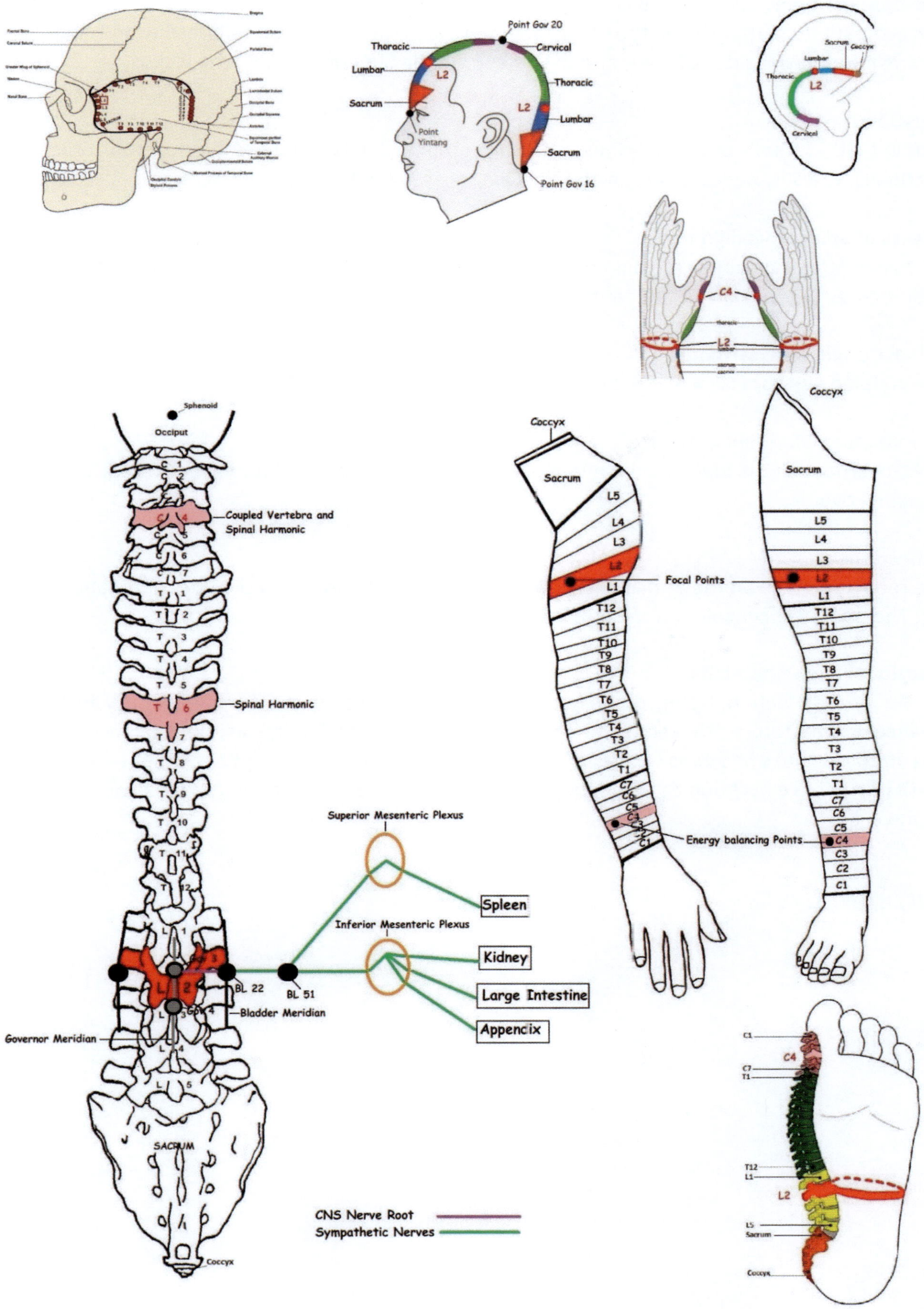

Reflections and Associations of Lumbar 2

Autonomic Nerves and Internal Organs
The sympathetic outflow from the L1-L2 root innervates the Kidney, Large Intestine and Appendix via the Inferior Mesenteric Plexus and the Spleen via the Superior Mesenteric Plexus.

Muscles Supplied
Muscles either totally or partially innervated from the L1-2 nerve root are Iliopsoas; Sartorius; Pectineus; Gracilis; Adductor group and the Quadriceps group of muscles.

Effects of Spinal Misalignment
L2 lesions often cause referred pain to the appendix and the ilio-caecal valve region of the abdomen as well as pain on the dermatome.

Spinal Couple and Harmonic
The coupled vertebra is C4 and the other harmonic influence is at T6

Acupuncture Meridian influence
The Governor and Bladder meridians influence this upper lumbar vertebra with Gov 3, Gov 4 and BL 22 acting over it.

Reflections
The reflected girdle on the arm and leg is approximately half way down the upper arm and upper leg. The normal Focal point on the arm is LI 14.

Emotional and Personality
L2 falls into the 'Action- Doing' group but is also to do with Movement, Family, Security and Finance. It is therefore affected with worry and stress regarding family members. In my experience this often leads to symptoms such as bowel irritation and referral through to the ilio-caecal valve (ICV). (If you have occasion to treat a positive ICV, always check the upper lumbar spine – it could be the culprit!)

Lumbar 1

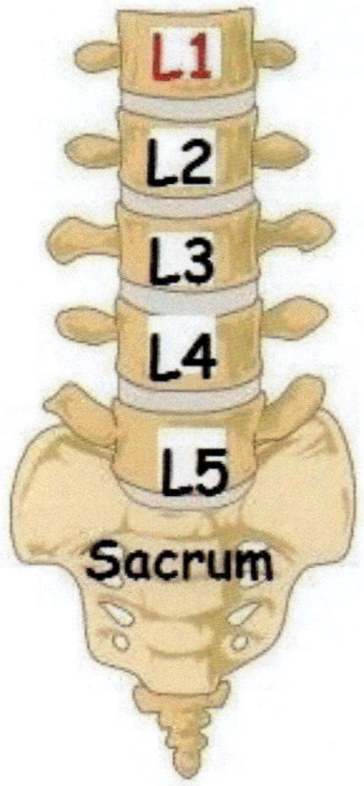

Figure 2.9 Position of L1 (anterior aspect)

Lumbar 1 is the most superior of the 5 lumbar vertebrae, sitting between L2 and the 12th thoracic vertebra.

Spinal Nerve and Dermatome

The nerve root leading from T12-L1 is the most superior of the lumbar plexus nerves and becomes the Ilioguinal nerve with a small branch to the Genitofemoral nerve. The dermatome is across the upper part of the lower back round to the inguinal and groin region with a narrow innervation to the skin at the very top of the medial aspect of the leg.

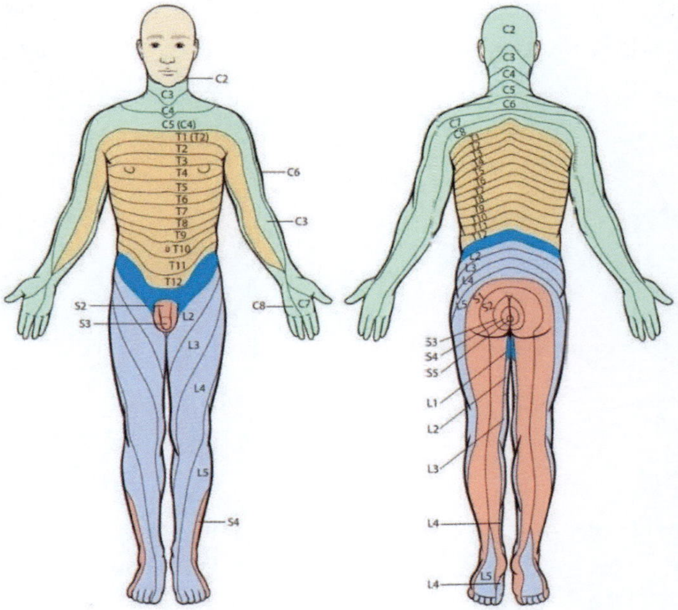

Figure 2.10 Dermatome of L1 (in blue)

Autonomic Nerves and Internal Organs

The sympathetic outflow from the paravertebral vertebral chain goes via the Coeliac (Solar) Plexus to supply the Spleen, Stomach and Suprarenals. There is also a link to the Small Intestine and Large Intestine via the Superior Mesenteric Plexus.

Muscular Supply

Muscles that re wholly or partially supplied by T12-L1 are the Rectus Abdominus, Obliquus Internus and Obliquus Externus Abdominus, Transversus Abdominus and Iliopsoas.

Effects of Spinal Misalignment

Some of the symptoms for a lesion with this vertebra are Irritable Bowel Syndrome (IBS), bloating, abdominal muscular weakness, groin pain, stomach conditions.

Spinal Couple and Harmonic

The coupled vertebra is C5 and the other spinal harmonic is at T7

Linked Internal Organs through the Energetic System

The Back-Transporting Point of BL 21 supplies the Stomach

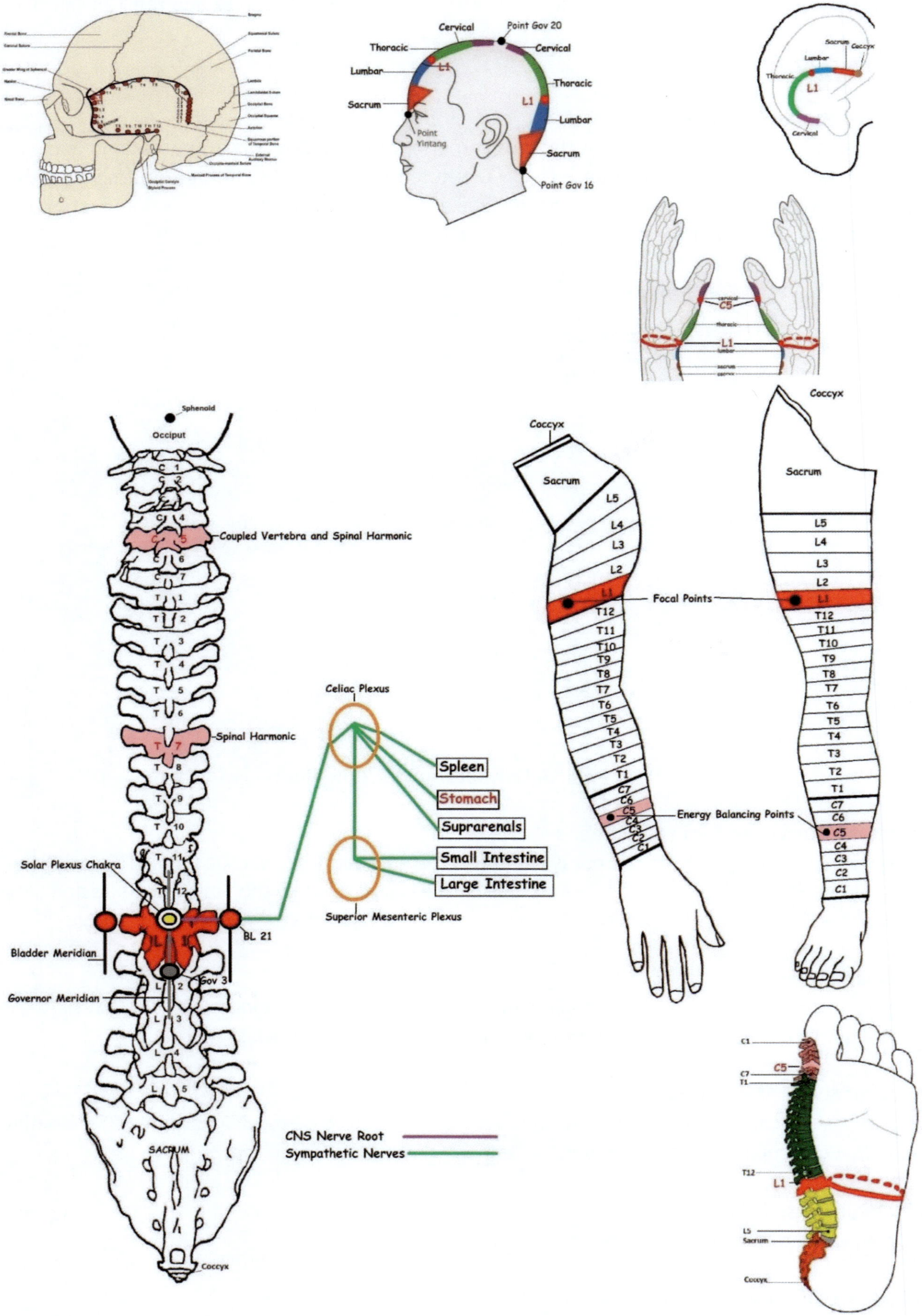

Reflections and Associations of Lumbar 1

Acupuncture Meridian Influence

As with other spinal vertebrae, the Bladder and Governor meridians affect this region. The important acupoints are BL 21 and a non-meridian point between T12 and L1 called Chi Chung that, although it sits on the Governor meridian and highly important, it isn't ranked as a Governor acupoint - very strange.

Posterior Major Chakra

The Posterior physical aspect of the Solar Plexus Chakra emanates from between T12 and L1 (Chi Chung). The associated minor chakra (8th major) is the Spleen chakra.

Reflections

These are as indicated on the above illustration

Emotional and Personality Links

L1 falls with the 'Action-Doing' part of the spine and as an individual vertebra is concerned with Communications and Relationships. Lesions at the level may lead to be a poor communicator and not able to form relationships. This may lead to depression, worry, anxiety, low self-esteem and to affect the pancreas endocrine gland. Naturally, it is a two-way thing, with these types of personality issues and emotional imbalance leading to a physical imbalance at L1.

Chapter Three – The Thoracic Spine

Twelve vertebrae make up the thoracic or dorsal part of the spine. It is the least mobile part of the spine due to the articulation of the rib cage that is fixed at the front by the sternum. It is vital to have protection of the heart, lungs and other major organs by the rib cage. Because of this lack of movement there are fewer problems of an accidental or traumatic nature associated with the thoracic spine. Prolapsed intervertebral discs are rarer than in the lumbar and cervical, but they do occur. The natural curve for the thoracic is one of convexity (kyphosis). It is also prone to scoliosis of either a 'C' or 'S' shape which may be congenital or acquired during the teen years and be of unknown aetiology (idiopathic scoliosis). Scoliosis may require surgical intervention, although mild curvatures may be managed with physical therapy. See the individual vertebra text for possible causes.

Thoracic 12

T12 is, obviously, the most inferior of the 12 and articulates with T11 and L1. T12 and T11 aren't as fixed as the others as the ribs are 'floating' in that they do not articulate with the anterior aspect of the chest. Figure 12.1 shows the anatomical position in a lateral view.

Spinal Nerve and Dermatome

The nerve roots that emanate from the lower thoracic spine travel around chest wall to supply the intercostal muscles as well as the abdominal muscles and serratus anterior. The T12 nerve is called the subcostal nerve. The Dermatome of the T12 is as shown in Figure 12.2 namely girdling the chest and back roughly at its level.

Autonomic Nerves
The sympathetic nerve outflow from the paravertebral chain goes to both the Celiac and Superior Mesenteric Plexuses supplying the Spleen, Pancreas, Fallopian tubes, Testes and upper part of the Small Intestine.

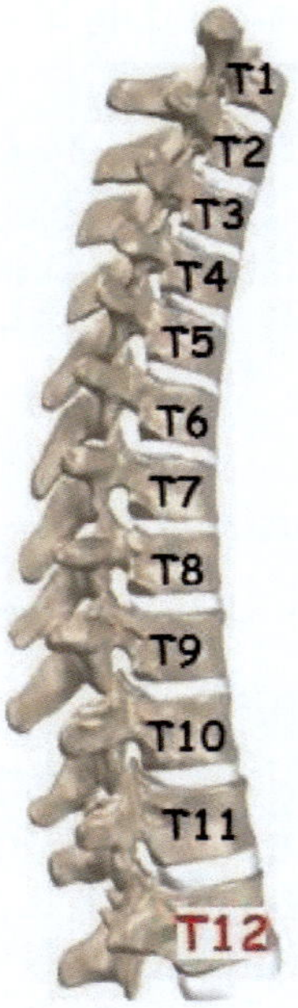

Figure 3.1 Position of T12 (lateral view)

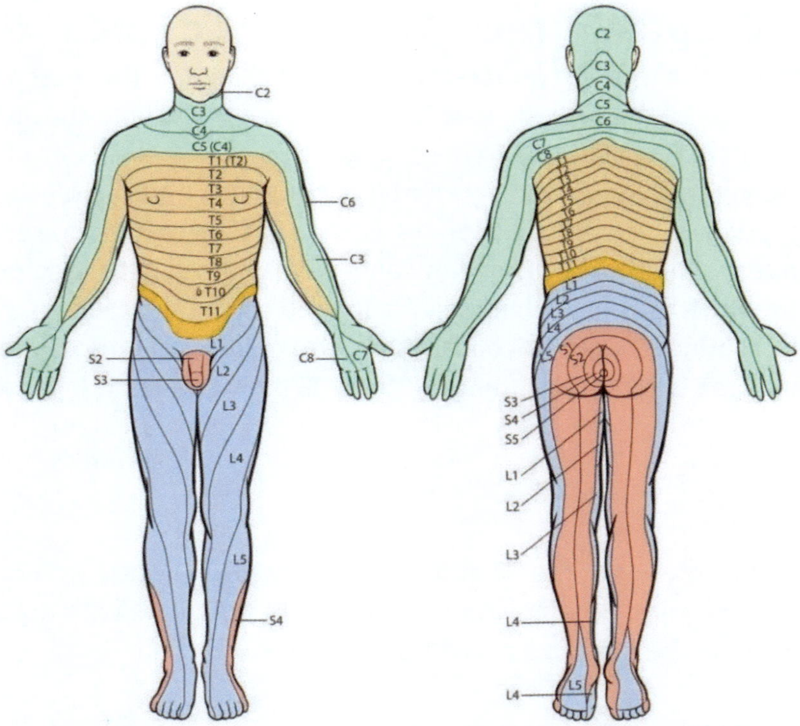

Figure 3.2 The Dermatome of T12 (in dark yellow)

Muscles Supplied
Intercostal muscle, lower part of Abdominus Obliquus and Rectus Abdominus plus a branch with L1 root that supplies the inguinal muscles.

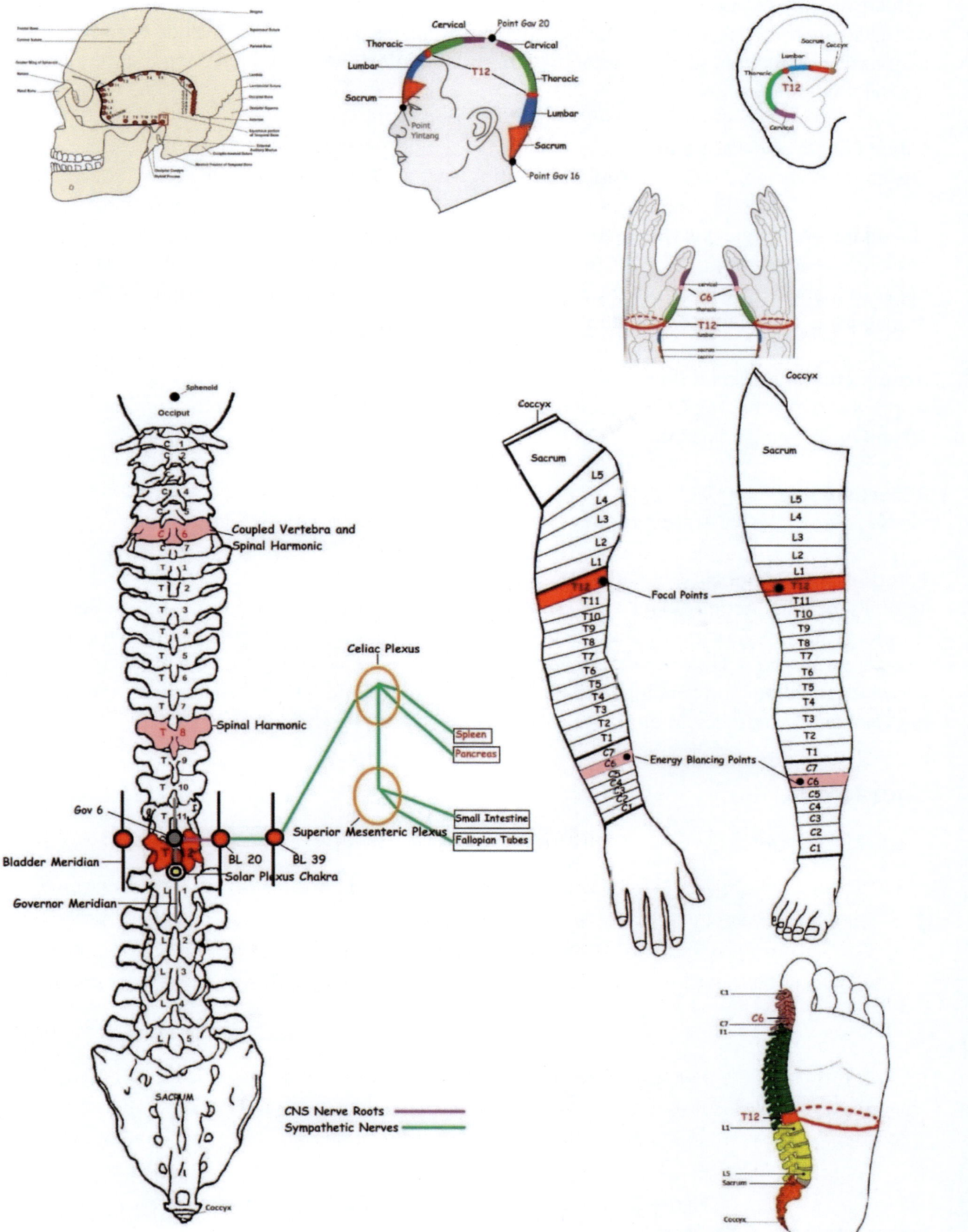

Reflections and Associations of Thoracic 12

Effects of Spinal Misalignment
As the sympathetic nerve flow is to the Small Intestine, lesions of T12 can include tiredness, lymphatic obstruction, some cases of diabetes, rheumatic diseases and anything that requires assimilation of food.

Spinal Couple and Harmonic
The coupled vertebra is C6 and the spinal harmonic is at T8

Linked Internal Organ via the Energetic System
The energy supply from T11/12 is to the Spleen and Pancreas. This in some small measure is because there is overflow from the Solar Plexus and Spleen chakras, but also that the BL 20 Back-Transporting and the outer line BL 39 supply these organs.

Acupuncture meridian influence
As previously stated, the Governor and Bladder channels are paramount with acupoints Gov 6, BL 20 and BL 39 being adjacent.

Reflections
Please refer to the illustration for their positions.

Emotions and Personality
T12 falls into the 'Action-Doing' region of the spine both in general and specific terms. Because of its energetic and sympathetic links to the Spleen/Pancreas as well as the Small Intestine, the key word is *assimilation*. Lesions at this level (mostly scoliosis) may be due to the inability to assimilate knowledge and our surroundings and how we move (or not move) forward in our society. A lack of joy, love and 'sweetness' in our life is also important at this level.

Thoracic 11

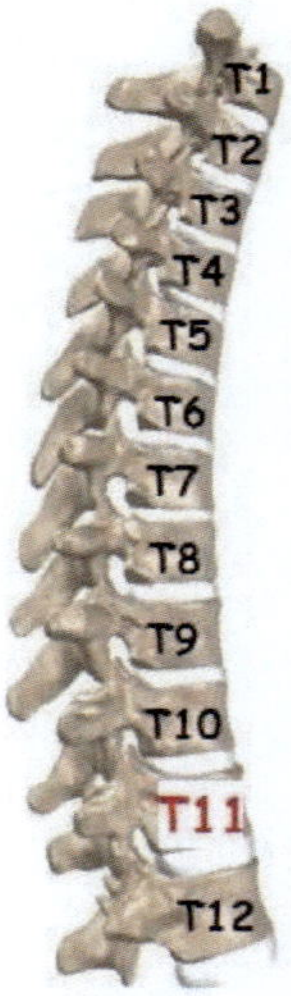

Figure 3.3 Anatomical position of T11 (lateral aspect)

Spinal Nerve and Dermatome
T10-11 nerve root becomes the intercostal nerve at this level and supplies the intercostal area around to the abdomen. The dermatome is as shown in Figure 12.4, namely girdling around the back and abdomen at its level.

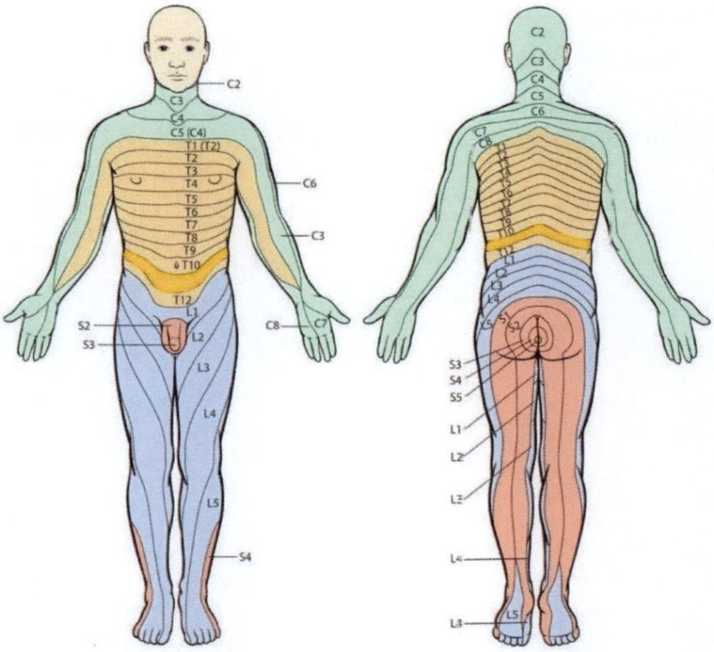

Figure 3.4 T11 dermatome (in dark yellow)

Autonomic Nerves
The sympathetic outflow from the paravertebral sympathetic chain travels via the Celiac and Superior Mesenteric Plexus to supply the Liver, Gall Bladder, Spleen, Small Intestine and Kidney.

Muscles Supplied
The Intercostal muscles and lower Abdominals as per T12

Effects of Spinal Misalignment
Lesions at this level remain rare except for long 'C' scoliosis with disc changes and obvious accidents or injuries. Some symptoms include bowel irritation, gall bladder colic, fatigue and kidney conditions.

Spinal Couple and Harmonic
The coupled Vertebra is C7 and the other Spinal Harmonic is at T9. The C7 -T11 couple is a very powerful one in the treatment of gall bladder conditions. This link is one reason why patients with gall bladder colic have pain referral to the side of the neck and shoulder.

Linked Internal Organ via the Energetic System
The Back-Transporting point at this level is BL 19 and its outer bladder line 'partner' BL 48. These send energy to the Gall Bladder organ. There is still an influence coming from the posterior Solar Plexus chakra that is linked with the Gall Bladder.

Acupuncture meridian Influence
The Governor meridian influence T11 by Gov 6 and Gov 7 and the Bladder by BL 19

Reflections
Please the illustration above for their position.

Emotional and Personality Links

Like T12 above, T11 lies within the 'Action-Doing' section of the spine at both general and specific modes. It is therefore associated with assimilation on a mental and emotional level. Energetic imbalance at an emotional level will affect the Gall Bladder and cause symptoms there such as gall bladder colic and calculi.

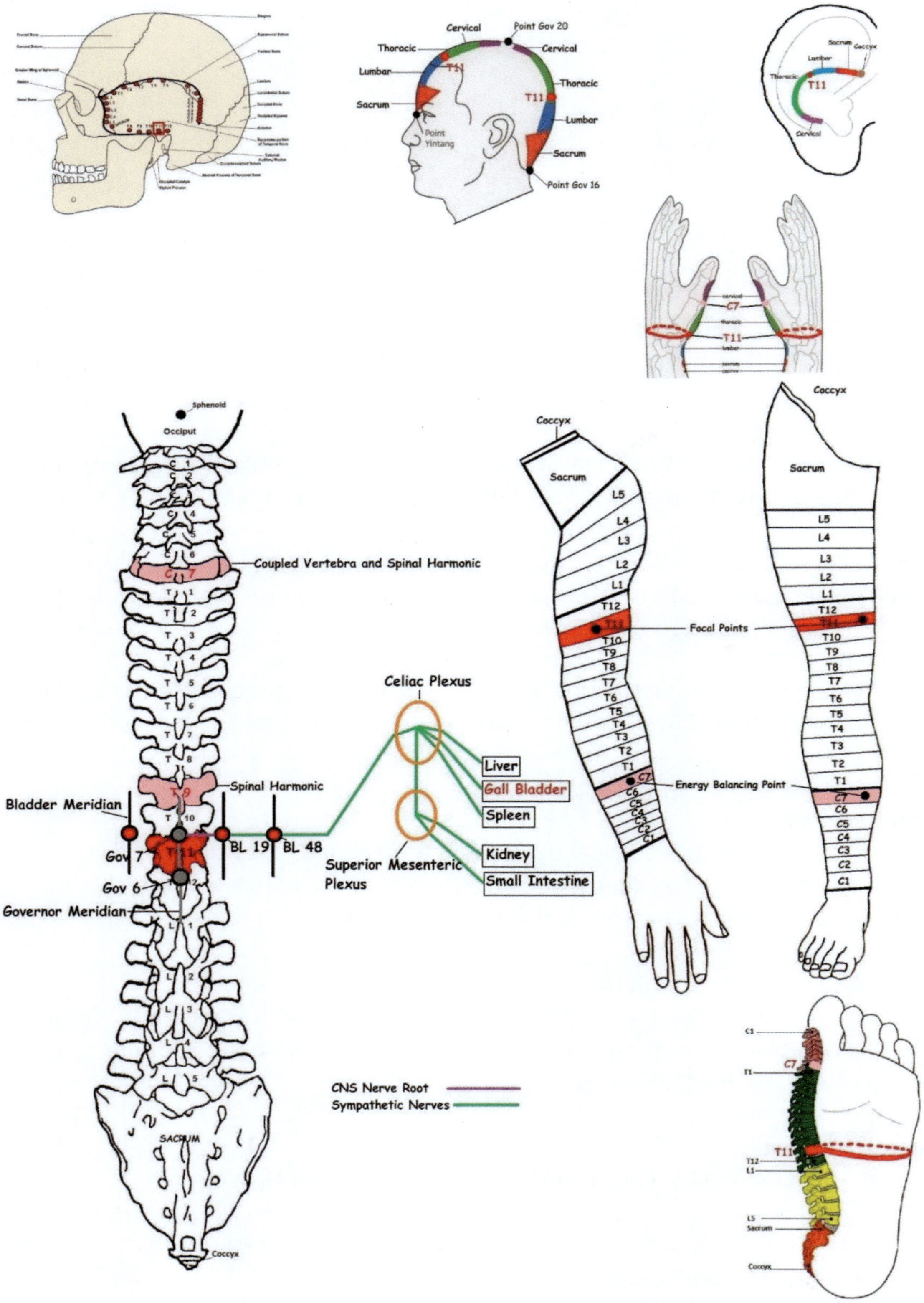

Reflections and Associations of Thoracic 11

Thoracic 10

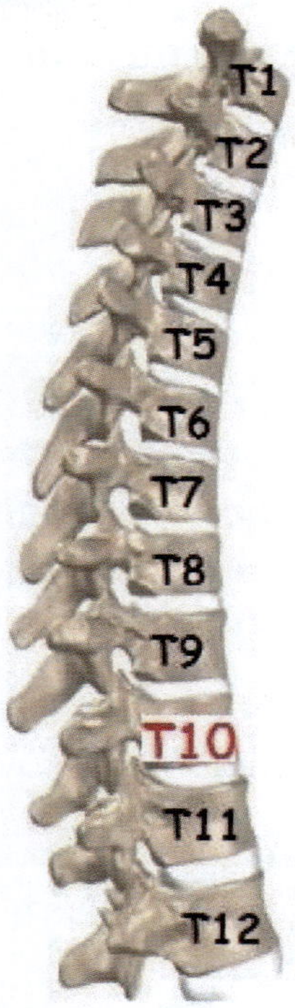

Figure 3.5 Anatomical Position of T10 (lateral aspect)

Spinal Nerve and Dermatome

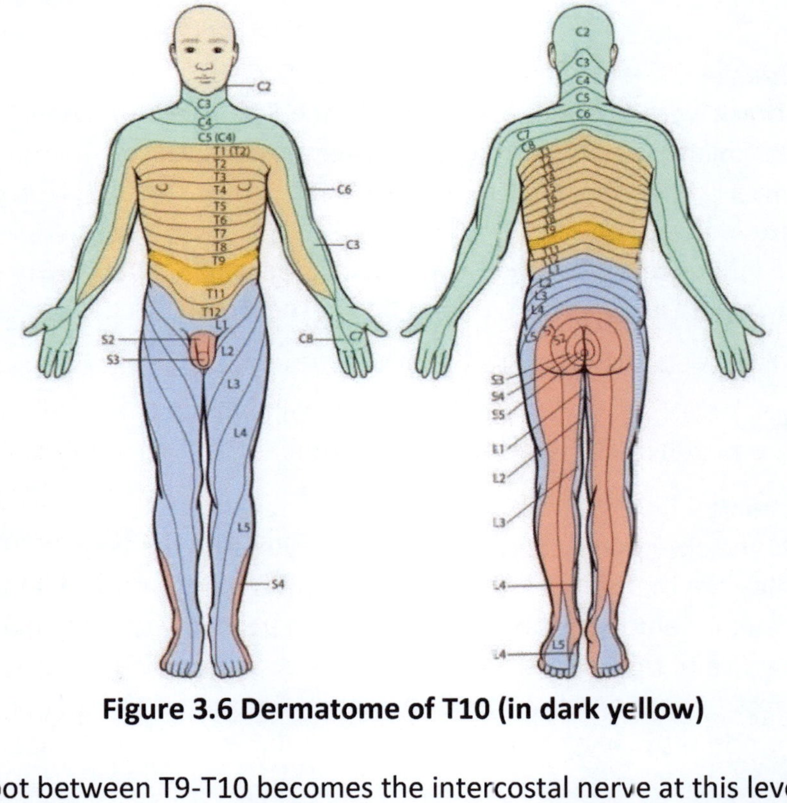

Figure 3.6 Dermatome of T10 (in dark yellow)

The spinal nerve root between T9-T10 becomes the intercostal nerve at this level and supplies the intercostal muscles at that level plus the fibres of rectus Abdominus and the obliquus abdominal muscles. The dermatome is as shown in Figure 3.6, namely the girdle around its anatomical level.

Autonomic Nerves
The sympathetic nerve outflow from the paravertebral sympathetic chain flows to the Celiac Plexus to supply the Gall Bladder, Liver, Spleen, Pancreas and Abdominal Blood Vessels. A branch then goes to the Superior Mesenteric Plexus which further supplies the upper part of the Small Intestine, Suprarenals and Kidney.

Muscles Supplied
As per T11 and T12

Effects of Spinal Misalignment
Lesions at T10 may be due to a long 'C' or 'S' scoliosis with or without rotation plus the obvious accident/injury. Severe lesions here can have profound consequences. The sympathetic nerve flow to the kidney may be affected as well as the abdominal blood vessels. This can produce kidney imbalance as well as chronic tiredness and arterial hardening. However, see below for the energetic and emotional implications.

Spinal Couples and Harmonics
This represents the only 'foursome' of spinal couples that includes the Sphenoid and Coccyx. The true coupled vertebra is T1. The energy balancing of this quartet is different to the usual trios and will be explained in Part Four.

Linked Internal Organ via the Energetic System
The Back-Transporting point of BL 18 and outer Bladder line point BL 47 are connected to the Liver by internal pathways. Influence is also felt at this level from the posterior Solar Plexus chakra.

Posterior Chakra Influence
Most of the lower thoracic vertebrae are influenced by the Solar Plexus chakra. Symptoms that affect the organs of assimilation and food processing are affected most.

Acupuncture Influence
As already stated, the influence is from the Governor channel and acupoints Gov 7 and Gov 8, and the Bladder meridian with its acupoints BL 18 and BL 47. There are also the Back-Shu points.

Reflections
As per the illustration

Emotional and Personality
T 10 is the uppermost vertebra that is linked with 'Action-Doing' in the general and specific modes. Emotion and Personality are therefore like T12 and T11 in that it is to do with assimilation of thought. This level though is amongst the most common to be involved in idiopathic roto-scoliosis (T7 – T10 range) giving rise to many physical symptoms such as migraine, chronic tiredness, diabetes, lymphatic obstructions and low immune system. Emotional and mental symptoms such as anger, rage, pent up emotions may be both the cause and the result of T10 imbalance.

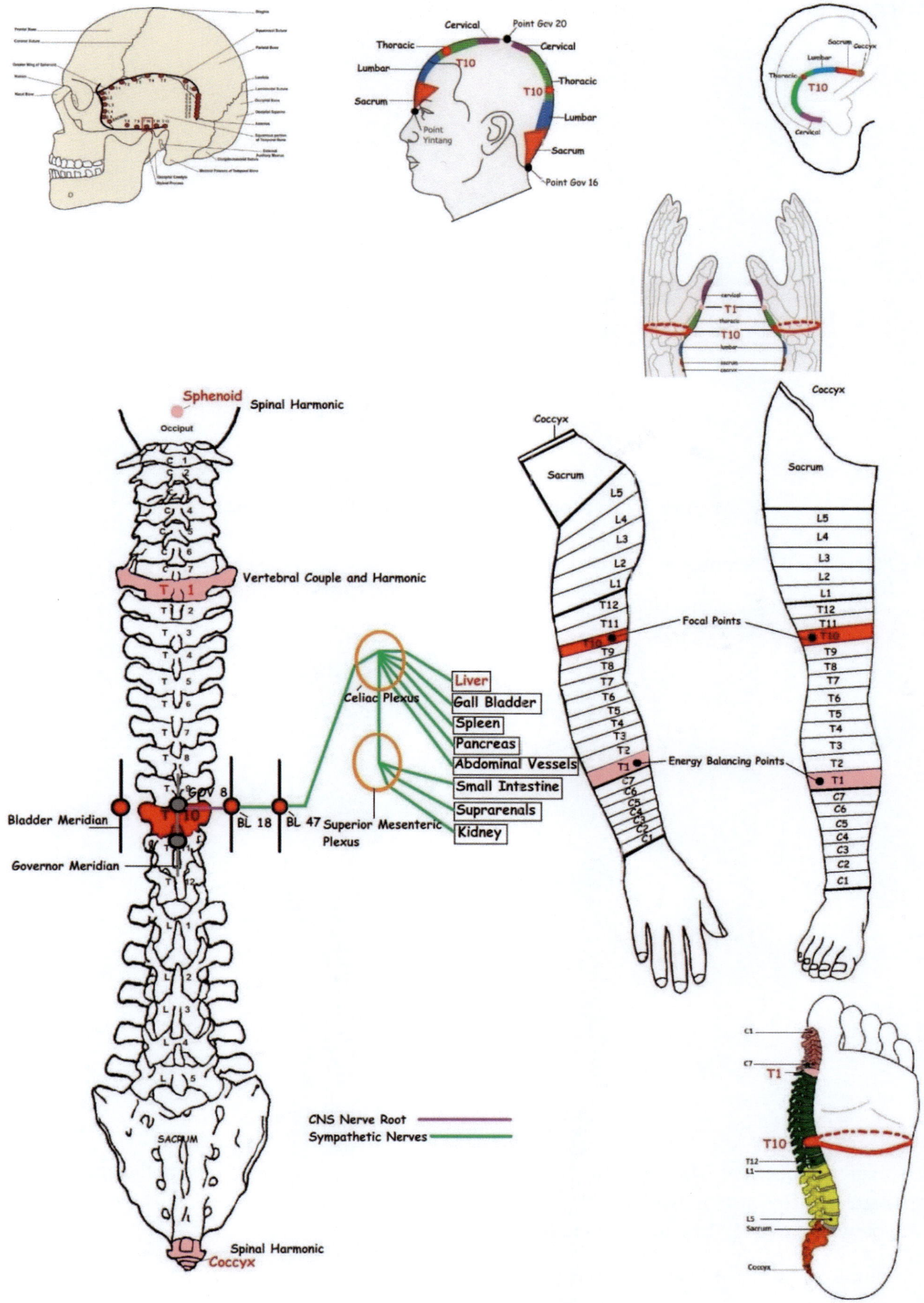

Reflections and Associations of Thoracic 10

Thoracic 9

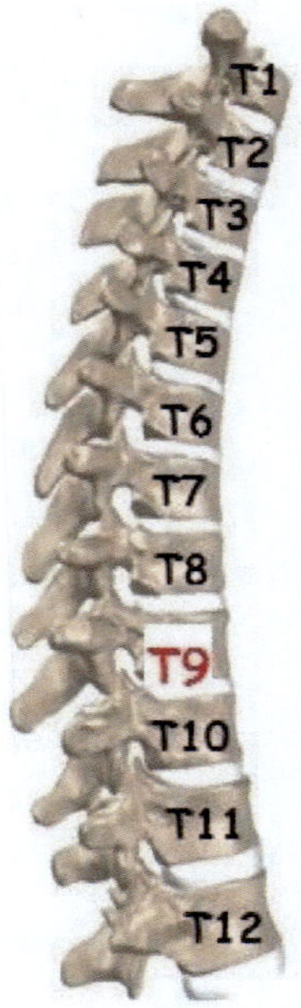

Figure 3.7 Anatomical position of T9 (lateral aspect)

Spinal Nerve and Dermatome

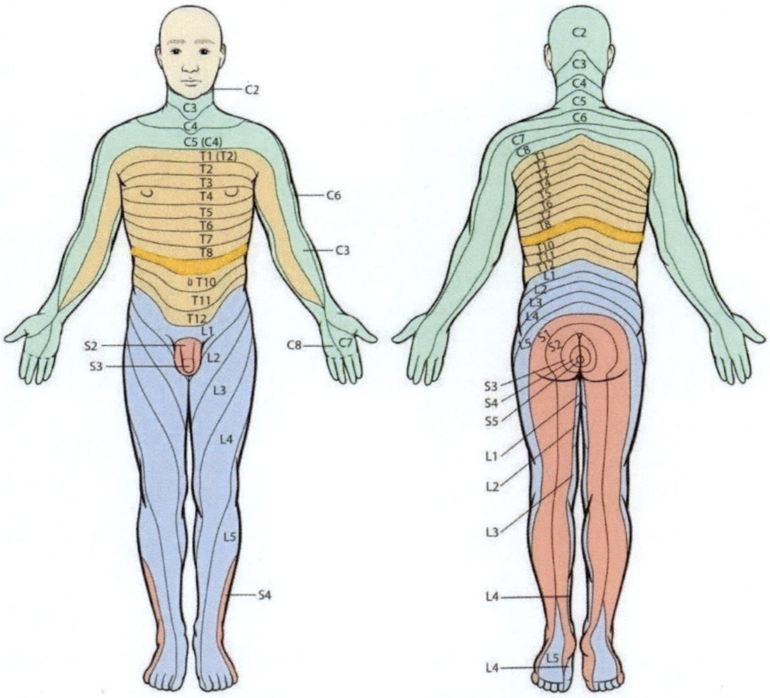

Figure 3.8 Dermatome of T9 (dark yellow)

The spinal root between T8-T9 becomes the intercostal nerve at this level and supplies the intercostal muscles at that level plus the rectus and obliquus Abdominus muscles. The dermatome is, as you would expect, to girdle around the torso at its level.

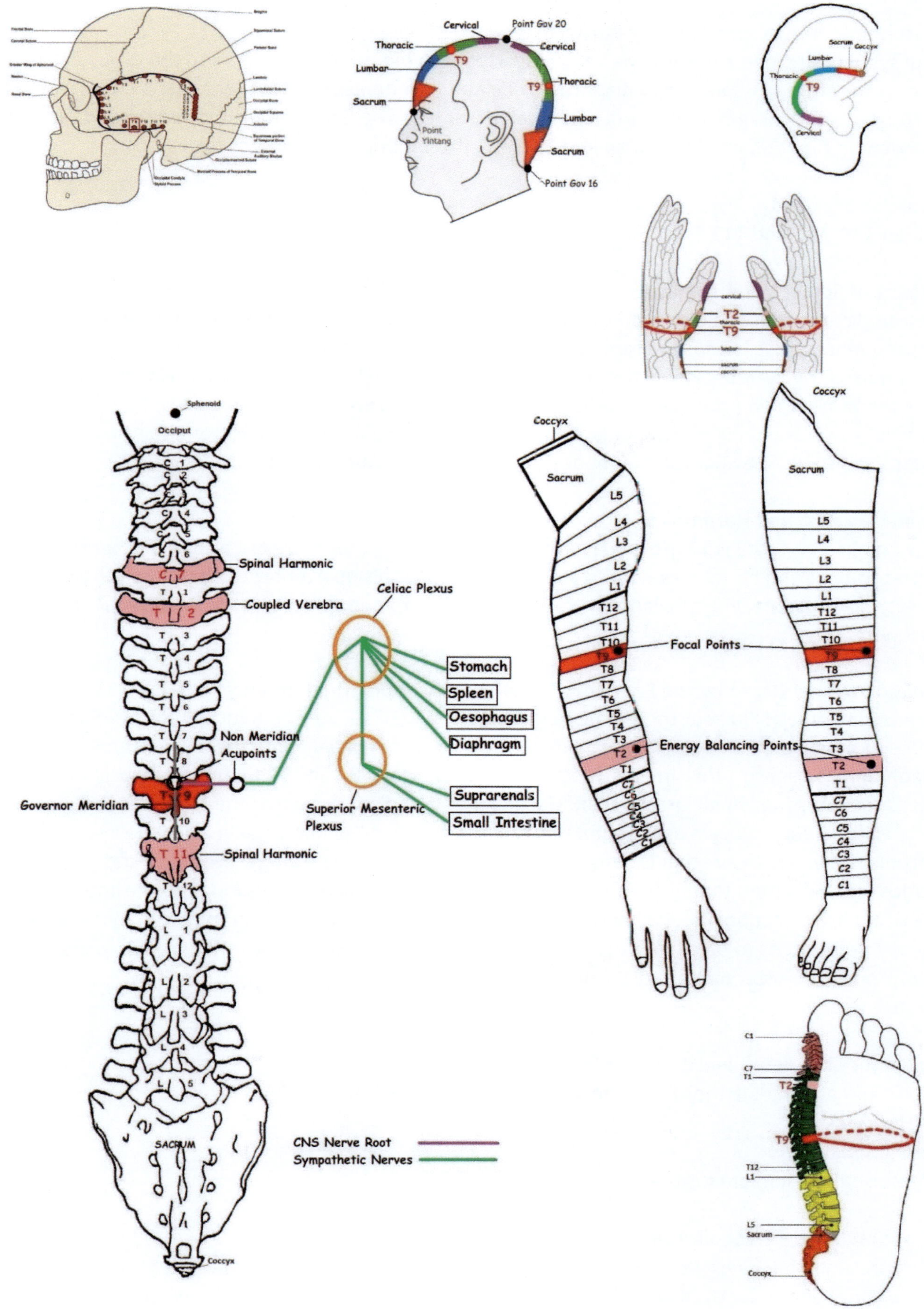

Reflections and Associations of Thoracic 9

Autonomic Nerves and links to internal organs
The sympathetic nerve outflow via the paravertebral sympathetic chain flow to the Celiac Plexus to supply the stomach, spleen and diaphragm plus the lower end of the oesophagus as it passes through the diaphragm at the cardiac sphincter. There is also links to the suprarenal glands and the duodenum (upper part of the small intestine) via the Superior Mesenteric Plexus.

Muscles Supplied
As per T10, T11 and T12

Effects of Spinal Misalignment
You would doubtless be surprised to read that misalignment of this vertebra can have severe consequences. Disc lesions are rare in the thoracic spine but, when they do occur, this is the most common as the vertebra lies in the centre of the most common type of congenital roto-scoliosis and therefore is compromised more than any other level. This level also has many 'bunched' spinal nerves at the beginning of the cauda equina. Therefore, lesions at this level tend to give radicular symptoms such as leg pain and numbness, muscular spasm and weakness.

Spinal Couples and Harmonics
The coupled vertebra is T2. However, this level is strange in that there are also two other levels that act as couples and harmonics – these are at C7 and T11. This quartet represents a very 'powerful' energetic foursome and imbalance with T9 may be due to energetic forces from the others – see below.

Linked Internal Organ by the Energetic System and Acupuncture Influence
There is no official link, but there is no doubt in my mind of seeing conditions at this level for many years of practice that lesions here can lead to severe oesophageal pain, Gourd symptoms and diaphragmatic spasm. This, in part, is due to the influence of C7 and T2 (and their association with the Large Intestine, Small Intestine and Gall Bladder meridians as well as the Throat chakra). As well as specific abdominal pain and spasm, this can also affect the whole body in giving nausea and chronic tiredness. This region is defined as a 'sacred' space in the esoteric literature and you will notice in the diagram that both the central line and the inner line 'Bladder' points are both non-meridian 'extra' acupoints. Traditional medicines such as acupuncture and shiatsu do not want any 'heavy' treatments to take place here as the originators realised that the inner economy could be compromised – osteopaths and physiotherapists
please note!

Posterior Chakra Influence
The upper and middle thoracic spine are influenced by the Heart chakra

Reflections
Please see the diagram for these

Emotional and Personality Link
T9 represents the lowest vertebra associated with 'Feelings-Emotions' in the general look at the spine and is also associated with these in the detailed picture. It is also within the influence of the posterior aspect of the Heart chakra, therefore is associated with the heart when it comes to

emotions and feelings. With traumatic affairs of the heart, such as breakdown of long term relationships or being jilted, this region of the spine is often affected, giving disparate symptoms as scoliosis, muscle spasms, indigestion, diaphragmatic spasm, tiredness and sudden allergic reactions when they did not exist beforehand. This region of the spine is also involved in 'lack of spirit and courage', affecting those people who shy away from conflict of any kind.

Thoracic 8

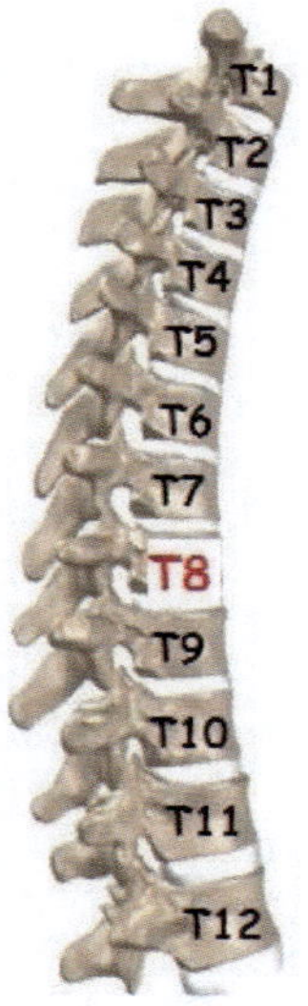

Figure 3.9 Anatomical position of T8 (lateral aspect)

Spinal Nerve and Dermatome

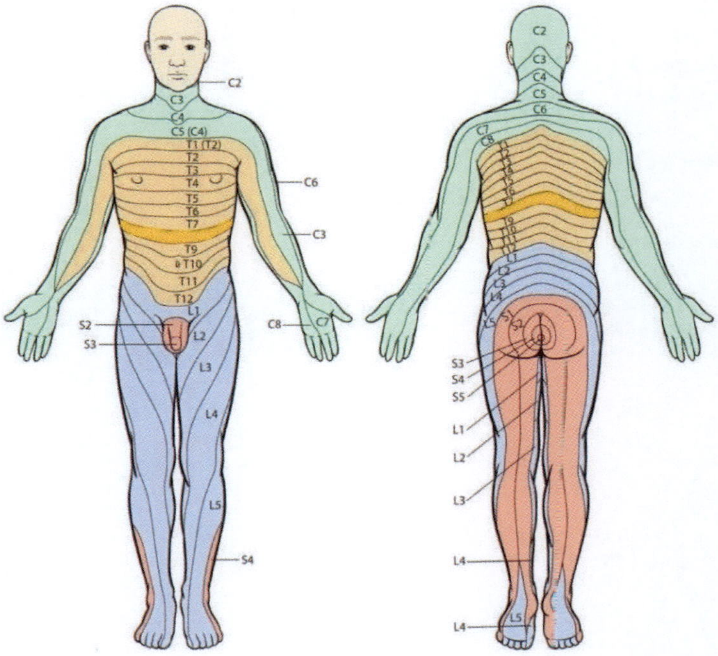

Figure 3.10 Dermatome of T8 (in bold yellow)

The nerve root of T7-8 becomes the intercostal nerve at this level and supplies the obliquus abdominal muscles and a section of the erector spinae. The dermatome girdles the torso at the level of the vertebra.

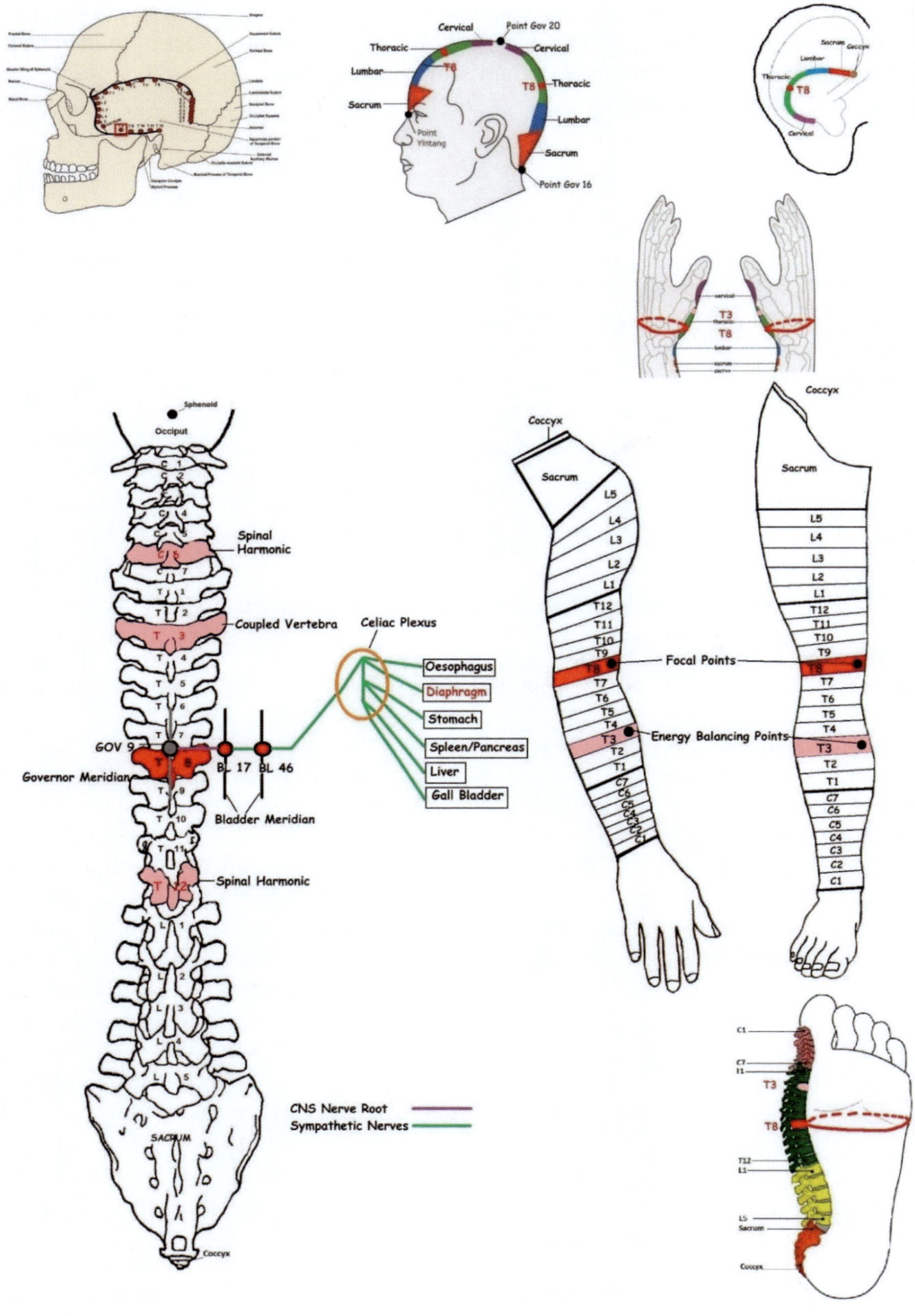

Reflections and Associations of Thoracic 8

Autonomic Nerve and Organs Supplied

The sympathetic outflow from T7-8 flows via the paravertebral sympathetic chain supplies the oesophagus, stomach, spleen, pancreas, liver and gall bladder via the Celiac Plexus. There is also a sympathetic supply to part of the diaphragm (see below)

Muscles Supplied

As per the other thoracic vertebrae

Effects of Spinal Misalignment

This vertebra is commonly affected by the many types of scoliosis (see description on T9) and may cause internal organic imbalance as well as hip and leg pain referral. Due to its relationship with the spleen, symptoms may also include lethargy and auto immune imbalance. Hiccoughs are often symptomatic of problems at this level.

Spinal Couples and Harmonics

The true spinal couple is T3, but there are spinal harmonics at C6 and T12, representing a powerful quartet in energy medicine treatments.

Linked Internal Organs by the Energetic System

The inner and outer Bladder line points of BL 17 and BL 46 give their energy supply to the Diaphragm. Although the diaphragm muscle is supplied by T7, T8 and T9, it is T8 that is the most powerful. In my humble opinion, more diaphragmatic spasms, Gourd, oesophageal spasm and other similar symptoms are caused by conditions affecting T7, T8 and T9 than any other reason – except stress related ones. Knowledge of this by doctors would save money in patients not having to buy indigestion remedies.

Acupuncture Influence

As with most of the other thoracic spine the Governor and Bladder meridians affect this vertebra

Reflections

The girdle reflected region on both the foot and hand is, naturally, around the centre of each. The diaphragm reflex is positioned in the middle of this line on the foot and hand. Also, on this line, at approximately the same point is acupuncture point KI 1.

Emotional Personality Links

T8 is linked with 'Feelings and Emotions' on both the general and detailed picture. It is also within the influence of the posterior aspect of the Heart chakra, therefore is associated with the heart when it comes to emotions and feelings. With traumatic affairs of the heart, such as breakdown of long term relationships or being jilted, this region of the spine is often affected, giving disparate symptoms as scoliosis, muscle spasms, indigestion, diaphragmatic spasm, tiredness and sudden allergic reactions when they did not exist beforehand. This region of the spine is also involved in 'lack of spirit and courage', affecting those people who shy away from conflict of any kind.

Thoracic 7

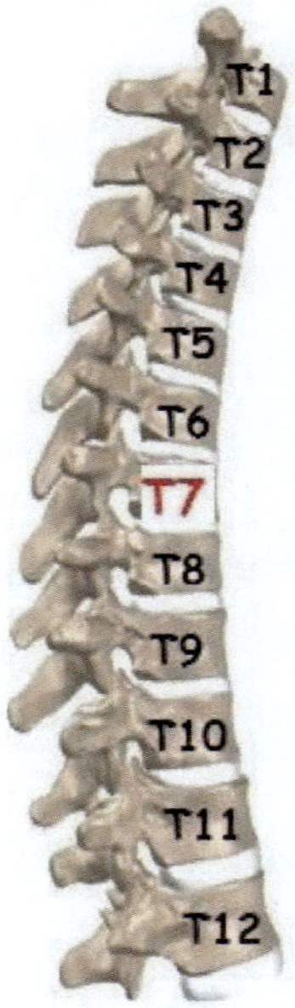

Figure 3.11 Anatomical Position of T7 (lateral view)

T7 and T6 represent the middle of the thoracic spine, and, as such are significant.

Spinal Nerve and Dermatome

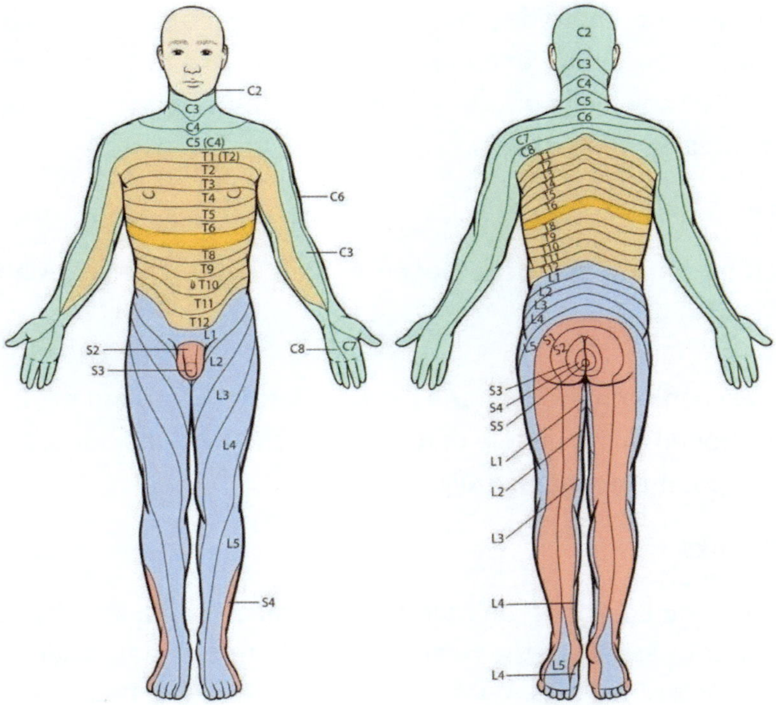

Figure 3.12 Dermatome of T7 (in bold yellow)

The nerve root of T6-7 becomes the intercostal nerve at this level and the dermatome girdles the middle of the chest.

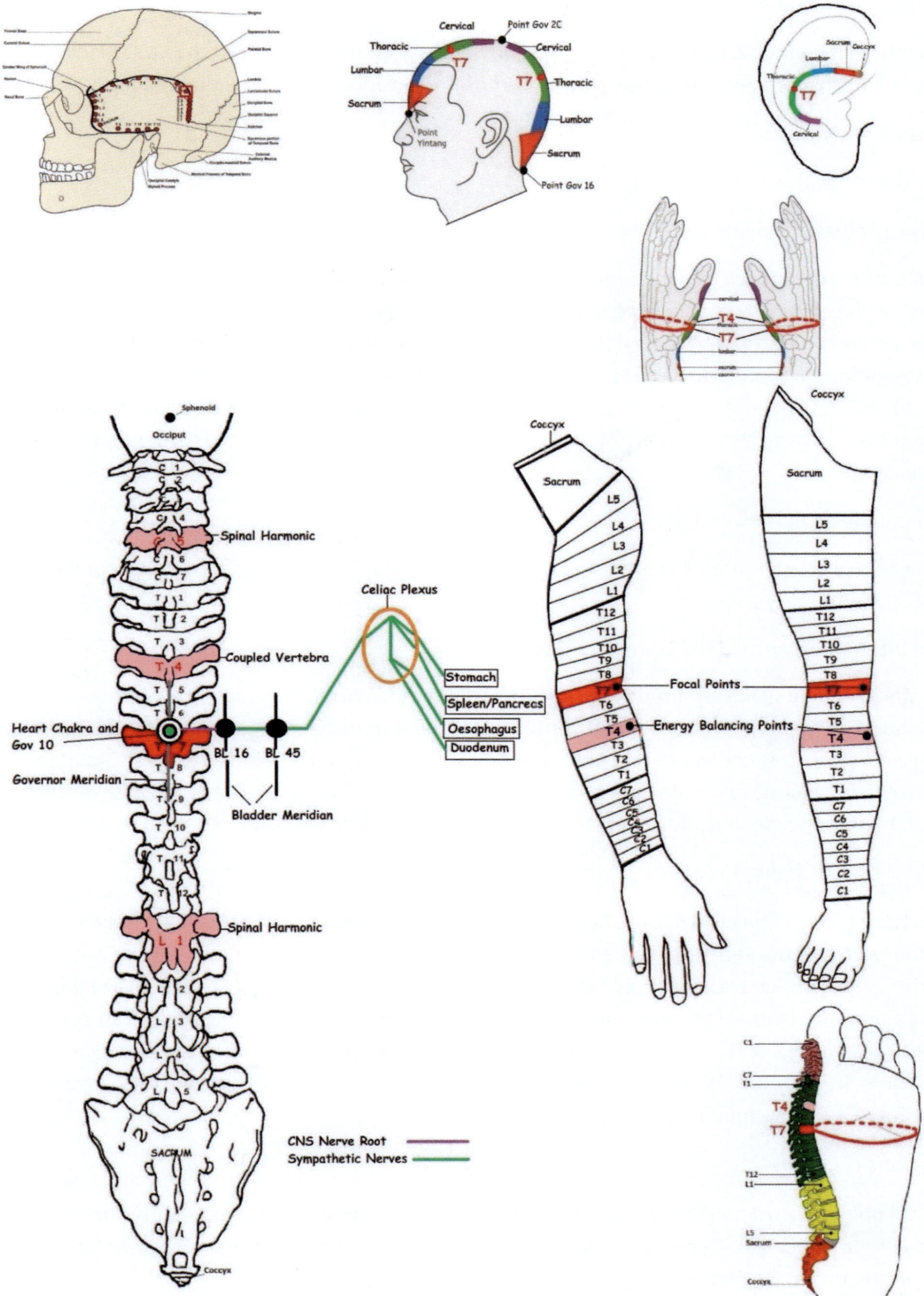

Reflections and Associations of Thoracic 7

Autonomic Nerve and Organs Supplied

The sympathetic outflow from T6-7 flows from the parasympathetic chain via the Celiac Plexus to supply the stomach, spleen, pancreas, lower part of the oesophagus and the duodenum.

Muscles Supplied

As per the other thoracic vertebrae

Effects of Spinal Misalignment

T7 falls within the classical scoliosis region and any deviation of the vertebra that impinges on the nerve flow may give rise to such symptoms as heartburn, dyspepsia and gastric reflux. In the chronic condition, as the main nerve flow is to the pancreas, it could be instrumental in the start of diabetes, although there also needs to be the correct chemical and emotional imbalance that accompanies it. Great pressure may be felt in the Solar Plexus region with anomalies at this level and give rise to sensations of 'butterflies' and anxiety that may not be sourced from emotional imbalance.

Spinal Couples and Harmonics

The main coupled vertebra (that is used in body reflexology) is T4. Other harmonic vertebrae are C5 and L1.

Linked internal organs via the energetic system

Although BL 16 and BL 45 are used extensively to treat internal organic imbalance, neither is a true Back Transporting point as it is often attributed to the Governor meridian as its energy focus. I have never understood this and yet to find anyone who can explain it to me. Similarly, Gov 10 is used extensively in respiratory problems associated with scoliosis and kyphosis but, strangely, is said to be forbidden to needle. It is, however, compensated by its affects with acupressure (see below)

Posterior Major Chakra influence

The posterior Heart Chakra is situated at Gov 10 (T6-T7). Its anterior equivalent is situated at Con 17 in the centre of the sternum. This a powerful point in that it has many emotional and physical symptoms that may be treated here. The Heart chakra is linked energetically to the Solar Plexus and, as a duo may be used for many internal organic conditions affecting the stomach, spleen, pancreas, liver, lungs and heart, circulation, middle aspect of the lymphatic system as well as the vagus nerve. Its emotional links are anxiety, tearfulness, affairs of the heart, being inconsolable, cannot forgive others but also excess compassion and empathy.

Reflections

The focal points of arm and leg reflex horizontal zones lie on the great toe and thumb sides. They are close together so a better way of energy balancing the reflected points may be with the foot to hand, or the arm to leg etc.

Emotions and Personality Links

T7 lies within the 'Feelings – Emotion' region of the spine both in the general and detailed picture. It therefore deals with affairs of the heart and love – also cowardice, diffidence and those that one would consider to be 'spineless'. The whole region from T5 down to T9 deals with 'affairs of the heart' but this vertebra is the central and most important one. Strong emotions that become chronic often lead to palpitations, angina as well as some cardiac conditions.

Thoracic 6

And so, we reach the upper half of both the thoracic spine as well as the whole spine if you include the two cranial bones. T6 and T7 represent the very centre of the spine and, as such, are pivotally significant.

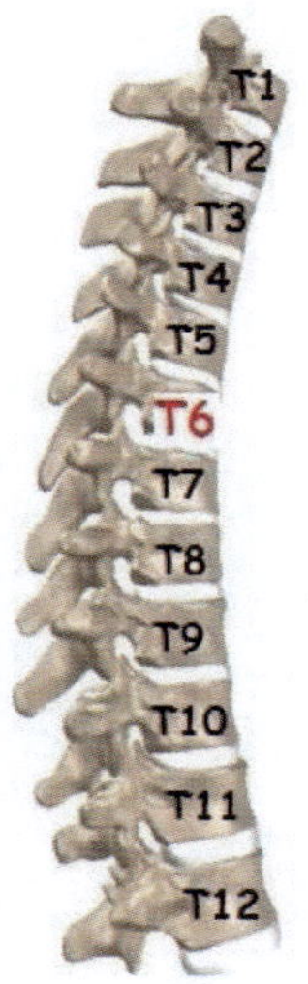

Figure 3.13 Anatomical Position of T6 (lateral view)

Spinal Nerve and Dermatome

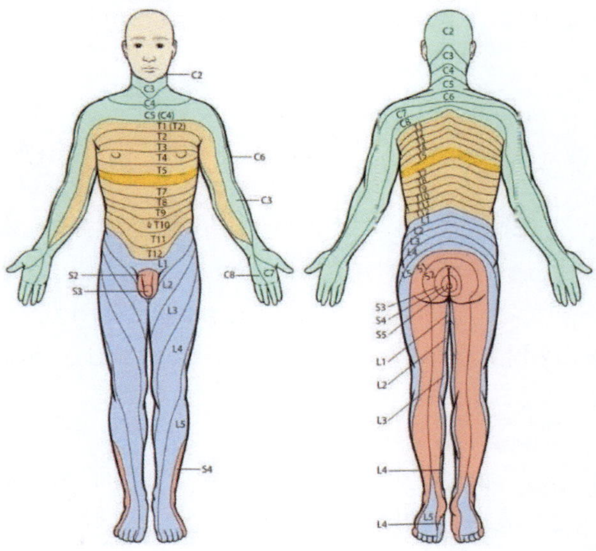

Figure 3.14 T6 Dermatome (in bold yellow)

The nerve root at this level becomes the intercostal nerve and the dermatome girdles the chest at this horizontal level

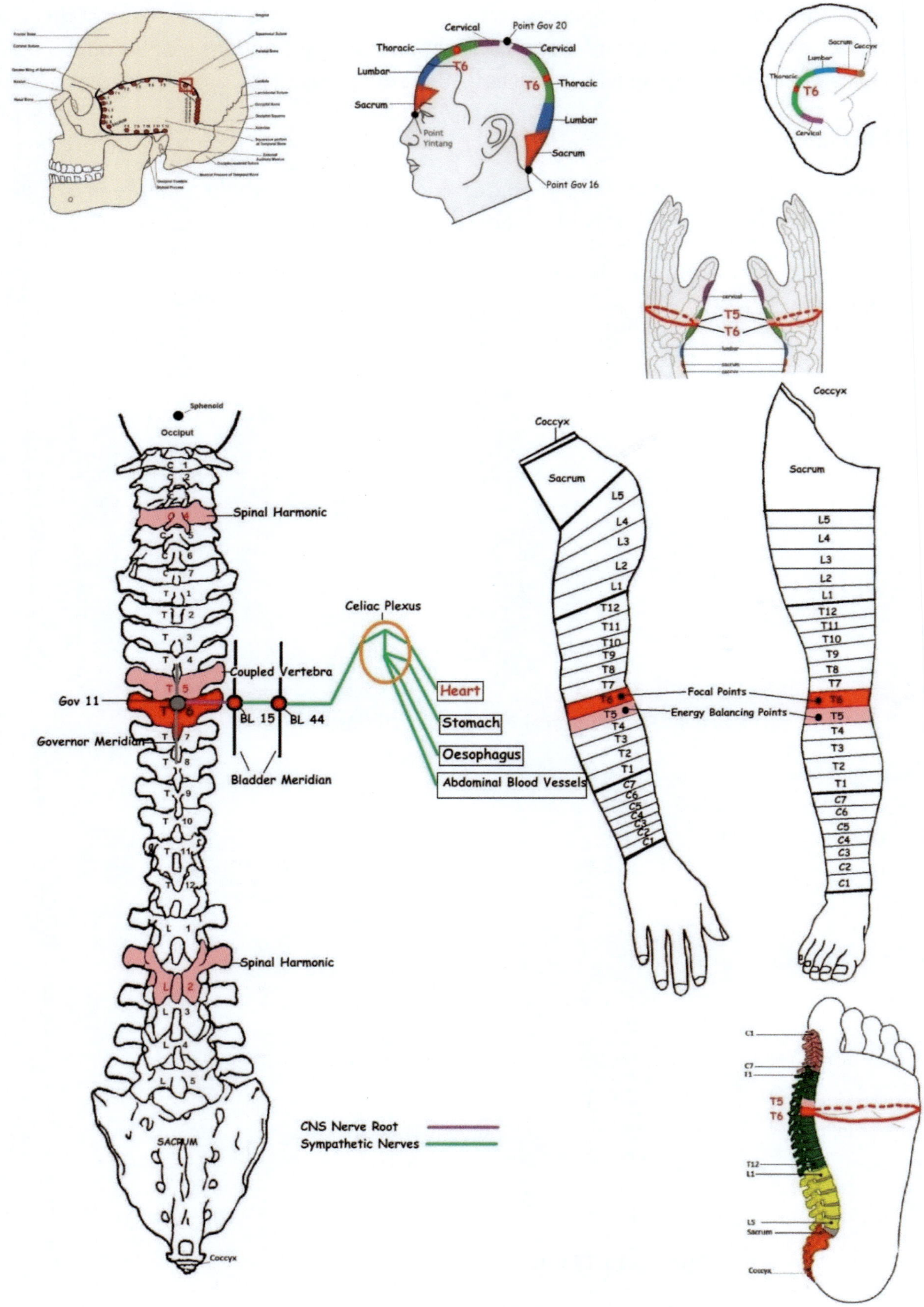

Reflections and Associations of Thoracic 6

Autonomic Nerves and Organs Supplied

The sympathetic outflow from T5 and T6 flows to the Celiac plexus via the sympathetic chain. The organs supplied are the heart, stomach, upper part of the oesophagus and the abdominal blood vessels.

Muscles Supplied

As per the other thoracic vertebrae

Effects of Spinal Misalignment

Misalignment due to acute trauma or chronic instability due to scoliosis or kyphosis may lead to some internal organic imbalance. These would include indigestion, dyspepsia, heartburn, cardiac sphincter spasm (upper oesophagus), diaphragmatic tension, nervous tension, anxiety syndromes, stomach ulcers, cardiac conditions including palpitation.

Spinal Couple and Harmonics

The true spinal couple is adjacent to T6, at T5. If this presents a problem when treating the foot or hand reflexes, then place the finger of one hand on the foot and the other on the leg (or hand and arm). This will be covered in Part Two. The spinal harmonics are C4 and L2.

Linked Internal Organ via the energetic system

The Back-Transporting Point at T5-T6 - BL 15 (and its outer Bladder Line partner BL 44), affect the Heart and, as such, are used, together with Gov 11 to treat conditions associated with the heart. These may be physical or emotional.

Posterior Major Chakra Influence

This level is strongly influenced by the Heart chakra, and some authorities place the posterior Heart chakra exactly at this level instead of T6-T7. Therefore, when using acupressure, it is wise to use a finger or hand spread on this area of the spine to confidently affect the chakra.

Reflections

As previously stated, the spinal couples are adjacent to each other. Therefore, in practice where the reflected point needs to energy balanced with its couple, you may balance one on the foot, the other on the hand, or a combination of the four areas.

Emotional and Personality Links

T6 lies in 'Feelings and Emotions' in both overall and detailed picture. It therefore deals with affairs of the heart as per its adjacent vertebrae. This level is also associated with acute and chronic anxiety, 'butterflies', sweating, panic attacks, palpitations and stress. As stated before this vertebra is also the midpoint of the spine and may be affected, giving physical symptoms, from family related tensions, especially if there is little communication in the family with subsequent tension. I have seen very many T6 lesions that have been caused by family tensions. When chronic unhappiness occurs, a burden is placed on the Celiac Plexus via the sympathetic nervous system. This, in turn, may produce anxiety syndromes of various types. As previously stated, T6 and T7 represent the centre of the spine and, emotionally, act the same as any other centred joints e.g. elbow and knee. This includes emotional symptoms of diffidence, not knowing which way to turn or being stuck in a rut.

Thoracic 5

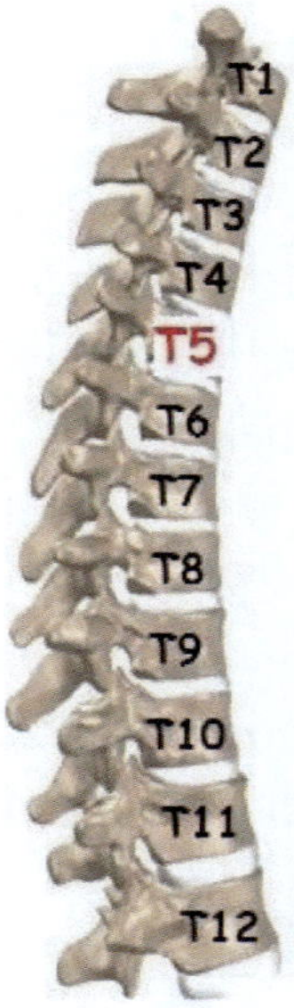

Figure 3.15 Anatomical position of T5 (lateral view)

Spinal Nerve and Dermatome

The nerve root between T4 and T5 becomes the intercostal nerve at this level and the dermatome girdles the trunk at this horizontal level.

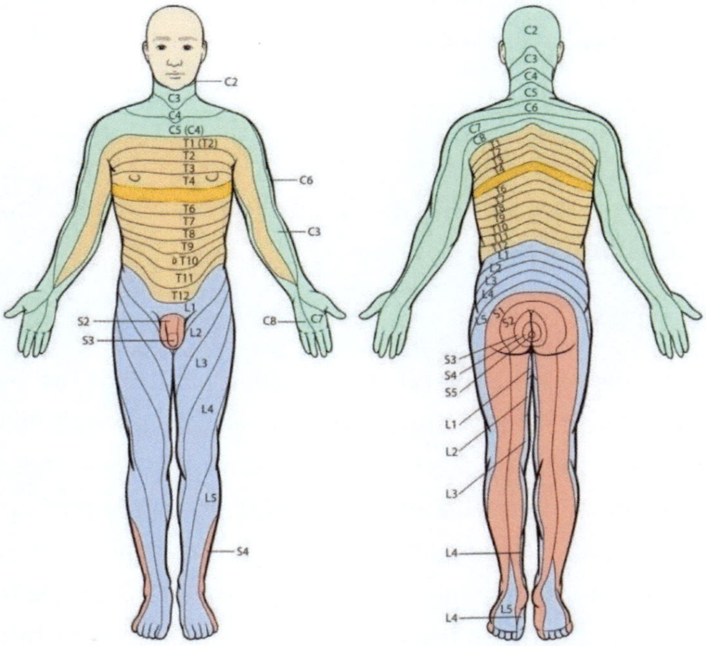

Figure 3.16 Dermatome of T5 (in bold yellow)

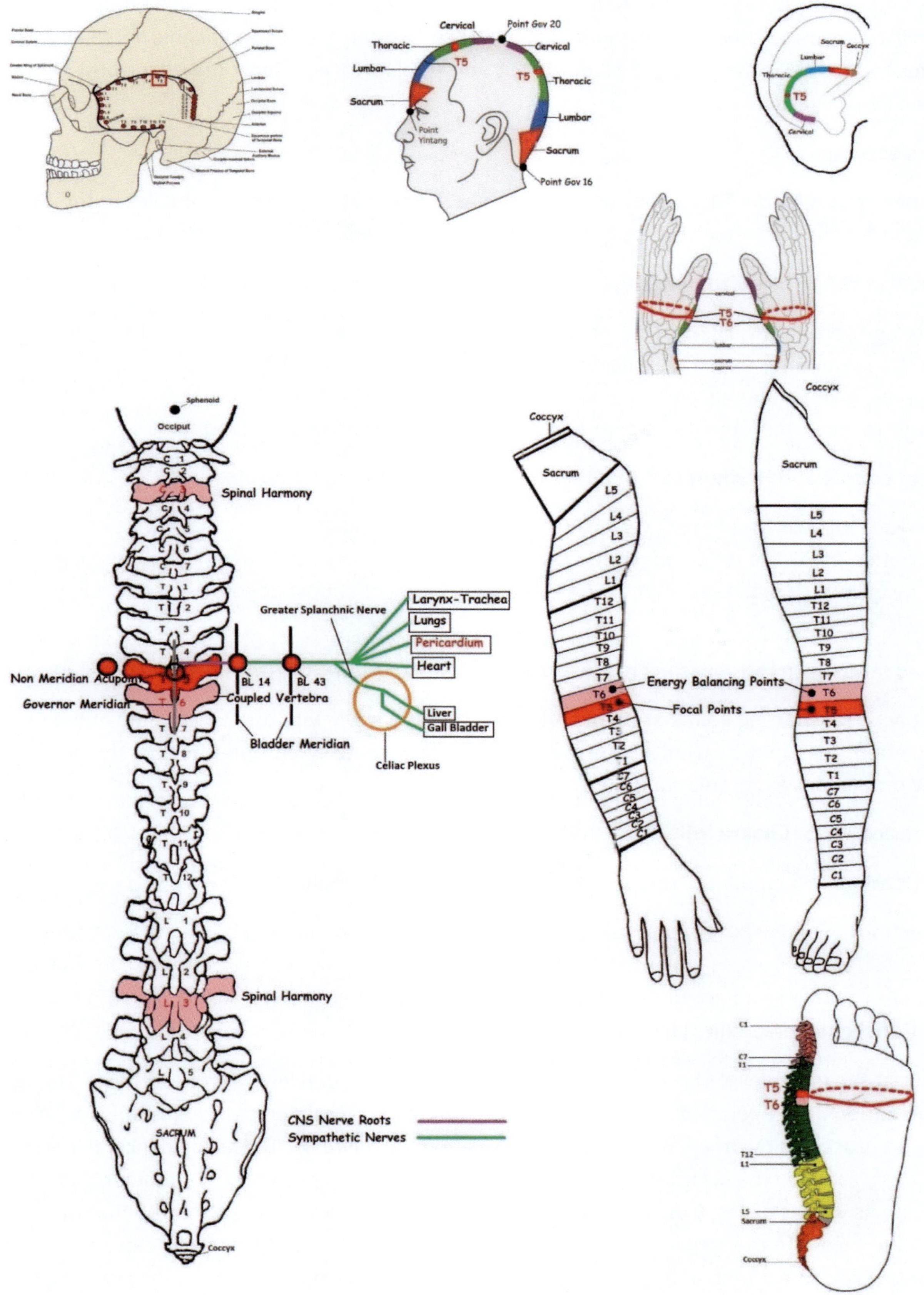

Reflections and Associations of Thoracic 5

Autonomic Nerve and Organs Supplied

The sympathetic nerve from T4-T5 flows via the paravertebral sympathetic chain either directly to supply the larynx, trachea, pericardium and heart; and via the greater Splanchnic nerve and Celiac Plexus to supply the liver and gall bladder. This vertebral level represents the uppermost influence by the Celiac Plexus.

Muscles Supplied

The motor nerve from T4-T5 becomes the intercostal nerve at that level. Anomalies to the nerve could affect the tranversus thoracis, serratus posterior as well as the Sacrospinalis.

Effects of Spinal Misalignment

Acute and chronic misalignments, ranging from scoliosis to road traffic accidents, may give disparate symptoms as the neural and energy supplies are so varied. These include acute liver and pancreas, fever, anaemia, poor circulation, lethargy and 'tired all the time' syndrome (TATS), chronic fatigue syndrome (CFS), poor blood circulation and respiratory conditions.

Spinal Couple and Harmonics

The true couple is its adjacent vertebra T6 and the harmonics are C3 and L3. As with the description of T6, the reflected points, zones and areas are very close together so need not be energy balanced on the same limb. This represents one of the most powerful vertebral harmonics there is.

Linked Internal Organs via the Energetic System

The Back-Transporting Points at BL 14 and BL 43 are associated with the Pericardium and Blood Circulation. They may be used with pressure or needle in acute symptoms affecting the pericardium or by using moxa in chronic conditions.

Posterior Major Chakra Influence

The Heart chakra influences this vertebra – same rules as T6 apply.

Reflections

Please see description of T6

Emotional and Personality Links

T5 lies at the lower level of both the overall and detailed vertebral level that represents 'Thought and Intuition'. The overall picture is 'Feelings – Emotions. Suppression of thoughts and intuitive thought processes by others may lead to complications at this level. These could include chest tightness, asthma type symptoms, muscular tension, circulation problems, general tension and lethargy as well as anger, frustration, anxiety, depression and low spirits. Also note that this vertebra is close to the centre of the thoracic spine and its harmonic twins being close to the centre of both cervical and lumbar spines. This is a 'perfect storm' for those folks who may be struggling with decision making and being stuck in a rut.

Thoracic 4

We are slowly creeping towards the very 'busy' part of the spinal column where nerve and energy flow proliferate.

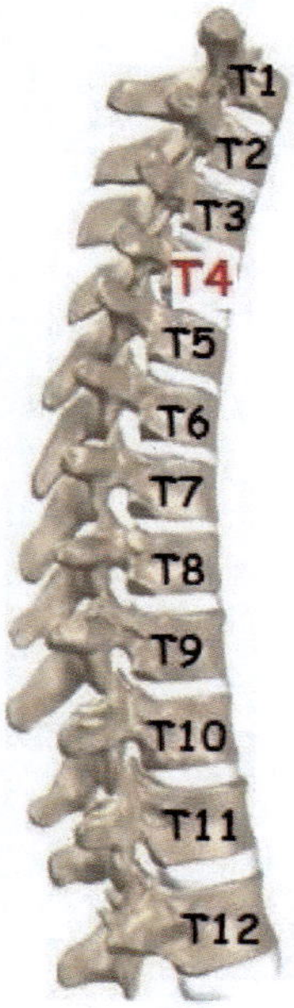

Figure 3.17 Anatomical position of T4 (lateral aspect)

Spinal Nerve and Dermatome

The spinal root from T3-T4 becomes the intercostal nerve that girdles the trunk at this level. The dermatome is around the trunk at roughly the level of the vertebra.

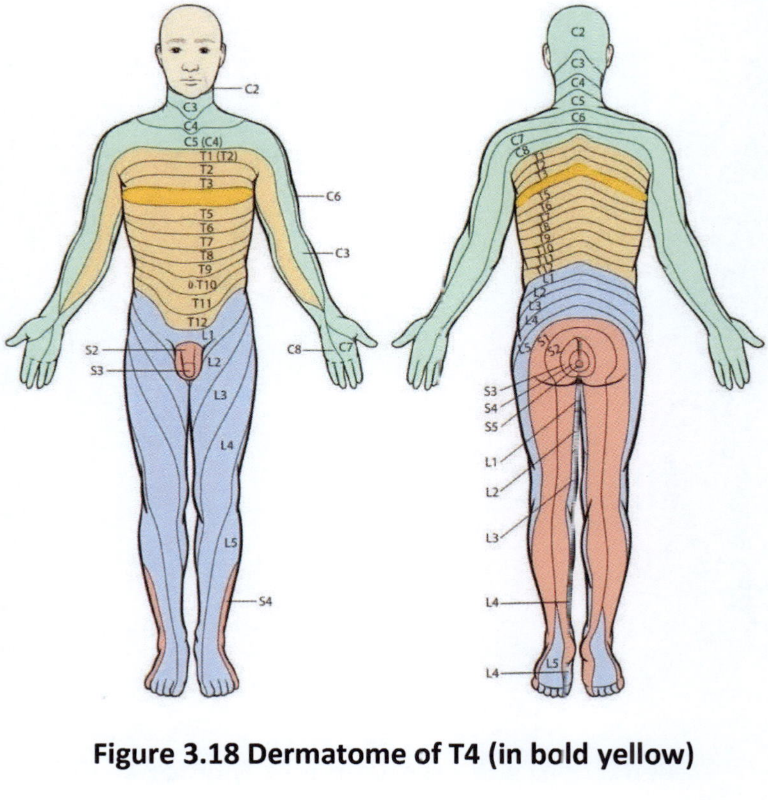

Figure 3.18 Dermatome of T4 (in bold yellow)

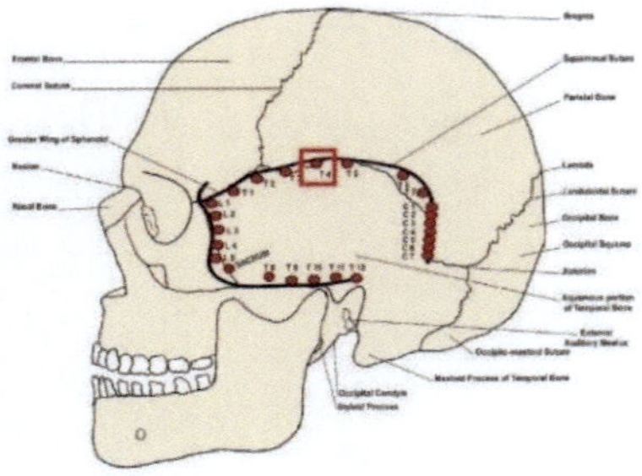

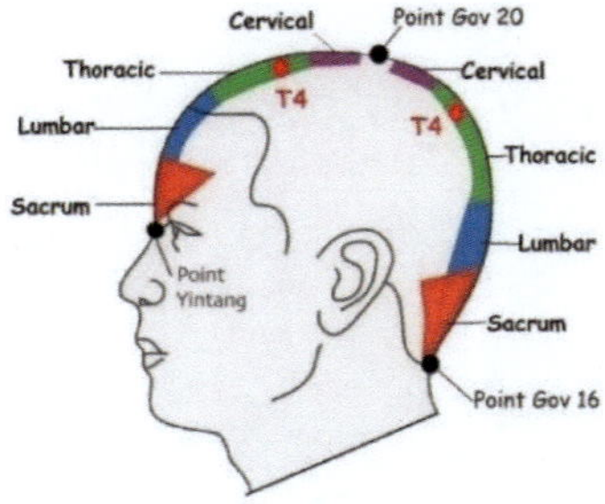

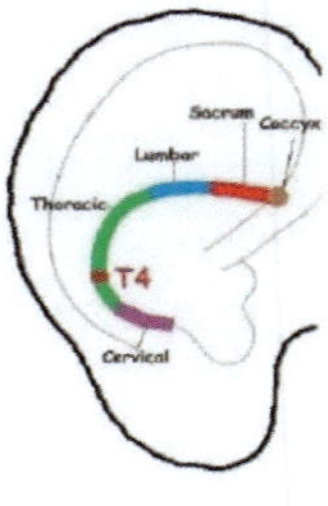

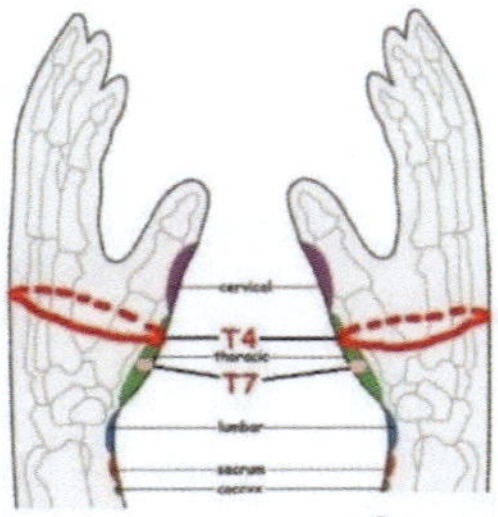

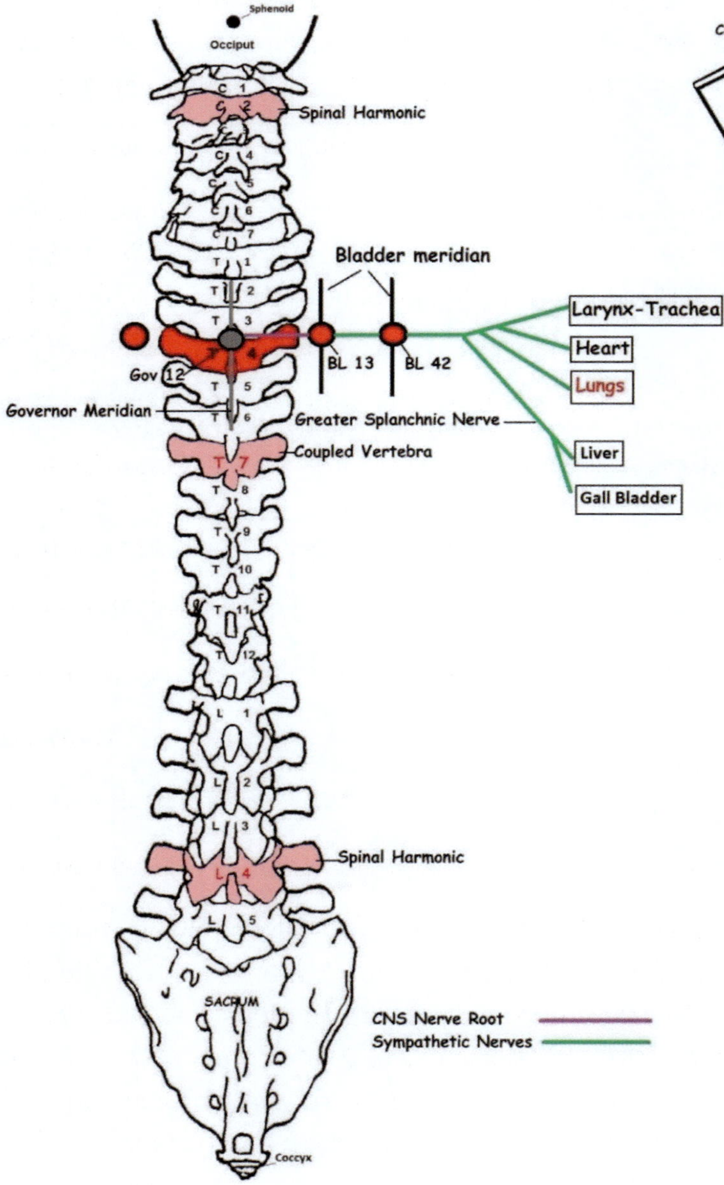

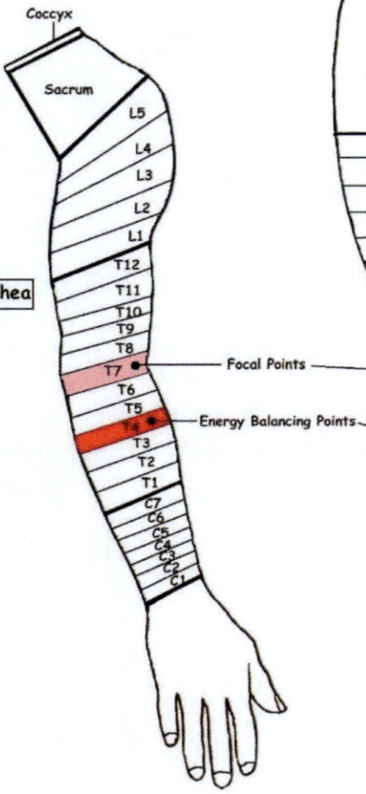

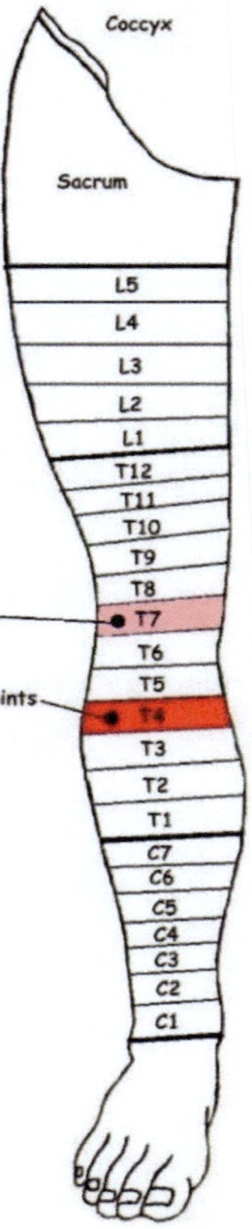

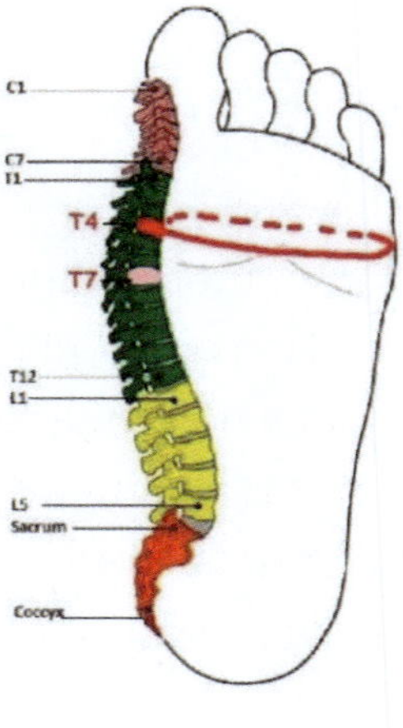

Reflections and Associations of Thoracic 4

Autonomic Nerve and Organs Supplied

The T3 – T4 level is the highest in the spine that does not include the Celiac Plexus. The sympathetic nerve flows via the paravertebral sympathetic chain to supply directly the larynx, trachea, heart and lungs and via the greater splanchnic nerve to supply the liver and gall bladder.

Muscles Supplied

Please see description for T5

Effects of Spinal Misalignment

As per T5, multiple and disparate symptoms are possible when this vertebra is affected either by spinal anomalies or trauma. Principle among these is the effect on the gall bladder, liver and common bile duct that may give rise to cholic pain or jaundice. Intercostal shingles is also quite common in susceptible patients with this lesion. Other symptoms can include chest tightness, dry and sore throat and circulatory problems. The very powerful Trapezius muscle may cause upper thoracic subluxations due to stress and subsequent muscle spasm.

Spinal Couple and Harmonics

The spinal couple is T7 with spinal harmonics at C2 and L4.

Linked Internal Organ via the Energetic Systems

BL 13 and BL 42 are the inner and outer bladder line points and are the Back-Supporting Points that energetically supply the Lungs. These points, together with Gov 12 are excellent acupoints by needle, pressure, magnets or moxa in the treatment of acute and chronic respiratory conditions.

Posterior Major Chakra Influence

This vertebral level is influenced by both the Heart and Throat chakras so will strongly influence the emotional aetiology.

Reflections

Please note that the reflected regions on the hands, feet and limbs are a little further apart from each other so the respective focal points may be utilised on the same part of the body.

Emotional and Personality Links

T4 lies within the 'Feelings – Emotion' in the overall picture and 'Thought - Intuition' in the detailed aspect. This means that some emotional symptoms may be caused by suppression of these. If this occurs as a child, it can produce an upper scoliosis. Tension in the throat region, tightness in the chest and breathing difficulties may also arise. As T4 is influence by both the Throat and Heart chakra, this may produce expression difficulties as well as affairs of the heart. Other emotional symptoms include anxiety, anger, rage, depression, melancholia, grief and bowel irregularities because of these imbalances.

Thoracic 3

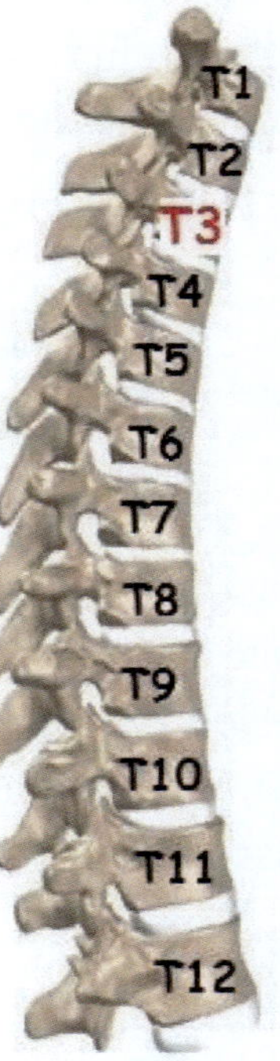

Figure 3.19 Anatomical position of T3

Spinal Nerve and Dermatome

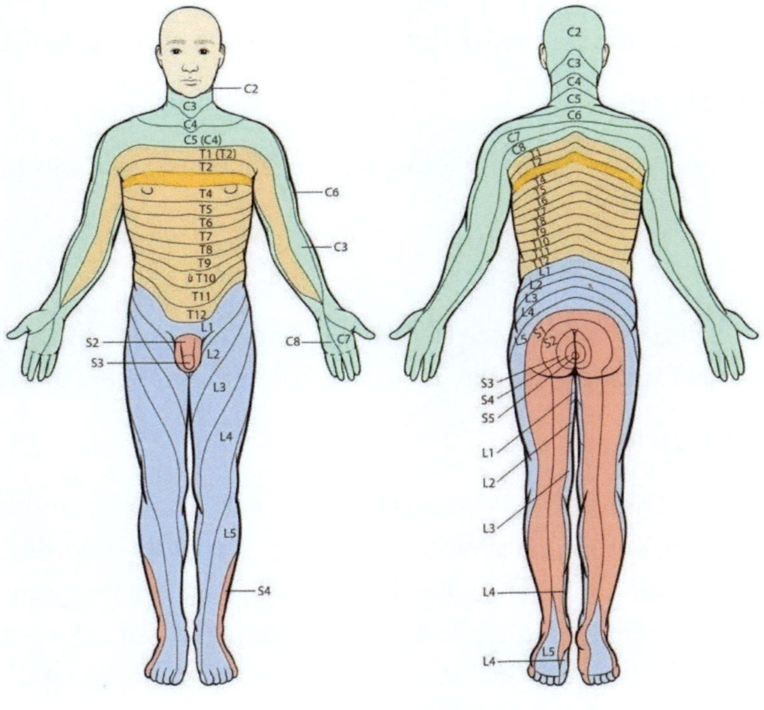

Figure 3.20 Dermatome of T3 (in bold yellow)

The spinal nerve between T2-T3 becomes the intercostal nerve at that level and the dermatome girdles the chest at the same horizontal level.

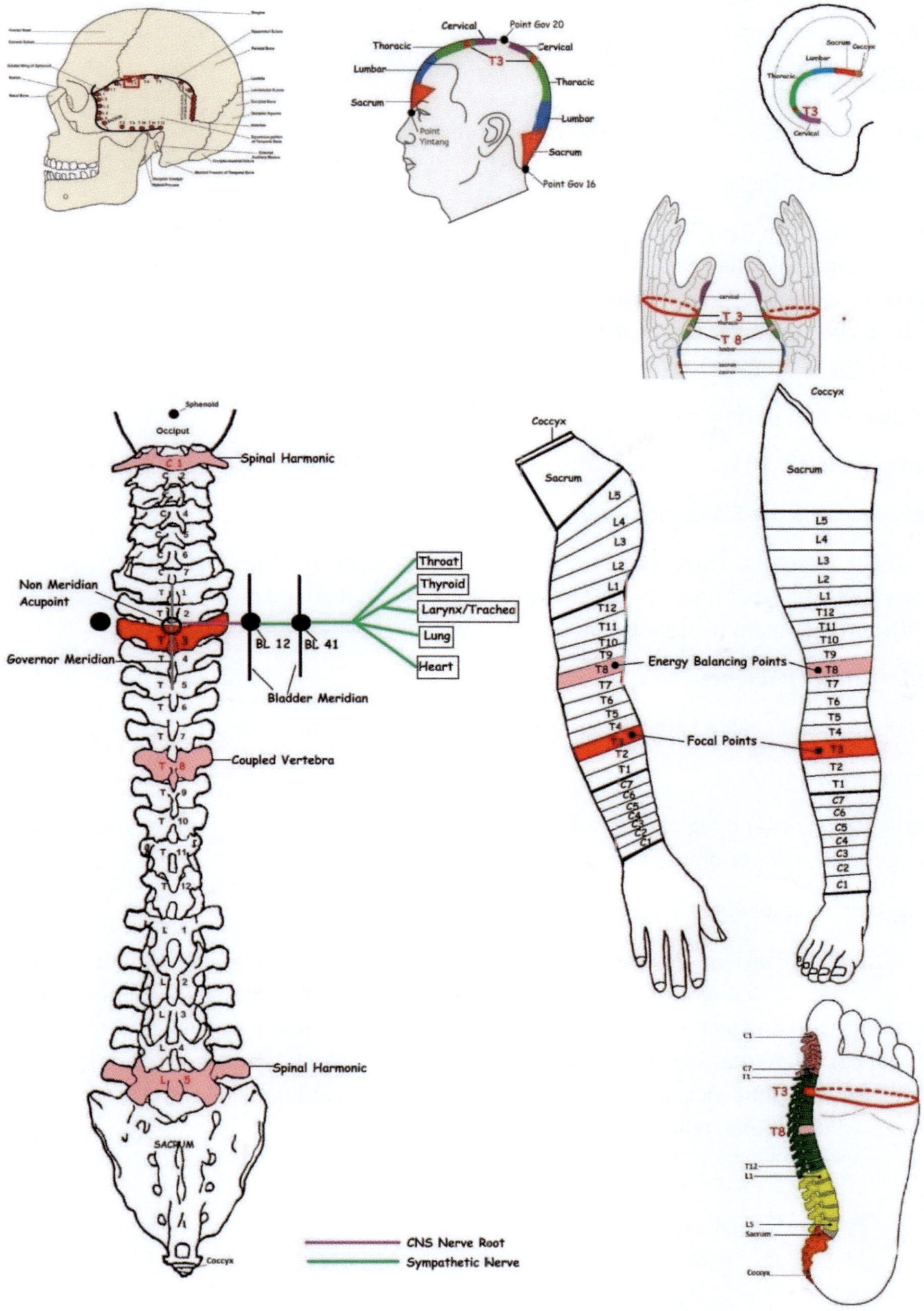

Reflections and Associations of Thoracic 3

Autonomic Nerve and Organs Supplied

The sympathetic nerves flow via the paravertebral sympathetic chain to supply the throat, thyroid, larynx, trachea, bronchial tubes, pleura, lungs and the upper aspect of the heart.

Muscles Supplied

Please see description for the other thoracic vertebrae

Effects of Spinal Misalignment

T3 is usually too high to be involved in a scoliosis, but it can be the upper end of a kyphosis and have strain placed on the vertebra with subsequent effects on the nerve and energy flow. It may be involved in trauma as in a crush injury. This vertebra deals with everything concerned with respiration and symptoms can be bronchitis, pleurisy, acute or chronic chest congestion, sore throat and thyroid imbalance.

Spinal Couple and Harmonic

The spinal couple is T8 and the two harmonic levels are at C1 and L5.

Linked Organs via the Energetic System

BL 12 and BL 41 are the acupoints associated with this vertebra, but they aren't true back Supporting Points. Treatment of these two points, though, is directed at lung energy and all the other associated organs mentioned above.

Posterior Chakra Influence

Although the Heart chakra has some influence at this level, it is the Throat chakra that is dominant

Reflections

The reflected points and regions are sufficiently far apart from each other that the focal points may be energetically balance on the same limb or digit.

Emotional and Personality Link

T3 lies within the 'Feelings – Emotion' area of the general spine and 'Thought – Intuition' as an individual vertebra. This vertebra is therefore physically affected by suppression of intuitional thought processes and by the inability to show emotions and feelings – hence its strong link with the Throat chakra. As a 2-way action, physical effects on this vertebra may lead to emotional imbalance such as diffidence, anxiety, shyness, stubbornness and tearfulness. These are the types of patients who cry when telling symptoms.

Thoracic 2

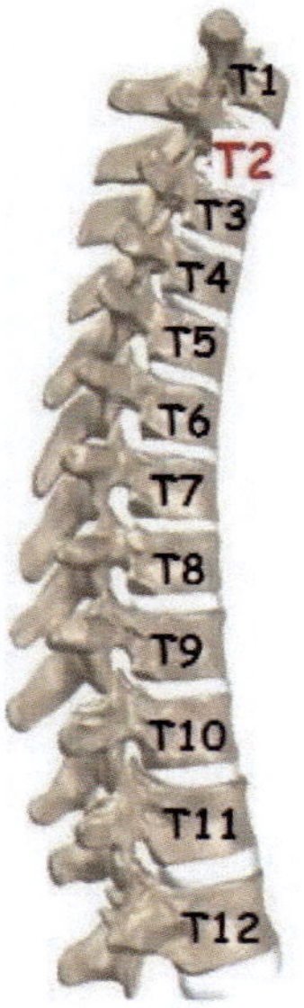

Figure 3.21 Anatomical Position of C2 (lateral aspect)

Please not how different the spinous process is compared with the middle to lower thoracic vertebrae

Spinal Nerve and Dermatome

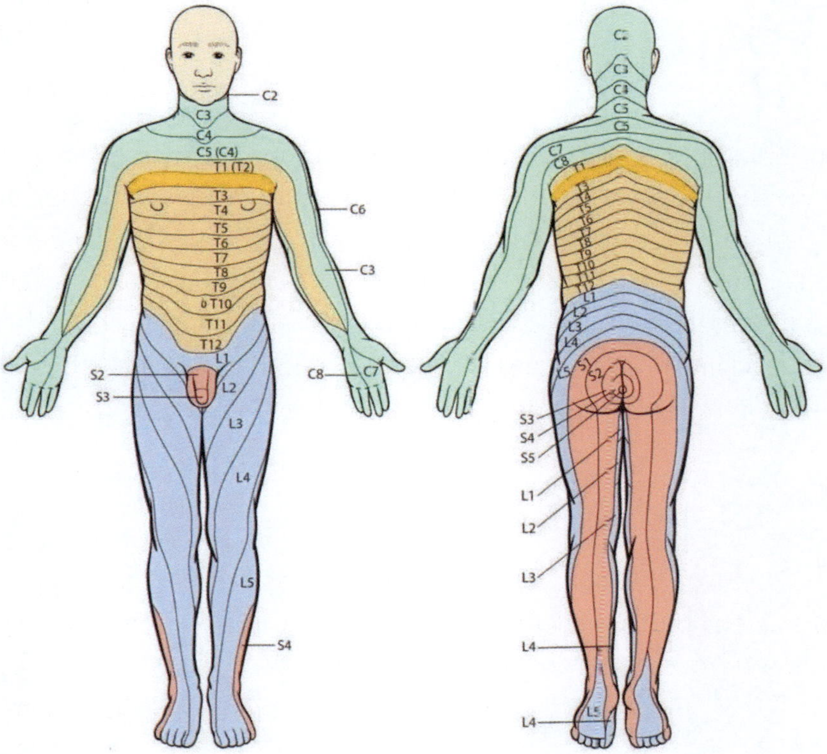

Figure 3.22 Dermatome of T2 (in bold yellow)

The spinal nerve emerging between T1 – T2 becomes the intercostal nerve at this level and the dermatome girdles the upper part of the chest.

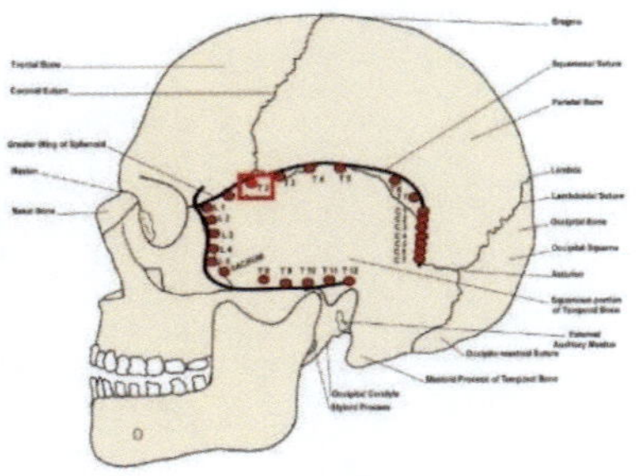

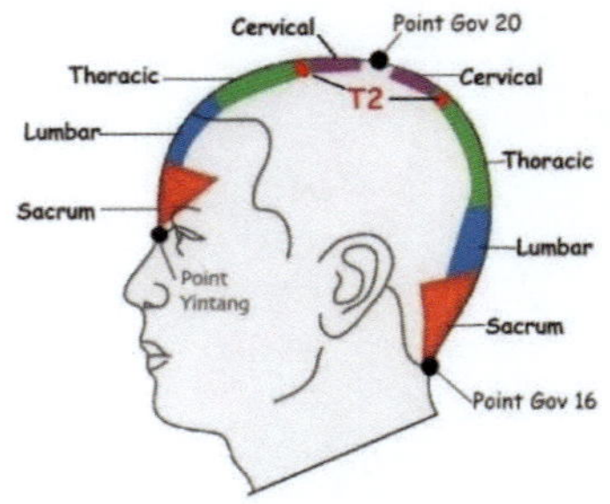

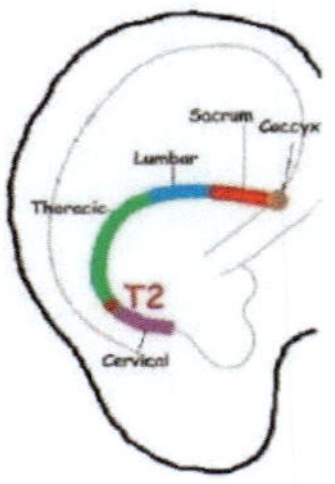

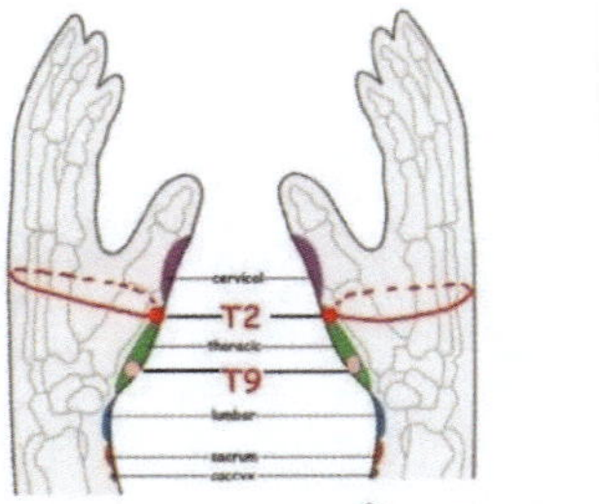

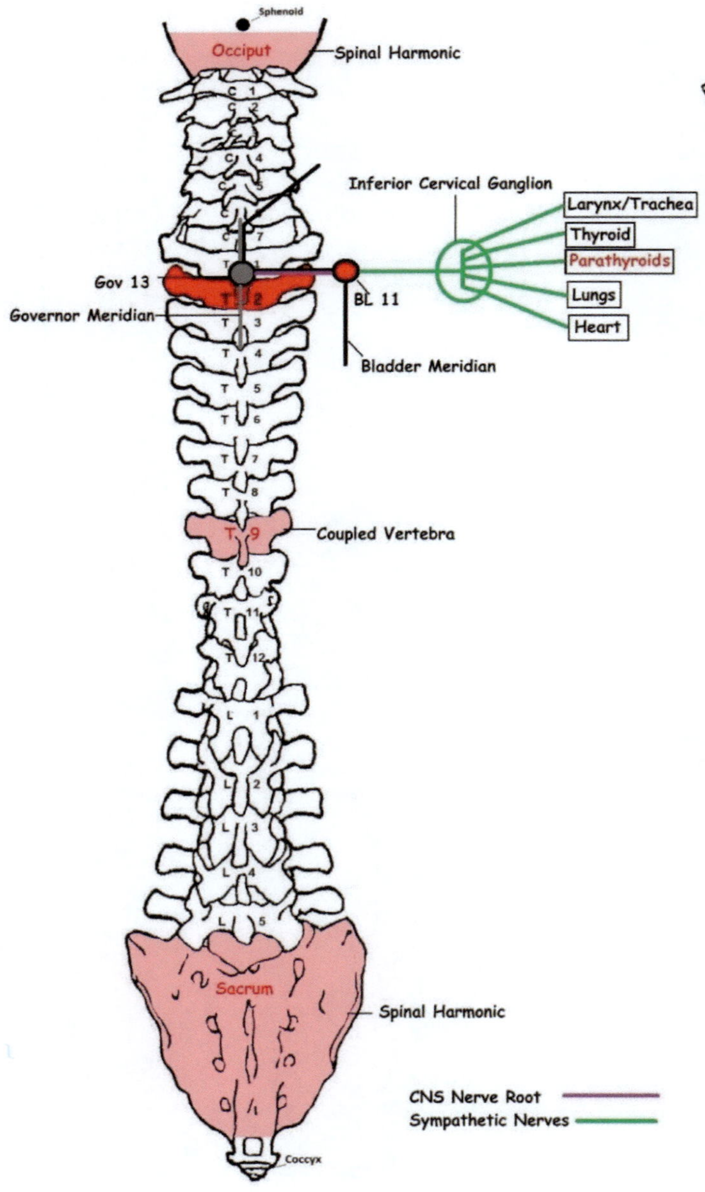

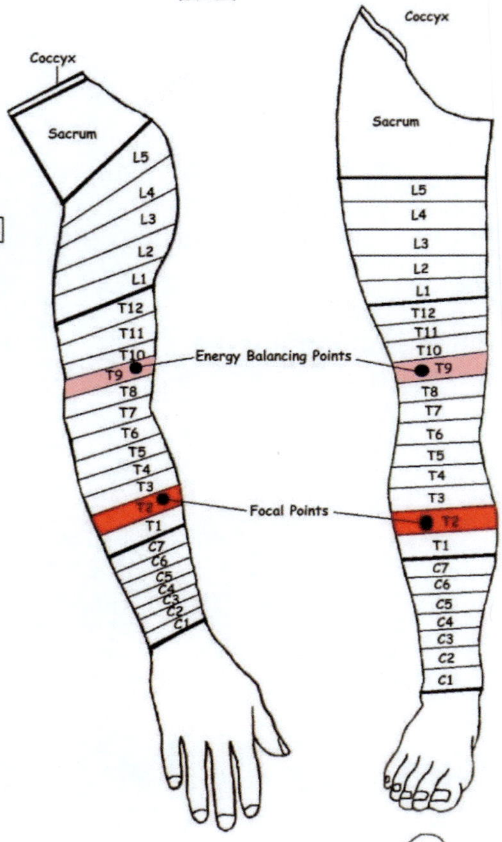

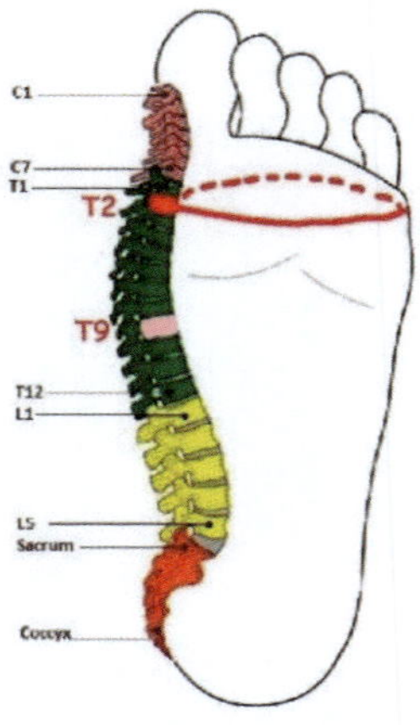

Reflections and Associations of Thoracic 2

Autonomic Nerve and Organs Supplied

The sympathetic nerve that emerges from T1-T2 flows via the paravertebral sympathetic chain to the Inferior Cervical Plexus. From there it supplies the heart, lungs, larynx, trachea, thyroid gland and parathyroid glands.

Muscles Supplied

These are the Transversus Thoracis, Intercostals, Serratus Posterior and the Sacrospinalis at this level.

Effects of Spinal Misalignment

Anomalies at this vertebral level may be caused by compression lesions (wear and tear arthritis), trauma or the effect of imbalances in other regions of the spine – mostly the sacrum and occiput. Symptoms vary widely depending on type and severity of misalignment. The main organ that seems to be affected is the heart, especially the atrium, pericardial sac and blood supply to the heart. This level is intrinsically linked to the thyroid and parathyroid glands and lesions can affect the production of thyroxin (thyroid) and affect the bony skeleton.

Spinal Couple and Harmonics

This is an extremely important quartet of spinal harmonics. The coupled vertebra is T9 and the two harmonic vertebrae are the occiput and sacrum. Whenever there is disharmony between these two (that is extremely common), there is always the tendency for T2 to be affected.

Linked Internal Organ via the Energetic System

The main acupuncture points at the T1-T2 level is Gov 13 and BL 11. This is not a recognized Back Supporting Point, but I disagree. In TCM terms this point is called the Sea of Bone. This is due to its influence on the parathyroid glands and their role in the regulation of osteoblasts. This point is therefore priceless in the treatment of non-unification of fractures, osteoporosis and any other chronic condition where bone is affected.

Acupuncture Meridians

The Bladder meridian deviates at BL 11 (inner bladder line) towards the spine where it lies with the Governor channel up to C6 where it deviates again towards the base of the occiput at BL 10.

Posterior Major Chakra Influence

The Throat chakra affects T2 although the Heart chakra has some influence

Reflections

As per the diagrams

Emotional and Personality Links

T2 lies within the 'Feelings – Emotion' region of the whole spine and 'Thought – Intuition' as an individual vertebra – see T3 for description of this 'duo'. T2 is affected by chronic stress due to its position in being just below the centre of the 'cross' in the parallelogram of forces that is the vertical spine axis and the horizontal shoulder to shoulder axis. As well as producing lethargy and extreme tiredness, heart conditions may be caused due to the ongoing stressful situation. It is particularly affected by the ‘release’ of the loss of a loved one if that relationship had been stressful.

Thoracic 1

This vertebra is hugely important in maintaining our general health, due to its many and various energetic links. It links with C7 at the base of the neck – it is therefore at a crossroads in the spine.

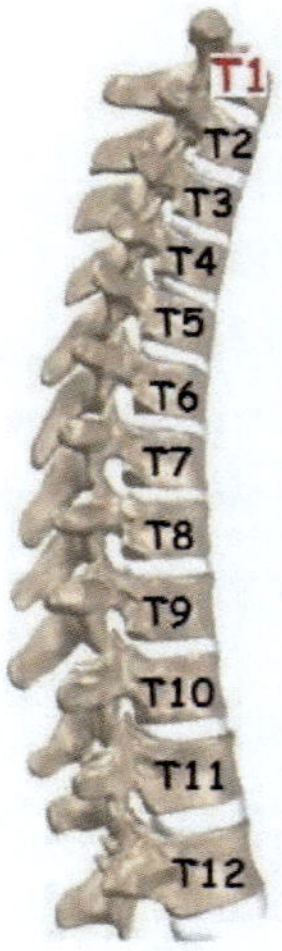

Figure 3.23 Anatomical Position of T1 (lateral aspect)

Spinal Nerve and Dermatome

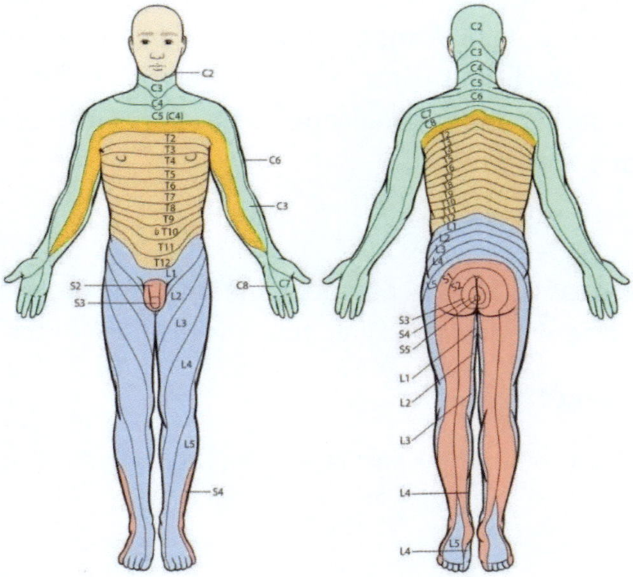

Figure 3.24 Dermatome of T1 (bold yellow)

The spinal nerve from C7-T1 (called C8-T1 nerve root) forms part of the lower end of the brachial plexus. It overlaps the first rib and can cause pain and paraesthesia if a lesion occurs. The C8-T1 nerve root is often called the inferior trunk of the brachial plexus and becomes the medial and posterior cord in forming an aspect of the ulnar, median and radial nerves. The dermatome forms a departure from the remainder of the thoracic spine in that it girdles the torso at its horizontal level but on the anterior aspect runs down the arms to as far as the upper part of the wrist on the antro-medial aspect of the upper and forearm.

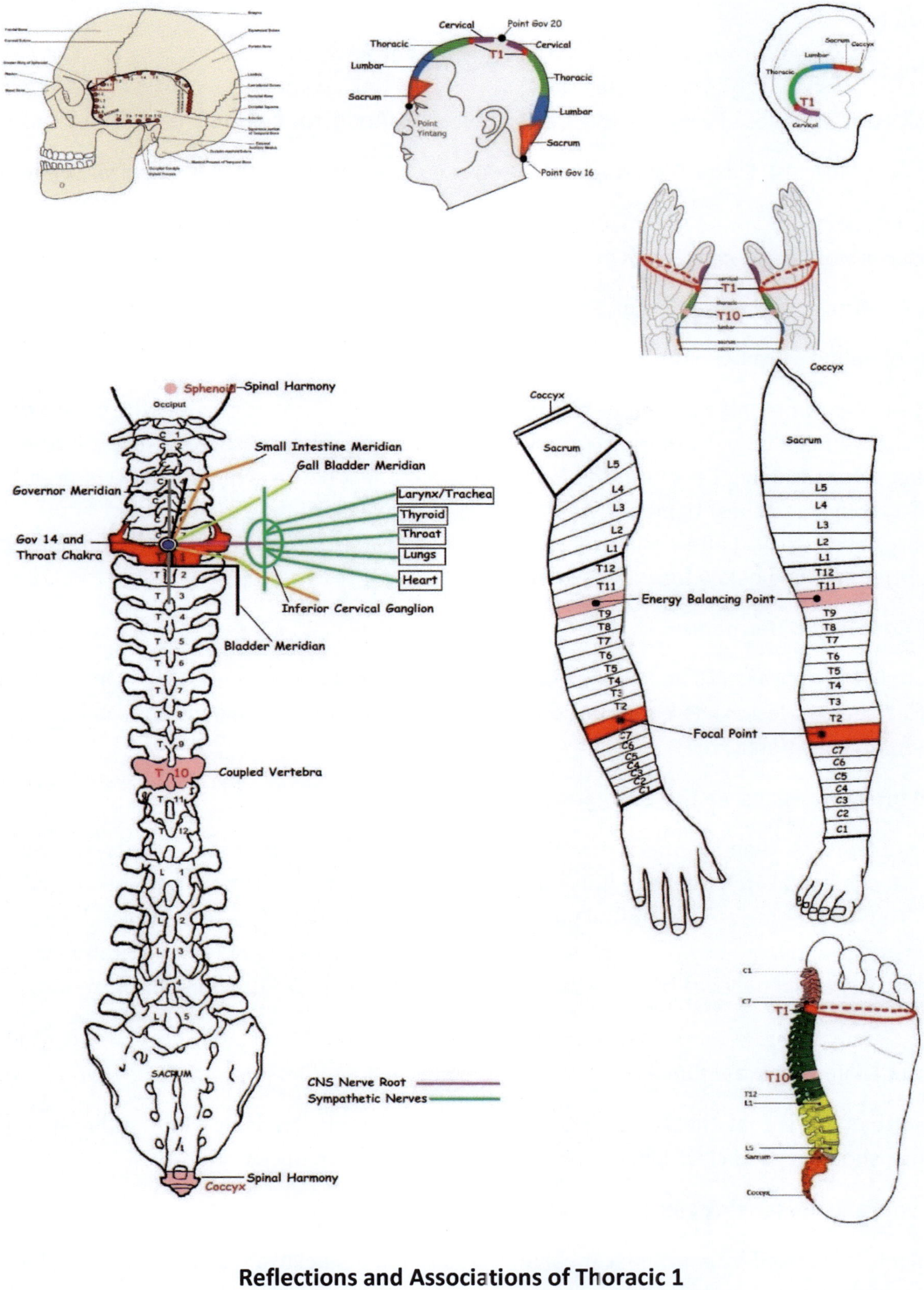

Reflections and Associations of Thoracic 1

Autonomic Nerve and Organs Supplied

The sympathetic nerve that flows via the paravertebral sympathetic chain and Inferior Cervical Ganglion supplies the larynx, trachea, thyroid, throat, lungs and heart. Some authorities insist that the oesophagus receives innervation from this level. I think it more probable that the upper aspect of the oesophagus by the pharynx has innervation, but not the cardiac sphincter end adjacent to the stomach.

Muscles Supplied

Intrinsic Hand Muscles: Flexor Pollicis Brevis; Interossei; Abductor Pollicis Brevis; Adductor Pollicis.

Lower Arm Muscles: Flexor Pollicis Longus; Pronator Quadratus; Flexor Digitorum; wrist extensors; wrist flexors;

Upper Arm Muscles: Triceps

Shoulder Muscles: Pectoralis Major; Pectoralis Minor

Effects of Spinal Misalignment

The T1 level is commonly affected by muscular tension (as in stress) as it falls in the centre of the 'cross' that is made up of the vertical spinal column and the horizontal shoulder and clavicle complex – thoracic inlet. Lesions at this level may affect the lungs to give symptoms of breathing difficulty, cough and chest tightness. As the C7-8-T1 complex is at the inferior aspect of the brachial plexus, lesions may also affect all the muscles shown above as well as paraesthesia/numbness on the dermatome. See below for other symptoms.

Spinal Couple and Harmonics

The coupled vertebra is T10 and the harmonics are both the sphenoid and coccyx. One can therefore see that lesions here may not only affect these other spinal regions but can be the recipient of lesions afar.

Linked Internal Organs via the Energetic System

There are no fewer than five meridians that affect this level – the Governor, Bladder, Gall Bladder, Small Intestine and Large Intestine (this meridian isn't shown in the diagram as it would make it too 'busy'. The latter three are by internal pathways. Lesions here, therefore, may affect the gall bladder, small and large bowel as well as the head. As this level is one of the most common treated by therapists, the knowledge of these two extra meridians increases the number of treatment regimens available.

Posterior Major Chakra Influence

The centre of the Throat Chakra sits at Gov 14 (C7 – T1). This chakra deals with the throat, large intestine, shoulders and clavicles on a physical level as well as many emotions.

Emotional and Personality Links

T1 is highly influenced by emotional imbalance. It falls in the 'Feelings – Emotion' part of the spine in the overall picture but in the 'Movement – Family – Security – Finance' aspect as an individual vertebra. Stress and worry affect this level, especially worry over loved ones, including personal and family finances. Emotional symptoms often affect the throat (dryness), shoulders (congestion and 'frozen'). In my experience of treating frozen shoulder, it is 80% emotional aetiology. Also, at this level are shyness, poor at making decisions, anxiety, heart irregularities and sadness – plus many more.

CHAPTER FOUR - The Cervical Spine

The cervical spine (neck) consists of 7 much smaller vertebrae than either the lumbar or thoracic spine. They are similar in shape apart from the top two. The spinous process of C7 is longer than those of C3-C6.

Cervical 7 This vertebra is hugely important in maintaining the general health in both physical and emotional make up as it forms, with T1, the centre of the parallelogram of forces that is represented by the vertical spine and the horizontal thoracic inlet.

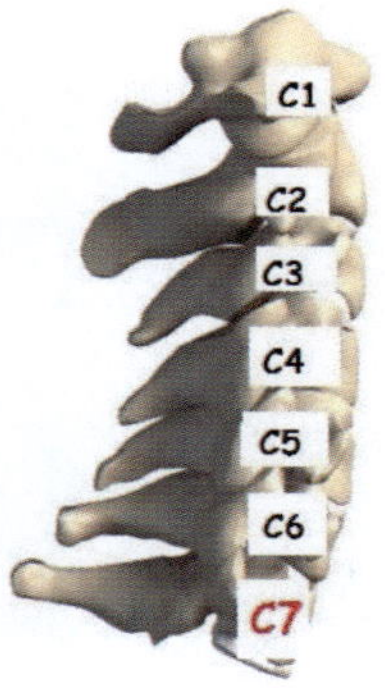

Figure 4.1 Anatomical Position of C7 (lateral aspect)

Spinal Nerve and Dermatome

The nerve root between C6-7 forms part of the brachial plexus and gives branches to the median, radial and ulnar nerves in supplying muscles of the arm and shoulder region.

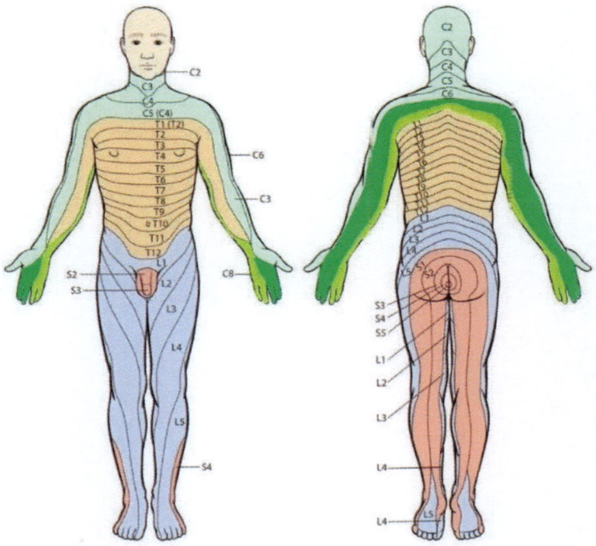

Figure 4.2 Dermatome of C7 (green) and C8 (yellow)

Both the C7 and C8 dermatomes are shown in the diagram above. They both cover the posterior aspect of the upper arm and forearm plus the medial aspect of the arm and the fingers (not thumb).

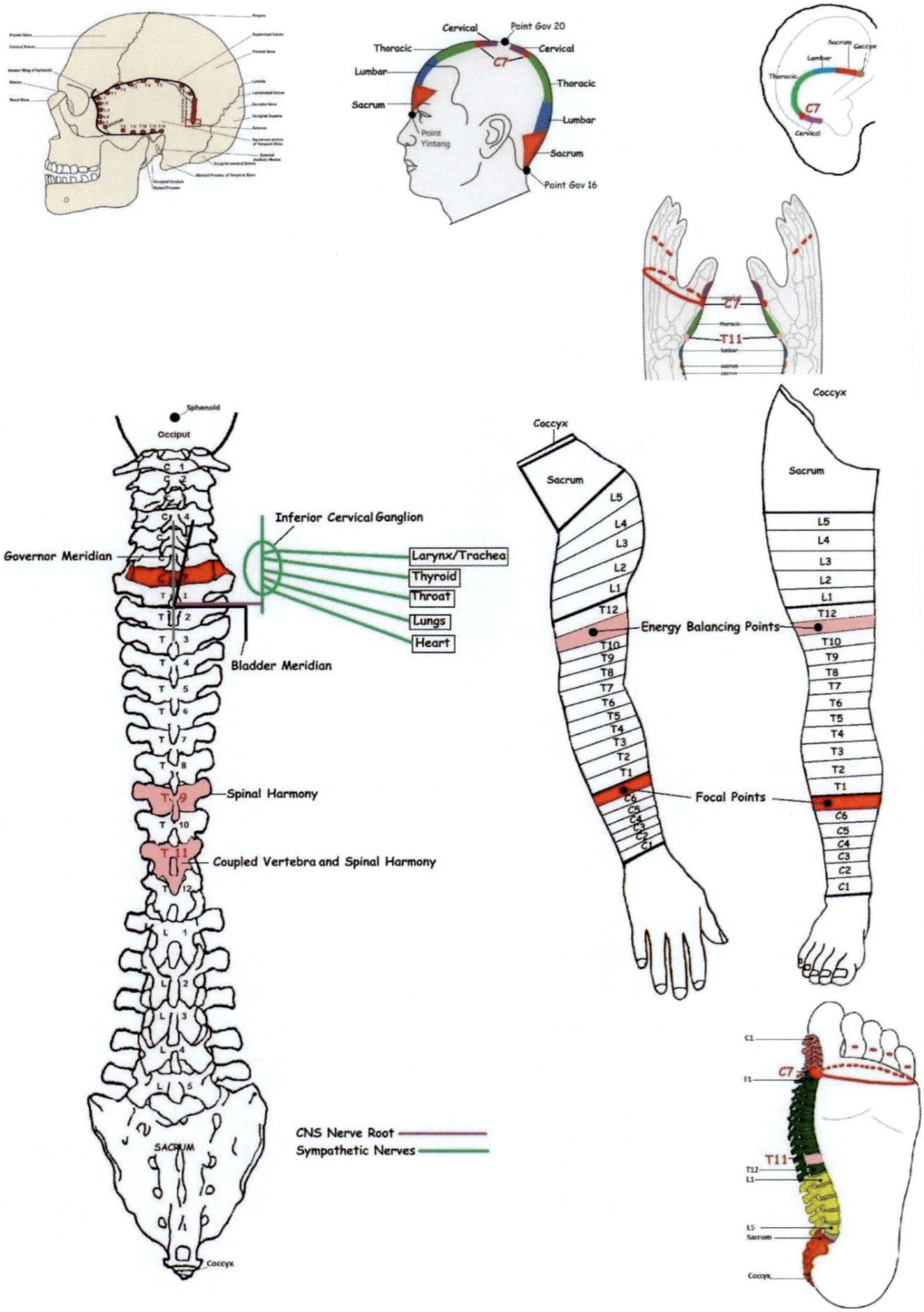

Reflections and Associations of Cervical 7

Autonomic Nerve and Organs Supplied

The sympathetic nerve flows from the nerve root and subsequent paravertebral sympathetic chain from T1 -T2 (as do all the cervical spine sympathetic outflows). The nerve enters the Inferior Cervical Ganglion to then supply the larynx, trachea, thyroid, throat lungs and heart.

Muscles Supplied

As per T1 (C8) supply plus Pronator Teres; Supinator; Serratus Anterior.

Effects of Spinal Misalignment

The C7 level is commonly affected by muscular tension (as in stress) as it falls in the centre of the 'cross' that is made up of the vertical spinal column and the horizontal shoulder and clavicle complex – thoracic inlet. Lesions at this level may affect the lungs to give symptoms of breathing difficulty, cough and chest tightness. The thyroid gland is associated with C7 and symptoms can include lethargy and immune system conditions, especially the susceptibility of catching colds. As the C7-8-T1 complex is at the inferior aspect of the brachial plexus, lesions may also affect all the muscles shown above as well as paraesthesia/numbness on the dermatome. Spinal lesions may give pain and numbness in the affected regions of the arm. See below for other symptoms.

Spinal Couple and Harmonic

The spinal couple is T11 and the harmonic is T9.

Linked Internal Organs via the Energetic System

Although there aren't any specific acupuncture points around C7 (except for non-meridian points on the central and inner bladder lines), the Governor, Bladder, Gall Bladder, Small Intestine and Large Intestine all affect C7 either by superficial or deep pathways.

Posterior Major Chakra and its influence

The Throat chakra is in command of C7, as its centre is at Gov 14 between C7-T1. This has energetic influence affecting the large intestine, lungs, shoulder and clavicles as well as affecting the emotions.

Reflections

Please note that the reflection on the temporo-sphenoidal line is at a different location to the thoracic spine, C7 being at the most inferior aspect of the temporal bone. The reflection on the hands and feet also divert from the regularity of the vertebrae below it. C7 is the highest vertebra that reflects all-round the foot and hand, C1-C6 are reflected mostly around the thumb or great toe. Other secondary reflected areas are also found on the fingers and toes – see diagram.

Emotional and Personality Links

C7 is highly influenced by emotional imbalance. It falls in the 'Feelings – Emotion' part of the spine in the overall picture but in the 'Movement – Family – Security – Finance' aspect as an individual vertebra. Stress and worry affect this level, especially worry over loved ones, including personal and family finances. Emotional symptoms often affect the throat (dryness), the thyroid gland (lethargy) and the shoulders that in turn give rise to shyness, diffidence, lack of self-esteem, low vitality and anxiety.

Cervical 6

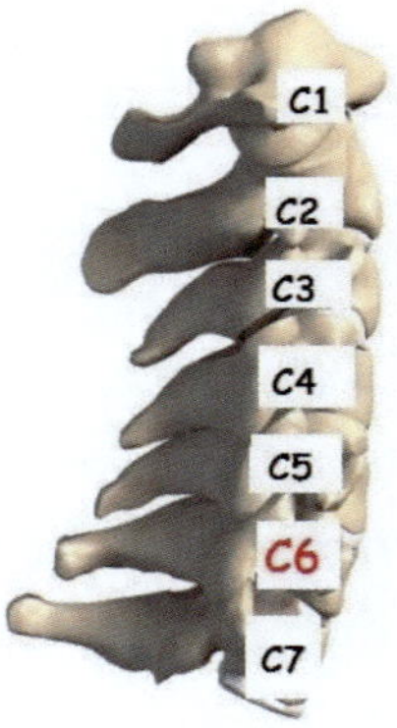

Figure 4.3 Anatomical Position of C6 (lateral view)

Spinal Nerve and Dermatome

The nerve root emerging between C5-C6 forms part of the brachial plexus that become the radial, median, ulnar, axillary, musculocutaneous and lower part of the phrenic nerve.

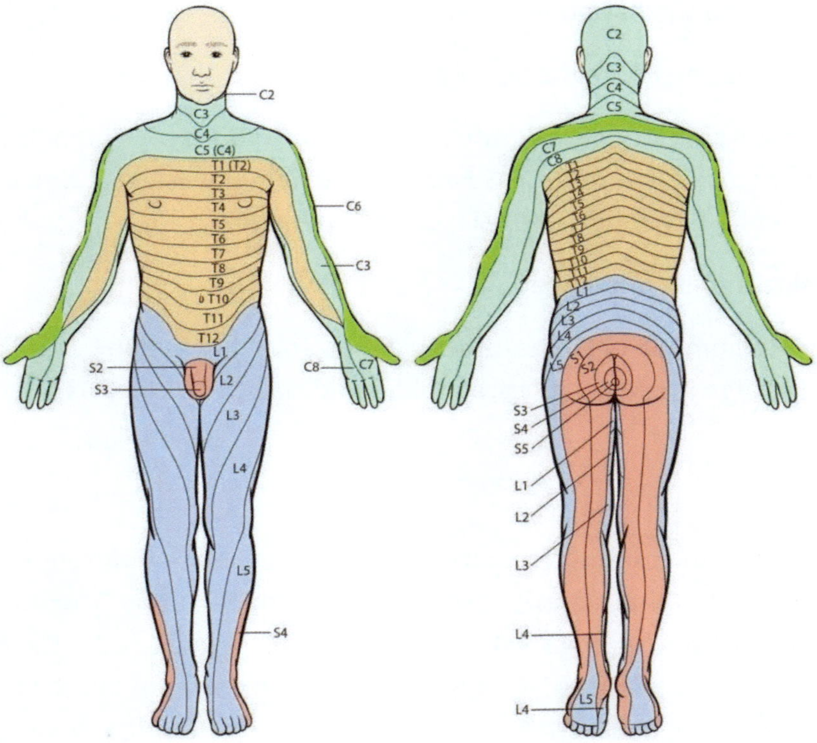

Figure 4.4 Dermatome of C6

The C6 dermatome is at its horizontal level on the spine and across to the shoulders on the posterior aspect, and down the very outside (medial aspect) aspect of the upper arms, forearms and thumbs. There is no dermatome region on the anterior aspect of the upper chest.

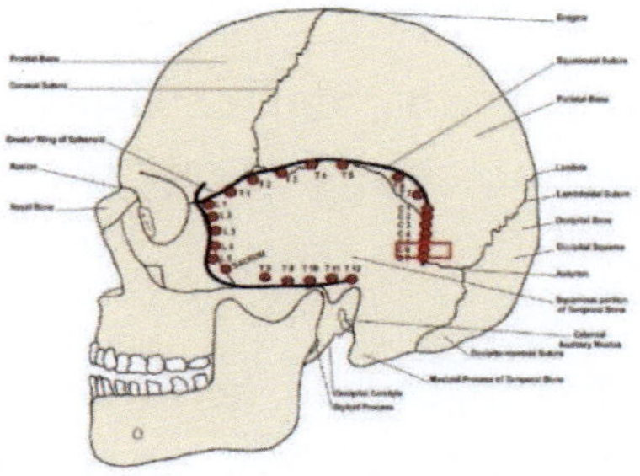

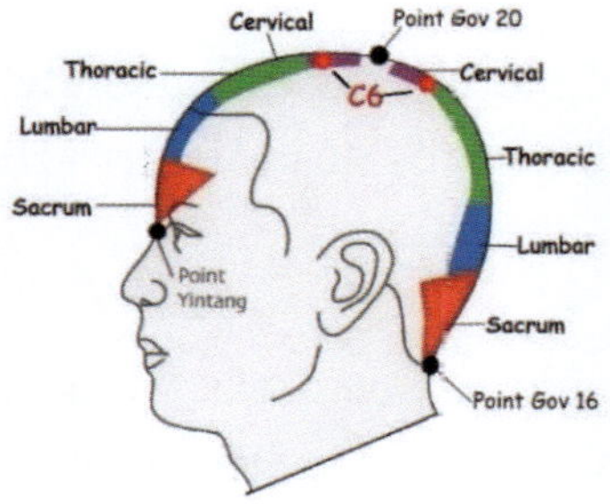

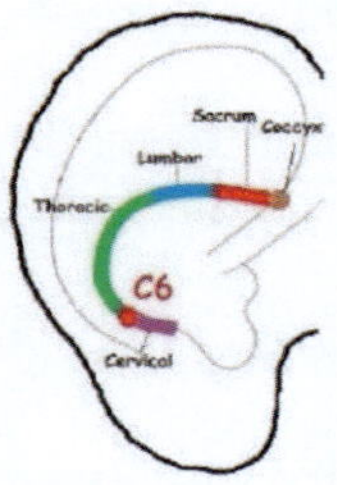

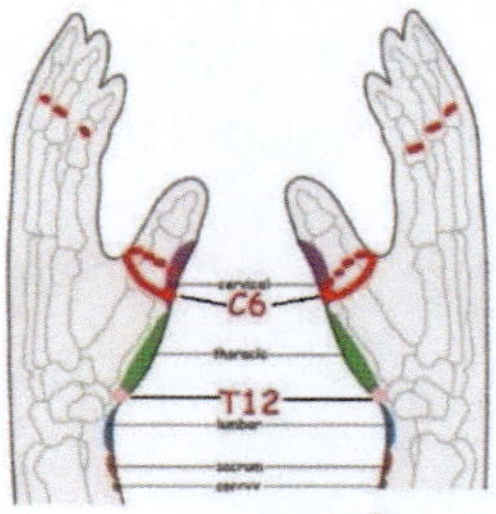

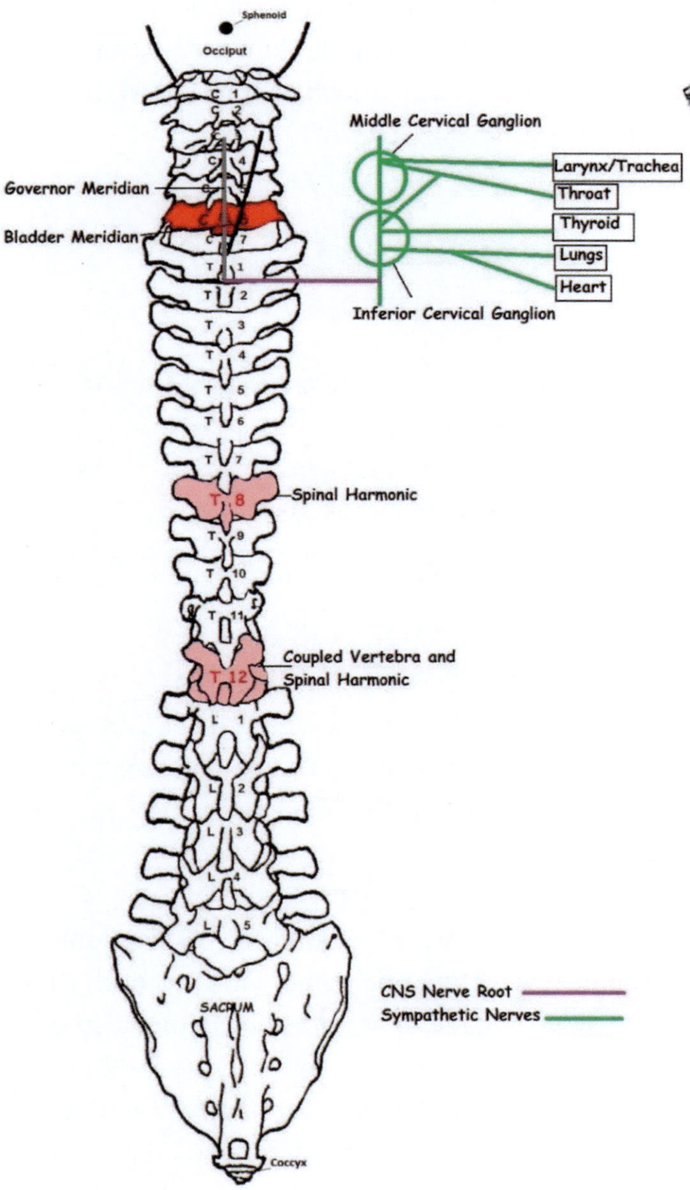

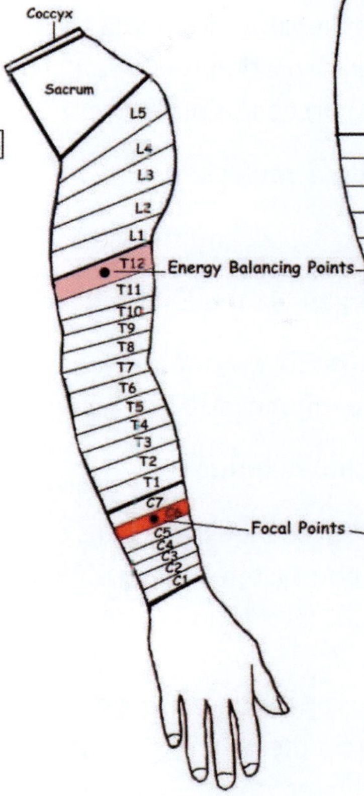

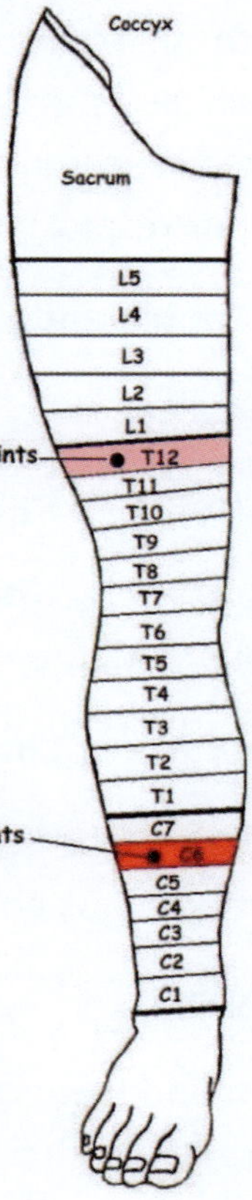

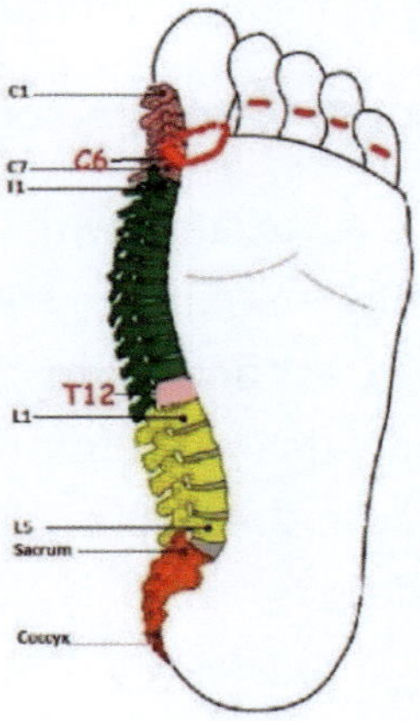

Reflections and Associations of Cervical 6

Autonomic Nerves and Organs Supplied

The sympathetic flow goes via the inferior cervical ganglion to supply the thyroid, lungs and heart and via a further link to the middle cervical plexus to supply the larynx, trachea and throat.

Muscles Supplied

These are the Supraspinatus; Infraspinatus; Pectoralis Major (upper section); Deltoid; Serratus Anterior; Rhomboid Major and Minor; Supinator; Biceps; Brachioradialis; Pronator Teres; Pectoralis Minor; Triceps; Extensor Carpi Radialis Longus and Brevis and Flexor Carpi Radialis.

Effects of Spinal Misalignment

This vertebral level is prone to acute trauma as in disc lesions, facet joint lesions and chronic conditions such as spondylosis. These would affect the muscles supplied and give radicular pain and paraesthesia to the dermatome. C5-C6 is the most commonly seen disc lesion in the neck region. This level also supplies the throat and tonsils by its sympathetic supply via the cervical ganglions. Therefore, constant irritation on C6 can give rise to throat symptoms such as sore throat, tonsillitis and upper respiratory conditions.

Spinal Couple and Harmonics

The spinal couple is at T12 and the harmonic is T8

Linked Internal Organ via the Energetic System

C6 is affected by the Governor and Bladder meridians but no other meridian (and subsequent internal organ) are influenced

Posterior Major Chakra Influence

C6 is ruled by the Throat chakra and, as such, also affects the Sacral, Shoulder and Navel chakras with their organs and systems being affected with any long-standing lesion.

Reflections

The foot and hand reflections take a departure from those vertebrae below this level. The reflected areas do not encircle the whole of the hand/foot but just circumvent the thumb and large toe. There are also reflected points on each of the fingers and toes, not thumb or great toe.

Emotional and Personality Links

C6 is associated with 'Feelings – Emotions' on the general spinal picture and with 'Movement – Family – Security – Finance' as an individual vertebra. This is the same combination as both C7 and T1. Stress and worry affect this level, especially worry over loved ones, including personal and family finances. Emotional symptoms often affect the throat (dryness), the thyroid gland (lethargy) and the shoulders that in turn give rise to shyness, diffidence, lack of self-esteem, low vitality and anxiety.

Cervical 5

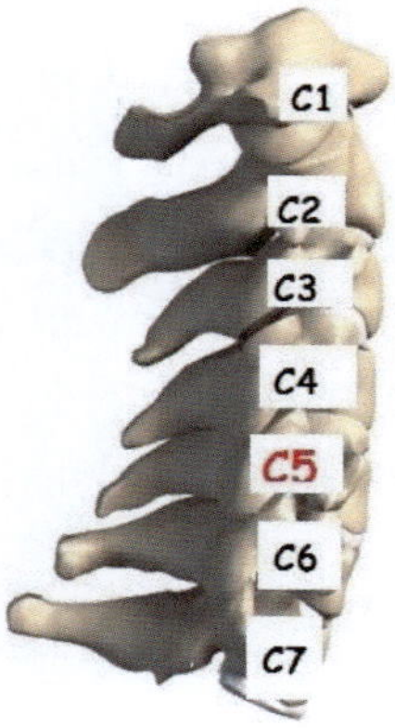

Figure 4.5 Anatomical Position of C5 (lateral aspect)

Spinal Nerve and Dermatome

The nerve root emerging from C4-C5 forms part of the brachial plexus (see description of C6). It also forms the lowest part of the cervical plexus giving filaments to the Accessory Nerve (XI cranial). Part of the phrenic nerve (nerve supply to the diaphragm) also comes from C4-C5.

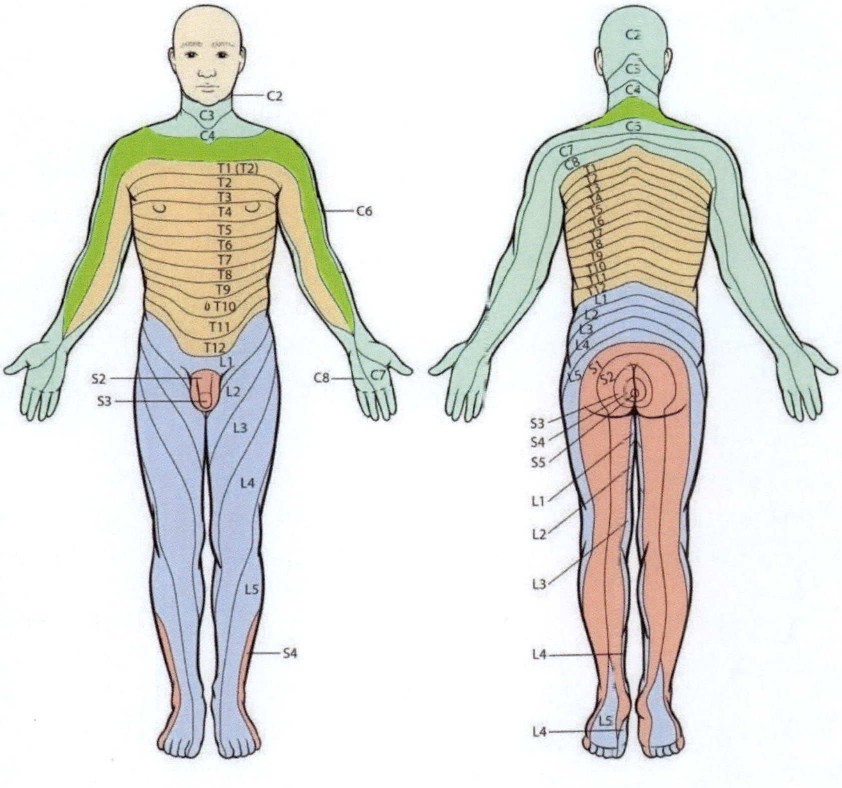

Figure 4.6 Dermatome of C5 (shown in green)

The posterior aspect of the C5 dermatome girdles the lower neck at its level. On the anterior surface, the dermatome is a line from shoulder to shoulder then down each antro-medial aspect of the arms to just above the wrist crease.

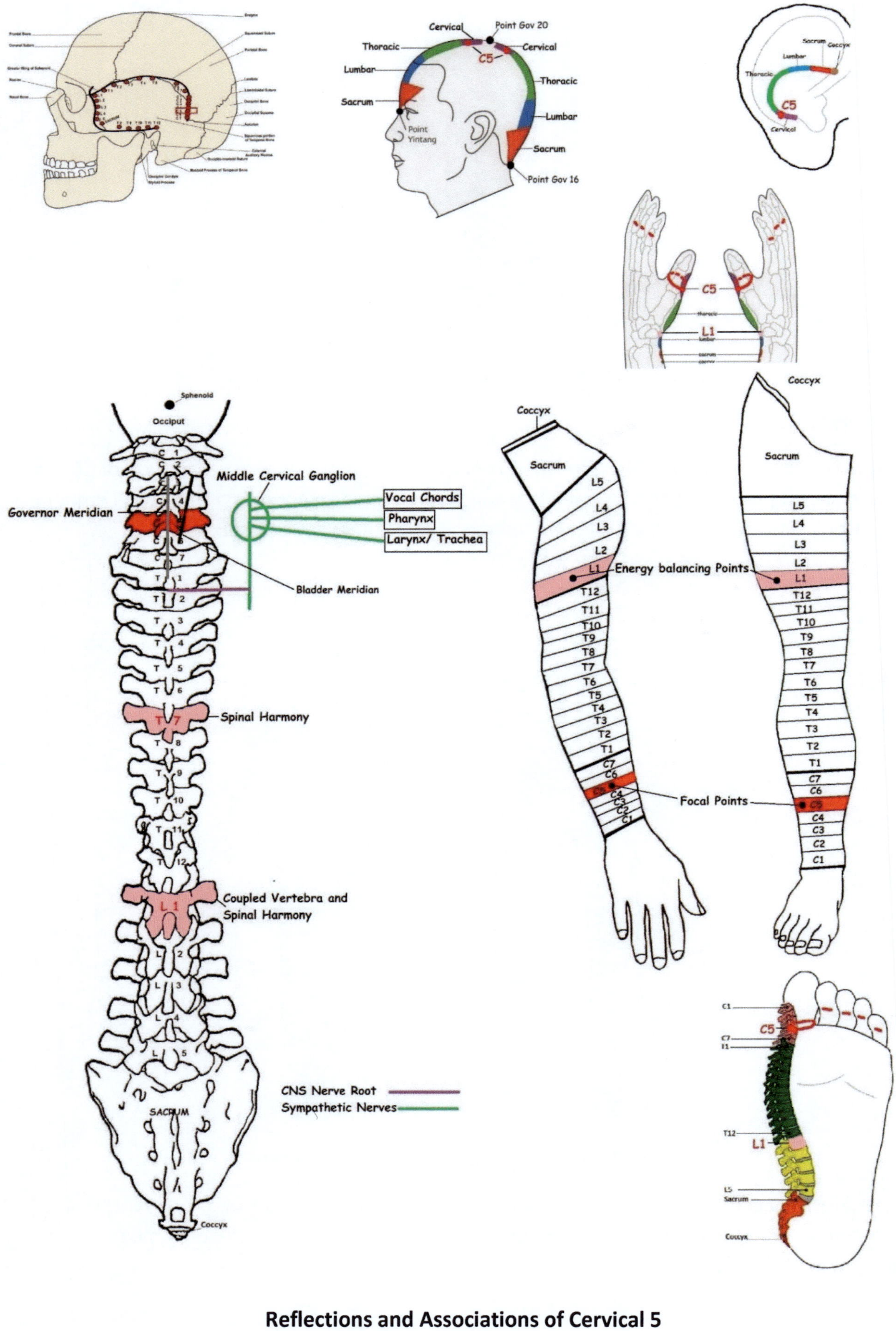

Reflections and Associations of Cervical 5

Autonomic Nerve and Organs Supplied

The sympathetic supply to internal organs is via the middle cervical ganglion that supplies the larynx, pharynx, vocal cords, throat, tonsils and trachea.

Muscles Supplied

These are the Supraspinatus; Infraspinatus; Pectoralis Major; Deltoid; Serratus Anterior; Rhomboid Major and Minor; Supinator; Biceps; Brachioradialis and Pronator Teres via the brachial plexus. Filaments to the Accessory Nerve (XI cranial) supplies the Sternocleidomastoid and the phrenic nerve supplies the Diaphragm.

Effects of Spinal Misalignment

As discussed earlier, this vertebral level is prone to acute trauma as in disc lesions, facet joint lesions and chronic conditions such as spondylosis. These would affect the muscles supplied and give radicular pain and paraesthesia to the dermatome. C4-C5 is a common disc lesion, though not as common as C5-C6. This level also supplies the throat and tonsils by its sympathetic supply via the cervical ganglions. Therefore, constant irritation on C5 can give rise to throat symptoms such as sore throat, tonsillitis and upper respiratory conditions.

Spinal Couple and Harmonic

The spinal couple is L1 and the spinal harmonic is at T7

Linked Internal Organs via the Energetic System

C5 is affected by the Governor and Bladder meridians, but no other meridian or internal organs seem to have energetic influence.

Posterior Chakra Influence

The posterior Throat chakra at C7-T1 influences C5. This level is at the upper end of its influence and there is also a small influence from the posterior Brow chakra.

Reflections

The reflections of C5 in the foot and hand are around the inferior aspects of the great toe and thumb respectively, with a further link to the toes and fingers.

Emotional and Personality Links

C5 is associated with 'Feelings – Emotions' on the general spinal picture and with 'Communication – Relationships' as an individual vertebra. Poor communication either by instability, insecurity or introvertness over a long period of time may affect C5. Emotional symptoms often affect the throat (dryness), the thyroid gland (lethargy) and the shoulders that in turn give rise to shyness, diffidence, lack of self-esteem, low vitality and anxiety. This level has an affinity on the vocal chords and tonsils.

Cervical 4

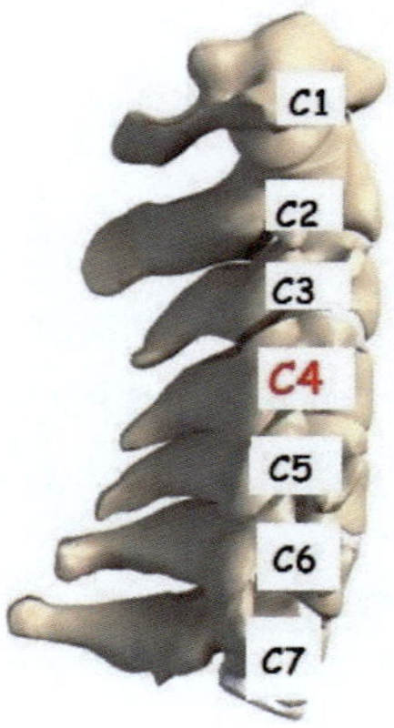

Figure 4.7 Anatomical Position of C4 (lateral view)

Spinal Nerve and Dermatome

The nerve root emerging from C3-4 forms part of the cervical plexus that lies deep to the jugular vein and the SCM muscle. This level becomes the three supraclavicular nerves and a branch to the omohyoid muscle. This level is also the central part of the phrenic nerve (diaphragm), gives a branch to the Accessory nerve (XI cranial), a filament to the Vagus nerve (X cranial) and Hypoglossal nerve (XII cranial)

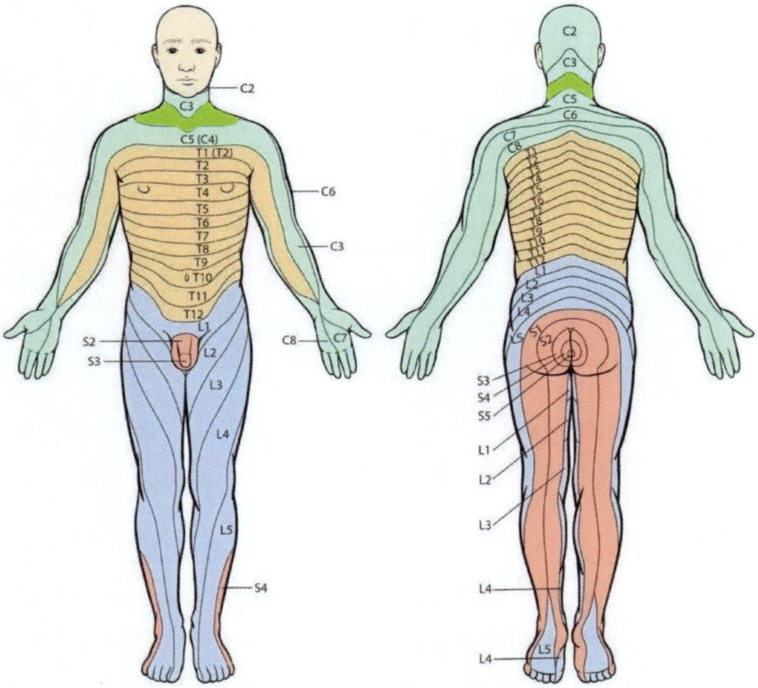

Figure 4.8 C4 dermatome (in green)

The dermatome on the posterior part of the neck is roughly centred around the vertebral horizontal level, whereas the anterior aspect is below the vertebral level.

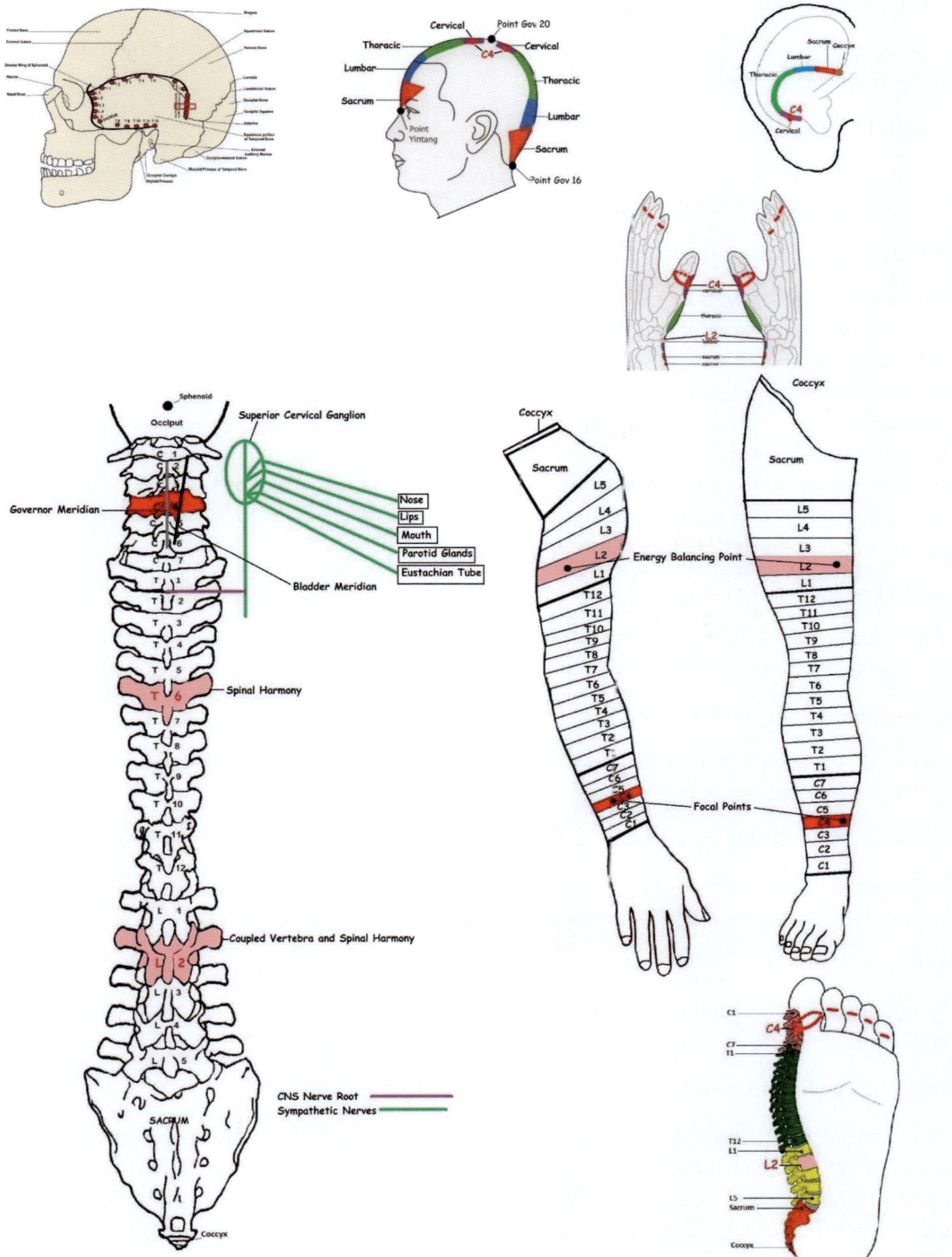

Reflections and Associations of Cervical 4

Autonomic Nerve and Organs Supplied

The sympathetic nerve supplies the nose, lips, mouth, parotid gland and eustachian tube via the Superior Cervical Ganglion

Muscles Supplied

These are the inferior aspect of the Omohyoid, Longus Capitis, Levator Scapulae, Scalenus Medius and the Diaphragm via the phrenic nerve.

Effects of Spinal Misalignment

This vertebral level covers many facial areas either by the sympathetic nerve supply, motor and sensory nerve supplies or energy flow. It is the nose and inner ears that seem to be worst affected with either acute or chronic misalignment. Physical therapists of all persuasions have encountered patients who have suffered from chronic catarrh, hardness of hearing or coryza, only to have those symptoms helped by the correct adjustment or mobilising of C4. My experience tells me that to ease these symptoms (if the vertebral misalignment is the true aetiology) the vertebra must be treated directly – it does not seem to work so well when treating through the reflections on the feet or limbs. Chronic congestion, inflammation or infection of the eustachian tube seems to be the culprit with hearing difficulties if caused by a lesion at C4.

Spinal Couple and Harmonic

The spinal couple is L2 and the harmonic is T6. This a powerful trio! Each of these roughly represents the 'centre' of their part of the spine – see Emotions.

Linked Internal Organ via the Energetic System

As per C5, although the Governor and Bladder channels affect this vertebra, there are no energetic referrals to internal organs.

Posterior major Chakra Influence

The posterior Brow chakra is in command of the upper cervical spine and there is wonderful symmetry and synchronicity with the facial area that are 'governed' by the Brow chakra.

Reflections

Please see description of the C5 reflection – C4 is obviously just superior to this on the great toe and thumb

Emotional and Personality Link

C4 is associated with 'Feelings – Emotions' on the general spinal picture, at its very upper end, and with 'Communication – Relationships' as an individual vertebra. Poor communication either by instability, insecurity or introvertness over a long period of time may affect C4. Emotional aetiology often affects the throat, eustachian tube, middle ear, nasal cavities, ethmoid that give rise to being either 'bunged up' all the time or suffer from painful sinusitis. These may arise from poor communication and not relating to others, shyness and insecurity. Together with C3 and C5, this vertebra also deals with tension in the diaphragm from ongoing stress. Diaphragmatic spasm can be life threatening although it is mostly just very uncomfortable and may require muscle relaxants (as well as cervical treatment) to help. This, in turn, may produce GORD, reflux, irritable bowel syndrome and asthma type symptoms.

Cervical 3

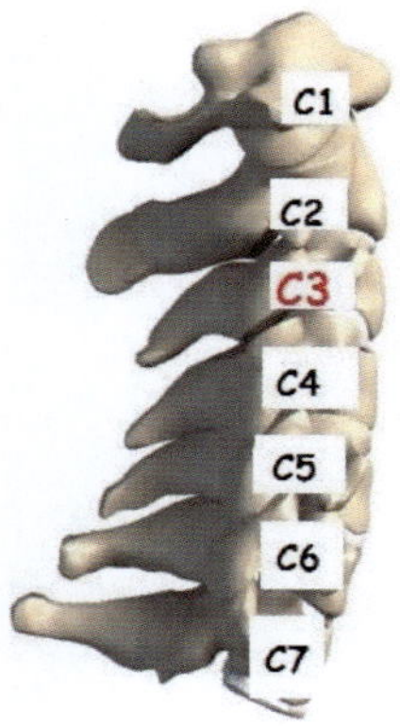

Figure 4.9 Anatomical Position of C3 (lateral aspect)

Spinal Nerve and Dermatome

The nerve root that emerges from C2-C3 forms part of the cervical plexus that lies deep to the jugular vein and the SCM muscle. This level becomes the 3 transverse cervical nerves, greater auricular nerve and lesser occipital nerve. This level also forms the upper part of the phrenic nerve (diaphragm), gives a branch to the Accessory nerve (XI cranial), a filament to the Vagus nerve (X cranial) and Hypoglossal nerve (XII cranial).

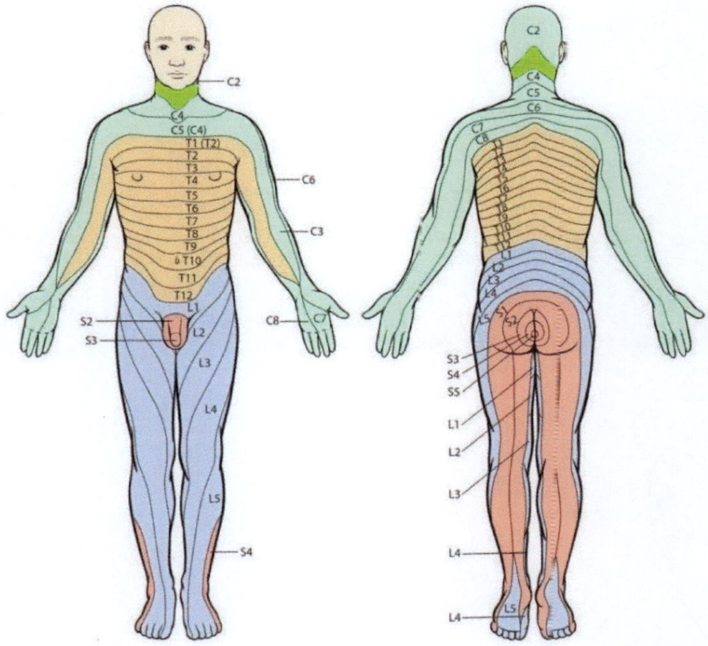

Figure 4.10 Dermatome of C3 (green)

As shown in the diagram, the C3 dermatome covers the whole of the throat region in the anterior aspect and the base of the skull around to the lateral side of the mid neck.

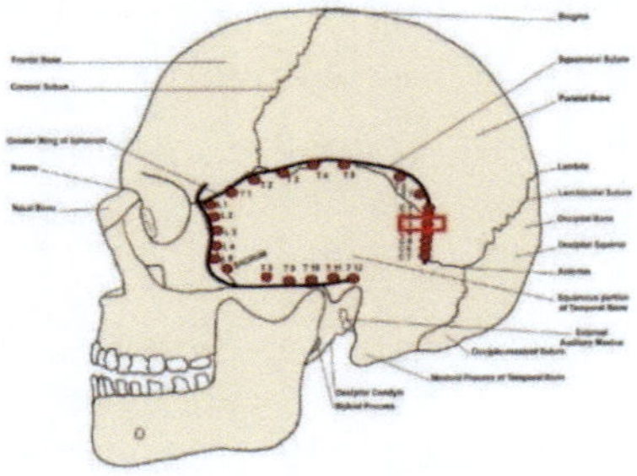

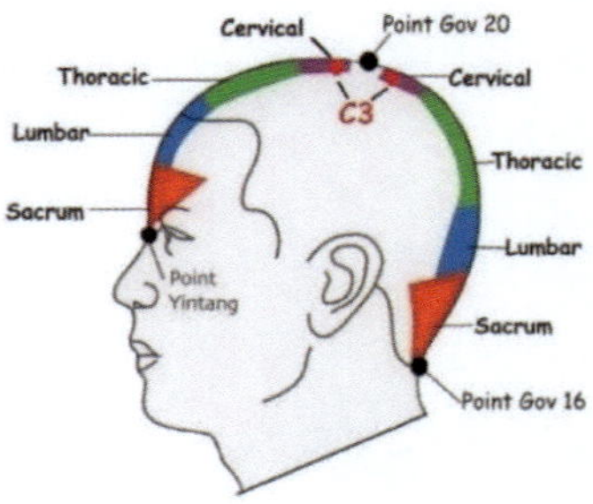

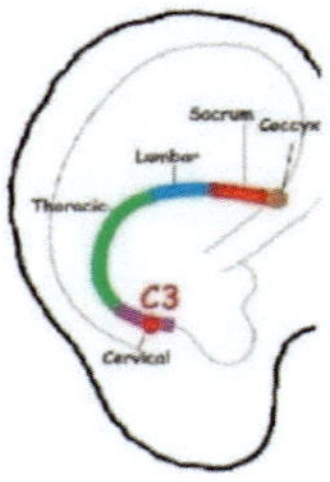

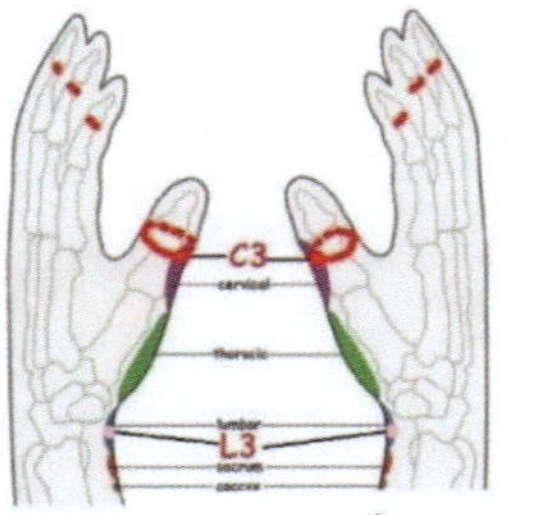

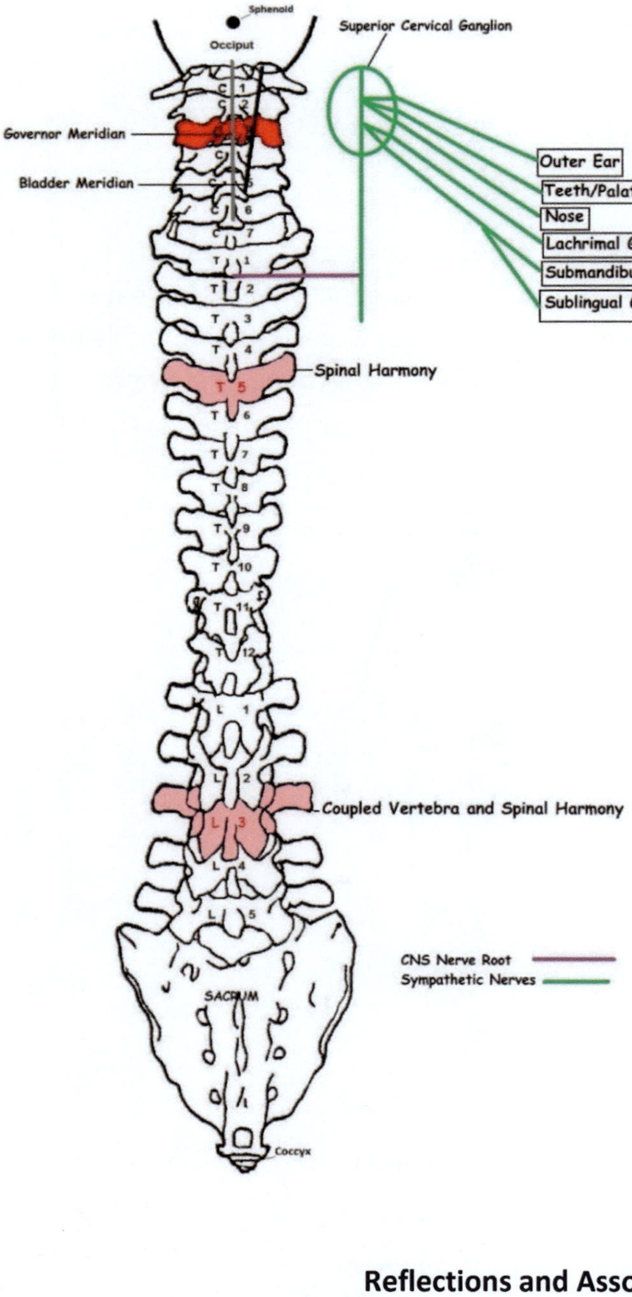

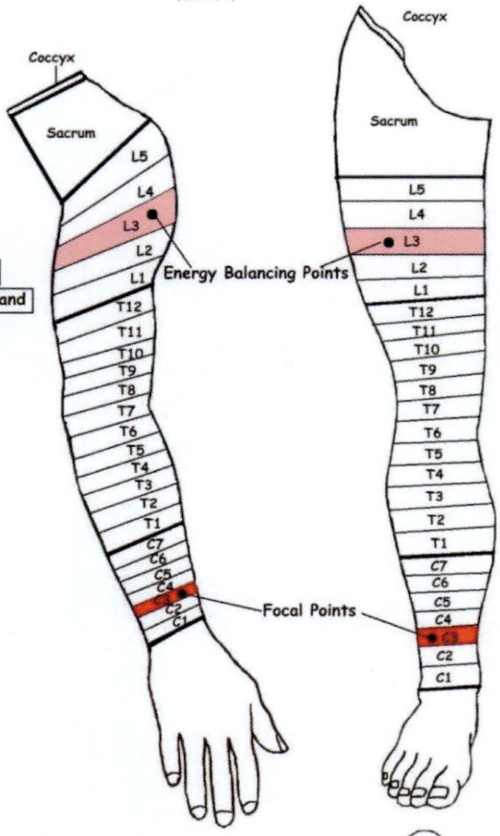

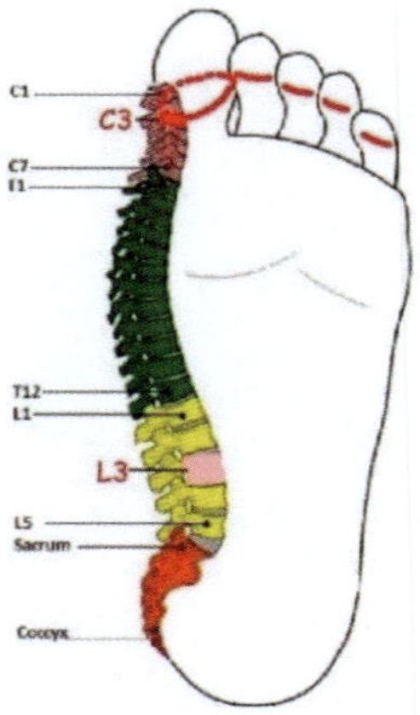

Reflections and Associations of Cervical 3

Autonomic Nerve and Organs Supplied

The Superior Cervical Ganglion is a direct link from the paravertebral sympathetic chain, linked from the nerve root from T1. The following are supplied – outer ear, mouth, part of the nose, lachrymal glands, submandibular and sublingual glands.

Muscles Supplied

These are the sensory nerves to both the Trapezius and SCM, the motor nerve to Longus Capitis, Longus Colli, Sternothyroid, Sternohyoid and Omohyoid. The Diaphragm is also supplied via the phrenic nerve.

Effects of Spinal Misalignment

Misalignment of this vertebral level usually affects the face, cheeks, facial bones and teeth. If this vertebra is subluxed with its C2 neighbour, the result is often headache, migraine and dizziness. The trigeminal nerve can also be affected and can give very acute and intense pain.

Spinal Couple and Harmonic

The vertebral couple is L3 with a further harmonic at T5

Linked Internal Organ via the Energetic System

As per most of the cervical spine, the Governor and Bladder meridians affect the vertebra but do not affect any internal organ.

Posterior Major Chakra

The posterior Brow chakra based at Gov 16 influences this vertebra

Reflections

Please see the illustrations

Emotional and Personality Link

C3 is associated with 'Thought and Intuition' in the general spinal picture and 'Action – Doing' as an individual vertebra. It is therefore often affected in many different emotional situations. C3 and its neighbour C4 are 'pivot' vertebrae and, as such, are affected by those times in our lives when we ae unsure as to which way to turn or we are at a crossroads in relationships or career. The example given earlier of trigeminal neuralgia will often occur during such times. Other symptoms to occur with emotional imbalance are catarrh, nasal conditions, sinusitis, adenoiditis, mouth ulcers, nose bleeds, herpes and cold sores, toothache and earache. General stress can often affect this level due to its association with T5 (heart) and L3 (kidney). Thus, if a situation in your life gives much fear and spiritual heartache, there is often a 'knock on' effect on the mid cervical region. It is therefore imperative that imbalance in the other vertebrae are addressed.

Cervical 2 (Axis)

The axis is situated between the atlas (C1) and C3 and, is arguably the strongest of all the cervical vertebrae. It provides a pivot around which the atlas and head moves and is a very atypically shaped vertebra.

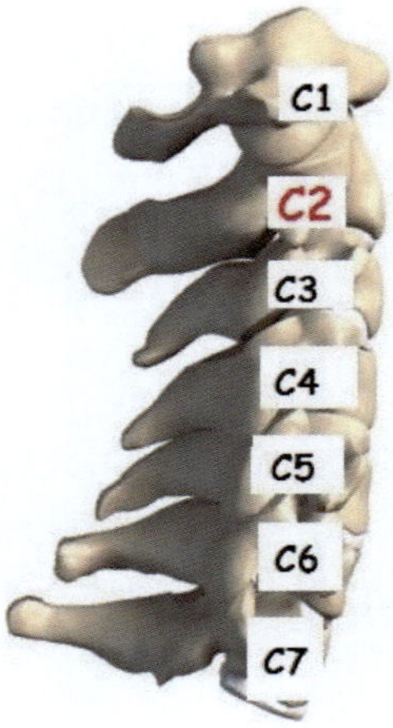

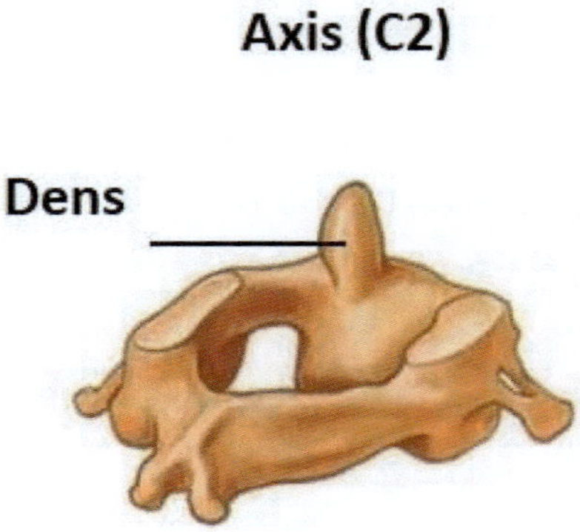

Figures 4.11 and 4.12 - Lateral aspect of C2 and showing the dens and bifid spinal process

Spinal Nerve and Dermatome

The nerve root that emerges between C1 and C2 is the upper part of the cervical plexus. Nerves here give communication to the Cranial Nerves XI (Accessory), X (Vagus) and XII (Hypoglossal). The dermatome

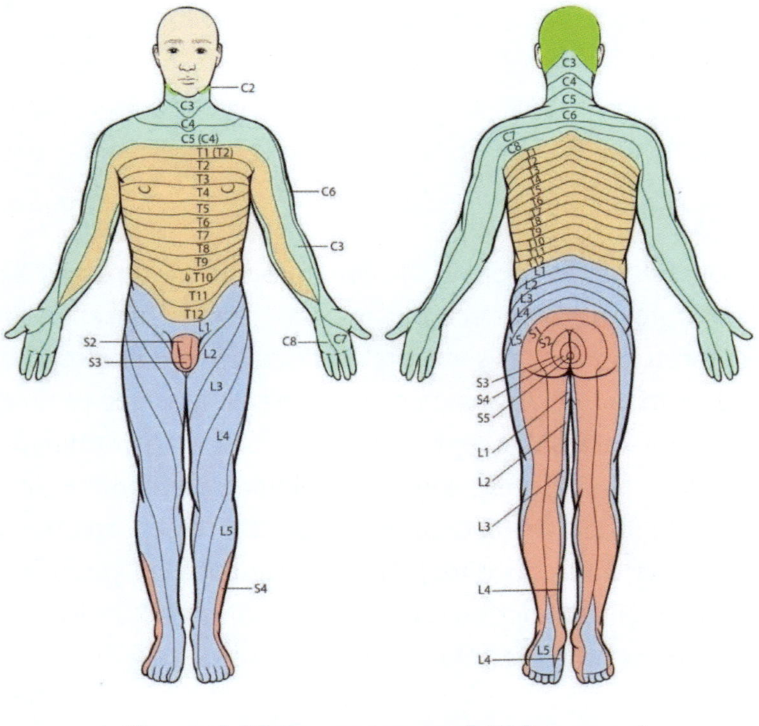

Figure 4.13 Dermatome of C2 (in green)

of C2 covers the whole of the posterior aspect of the head as well as a narrow strip on the anterior aspect of the neck.

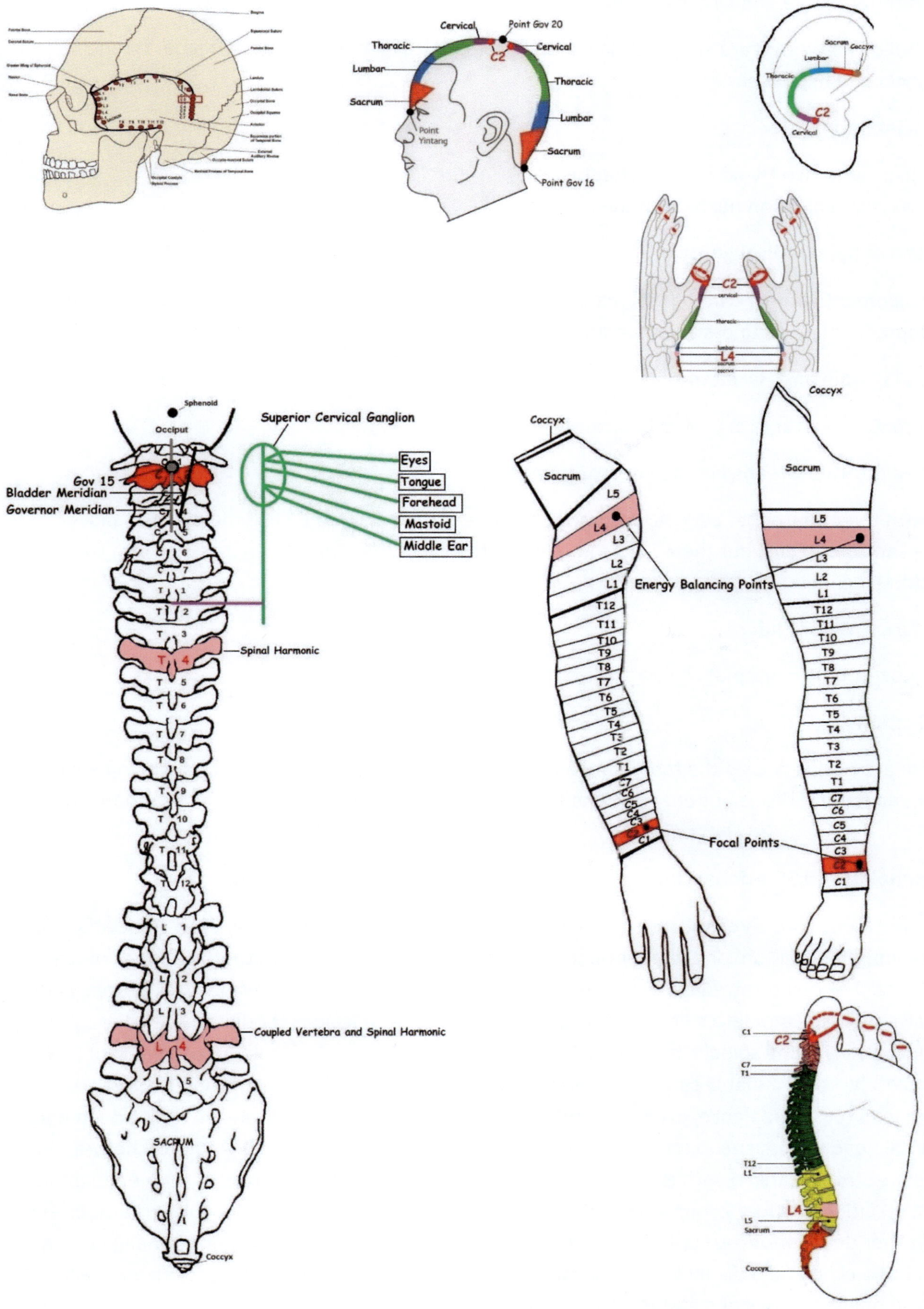

Reflexions and Associations of Cervical 2

Autonomic Nerve and Organs Supplied

The following organs are supplied via the superior cervical ganglion – eyes, tongue, forehead, mastoid and middle ear.

Muscles Supplied

These are the two Hyoid muscles, Rectus Capitis Lateralis, Longus Capitis, Rectus Capitis Anterior and a communication nerve with the vagus nerve.

Effects of Spinal Misalignment

Misalignments at this crucial level may give sinus pain, altered hearing, earache, fainting spells, diplopia, vertigo, dizziness and pain around the eyes.

Spinal Couple and Harmonic

The coupled vertebra is L4 with a further coupled vertebra at T4.

Linked Internal Organs via the Energetic System

As with the other upper cervical vertebrae, the energetic supply of C2 are the Bladder and Governor meridians, but there is an influence of the Large Intestine, Small Intestine and Gall Bladder channels.

Posterior Major Chakra

The posterior Brow (Ajna) chakra at Gov 16 influences the axis

Reflections

These are positioned on the foot, hand and skull at the anatomical positions one would expect. The foot and hand reflexes not only traverse the great toe and thumb but onto the toes and fingers as well.

Personality and Emotional Links

This vertebra is hugely significant in being affected by emotional imbalance. C2 is associated with 'Thought and Intuition' on the general picture and with 'Feelings and Emotion' as an individual vertebra. The obvious traumatic emotional consequence of a severe C2 lesion is, of course, a life of paralysis with a complete spinal cord lesion. Much less severe lesions though may lead to similar symptoms involving spinal cord 'shock' that initially 'apes' paralysis. Similarly, anyone who feels completely 'stuck', unable to move forward and 'paralysed' with fear about their situation will often lead to C2 imbalance, predominantly initiated by strong muscular tension of the deep upper cervical head flexors and extensors as well as the upper fibres of trapezius. As stated before, the eyes are strongly linked with the axis. I have personally seen many examples of poor eyesight in a child resulting in upper cervical (specifically axis) lesions. Sadness, loneliness, guilt, traumatic events and other deep emotional upheavals may cause atlas imbalance. The emotional imbalance may occur as a child and only become symptomatic as an adult. Symptoms would include headache, migraine, diplopia, vertigo and altered hearing as well as tinnitus.

Cervical 1 (Atlas)

The atlas is the uppermost of all the cervical vertebra and articulates with the occiput and axis. It is the most atypically shaped of the whole of the spinal column. There is no vertebral body and is a ring of bone. The atlas is a hugely significant vertebra both physically and energetically.

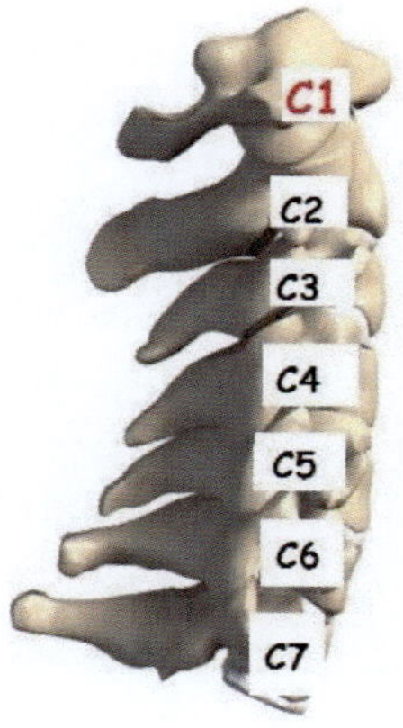

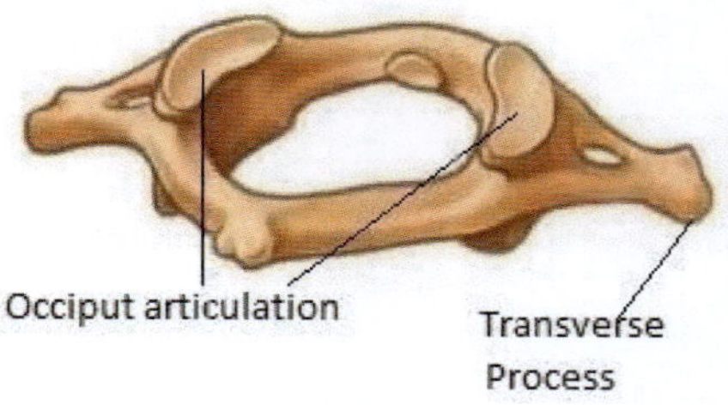

Atlas (C1)

Figure 4.14 and 4.15 Position of C1 (lateral aspect) and vertebra in detail

Spinal Nerves and Dermatome

C0 -C1 (occipito-atlas) nerves form the very upper part of the cervical plexus. Nerves from here communicate with Cranial Nerves XI (Accessory), X (Vagus) and XII (Hypoglossal). There are also muscular branches to the Capitis Lateralis and Anterior and Longissimus Capitis. There is no dermatome from this level.

Autonomic Nerves and Organs Supplied

The following are supplied via the superior cervical ganglion – facial bones, inner and middle ear and eyes. Due to the complex relationships in this region with the 3 cranial nerves mentioned and the cerebro-spinal fluid, the atlas will also affect the brain (especially the pituitary region) and affect the blood supply to the head and scalp. The atlas also affects many of the body's internal organs via its link with the vagus nerve (X cranial). Therapists please note that this is *the* most important and yet fragile area of the whole spine and extreme caution will be required with any type of local bodywork. Expert training in your specific therapy is essential when dealing with this region.

Muscles Supplied

Nerves from C0-C1 supply the Rectus Capitis Longus, Rectus Capitis Lateralis, Rectus Capitis Anterior, Rectus Capitis Posterior Major and Minor, Inferior Oblique and Longissimus Capitis. Please note that there is a direct link from the Rectus Capitis Posterior Minor with the dura mata – hence aggravation at this region will give pain and congestion around the head.

Effects of Spinal Misalignment

As already intimated, if there are any lesions of the atlas, however minor, there can be several disparate symptoms that ensue. In my experience of dealing with hundreds of atlas lesions, I can affirm that the most common cause of atlas is by having problems with L5 – its vertebral couple.

When the lower lumbar spine is out of alignment for any time the atlas *will* be affected. The upper cervical lesion has therefore to be viewed holistically and treated accordingly. Symptoms that may be presented by direct or indirect atlas lesions are headaches, migraine, insomnia, neurasthenia, amnesia, vertigo, dizziness, lethargy, hypertension and many of the emotional conditions discussed later.

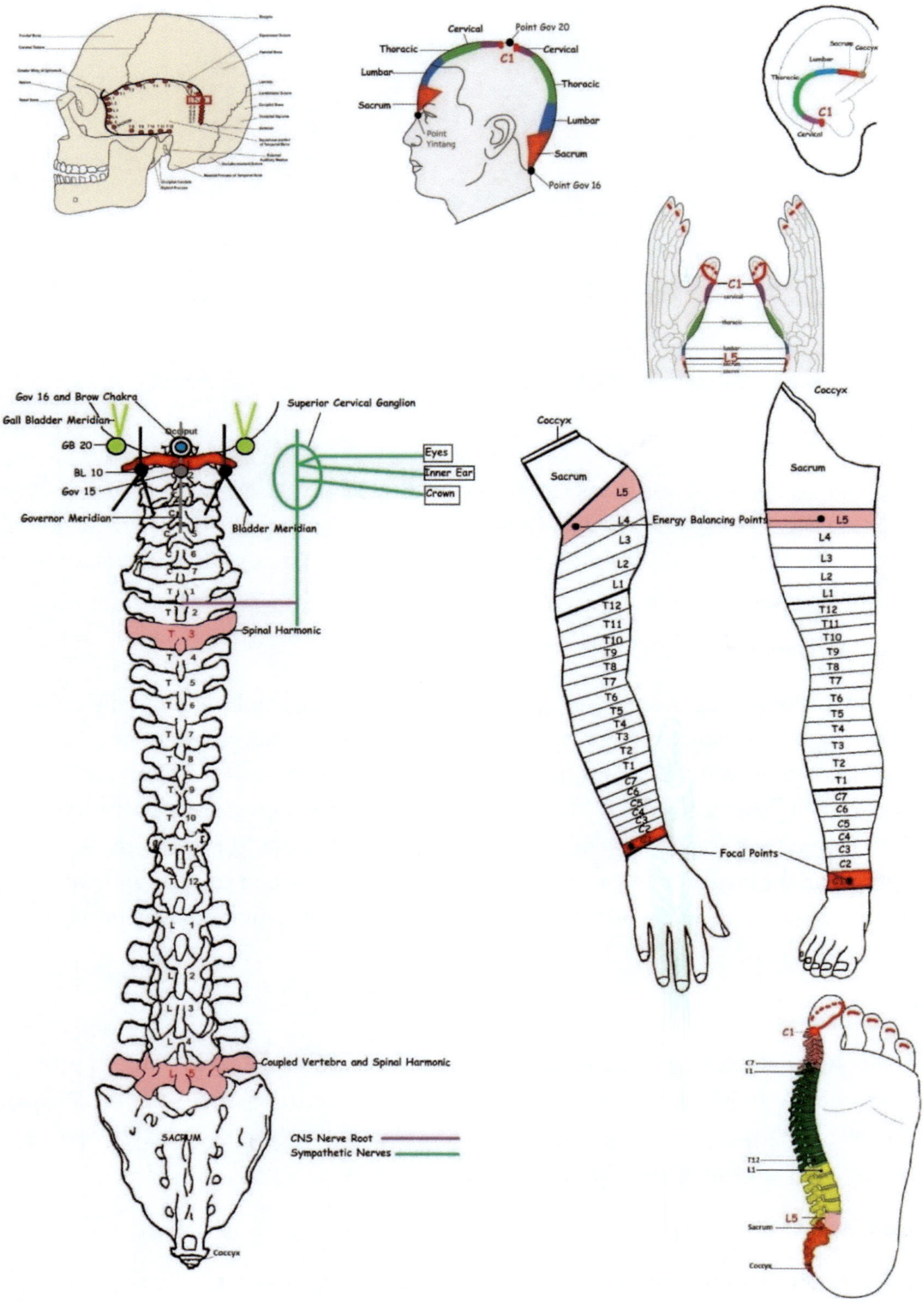

Reflections and Associations of Cervical 1

Spinal Couple and Harmonic

As intimated earlier, the spinal couple is L5 with the further harmonic vertebra at T3.

Linked Internal Organs via the Energetic System

The main energetic influences on the atlas are from the Bladder and Governor meridians, plus the Gall Bladder, Small Intestine and Large Intestine. Therefore, all the internal organs associated with these meridians will affect internal organs via the deep meridian channels. Specific acupoints that are used locally are BL 10, GB 20, Gov 15 and Gov 16.

Posterior Major Chakra

The posterior Brow chakra at Gov 16 directly affects the atlas. There is also a degree of influence from the Crown chakra at Gov 20.

Reflections

These are like C2 description and as per the diagrams

Personality and Emotional Links

The atlas is concerned with 'Thought and Emotion' both in the overall and individual pictures. As previously intimated, when these are suppressed as a child or teenager, this may give symptoms such as anxiety, nervousness, hyperactivity, nervous headache and visual disturbances. Other conditions may include nervous breakdown, amnesia and migraine. Other aspect of anomalies of the atlas and sub occipital region are the more 'spiritual' ones. If the child's intuition, spirituality or intellect are suppressed, this could give rise to atlas and occipital lesions in later life. This is due to the influence of the Crown chakra on this region. Suppression of intuitive gifts (e.g. natural healing, angelic realm contacts etc.) will certainly affect the sub occipital region in later life. It is sometimes difficult to ascertain the true cause of a lesion and certain questioning of the patient may be difficult, but if they do open to you and express their problems as children or adolescents, this can open a new world of understanding of the true cause of some physical conditions.

CHAPTER FIVE – The Occiput and Sphenoid

The Occiput

The occiput is positioned at the posterior aspect of the skull and articulates with the parietal and temporal bones in the skull and the atlas. Through its foramen magnum, the cranial cavity and vertebral canal are connected. The Occiput is hugely important in bodywork and acupressure. It is the main vehicle of assessment through craniosacral therapy and cranial osteopathy, where the hands of the therapist are placed on the occiput to ascertain to rate and rhythm of the cerebro spinal fluid. This is known as the vault hold. It is also an important player in such therapies as Cranio-Sacral reflextherapy, Occipito-Cranial Therapy acupressure and acupuncture. Its link and association with the Sacrum is of paramount importance.

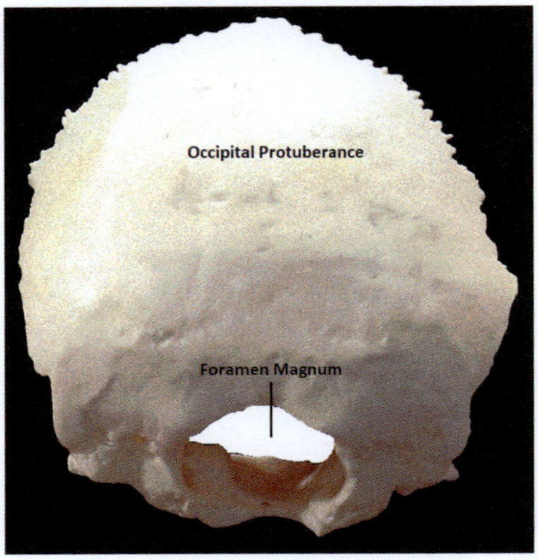

Figure 5.1 The Occiput Bone

Effects of Misalignment

Injury of any magnitude will often affect the atlanto-occipital joint and jeopardise the position of the atlas. Fracture and other accidental injury to the occiput may affect the eyes, due to the area of brain that it protects having links with the visual cortex. Long standing misalignment will start to affect the lower back and pelvis due to its correlation with the sacrum. The occiput is often affected through childbirth if this region of the skull is pulled with undue enthusiasm. General misalignment symptoms include headache, migraine, incoordination and unsteadiness, vertigo, thermal imbalance and lethargy.

Spinal Couple and Harmonics

The spinal couple is the Sacrum with a further harmonic at T2

Energetic influence

The main meridian influences are the Governor, Bladder and Gall Bladder (see diagram). The main acupoints are Gov 17, Gov 17, Gov 18, BL 9, BL 10, GB 11, GB 12, GB 19 and GB 20.

Posterior Major Chakra

The main influence is from the posterior Brow chakra at Gov 16, but there is also quite a lot of influence from the Crown chakra at Gov 20.

Reflections

Foot and Hand – the reflex is to be found on the lateral aspect (inside) of the middle of the great toe and thumb but its influence traverses around these two digits

Skull – The skull reflex is positioned over the frontal bone

Arm and Leg – The reflexes are on the heel of the hand and the heel of the foot

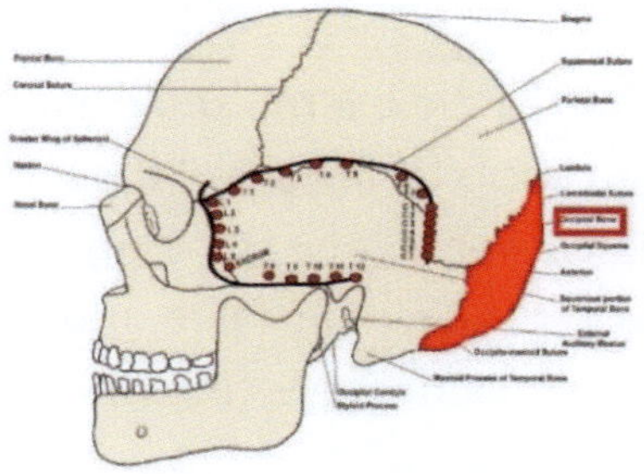

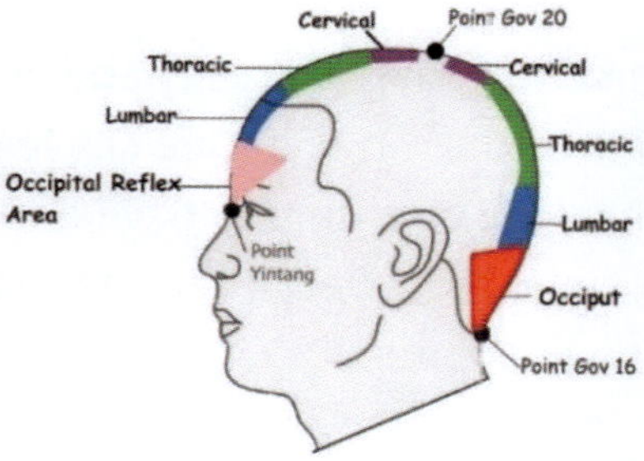

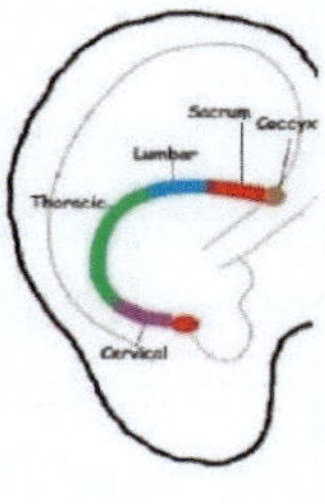

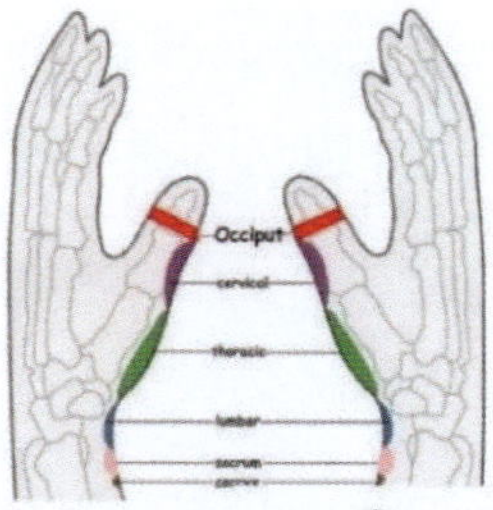

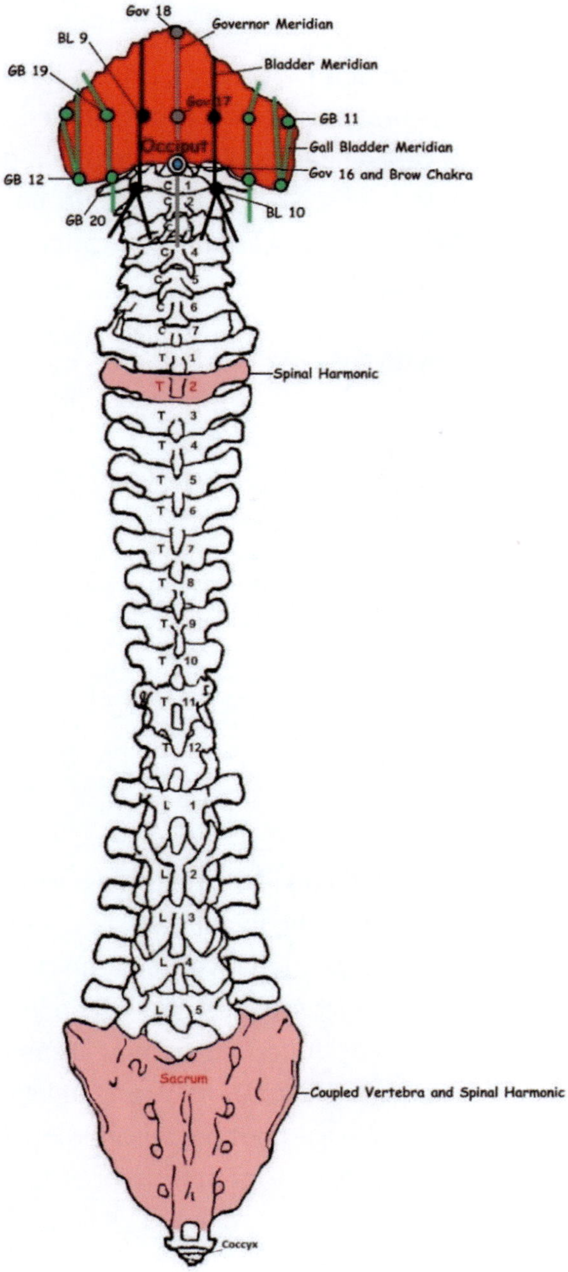

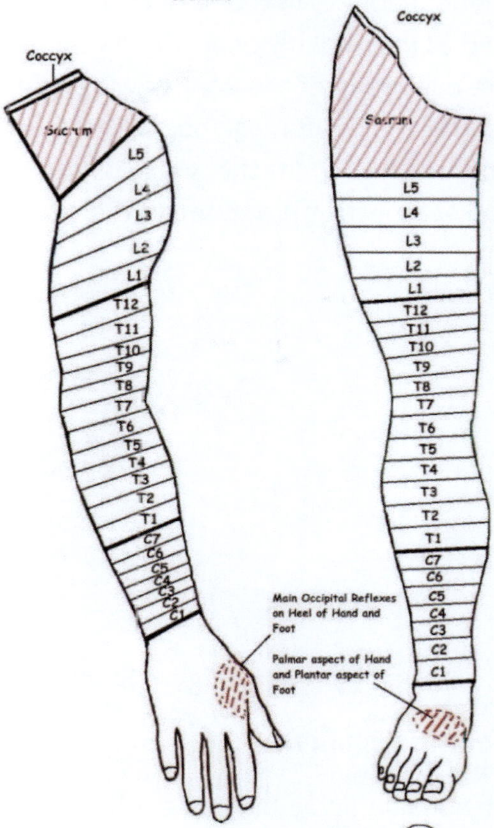

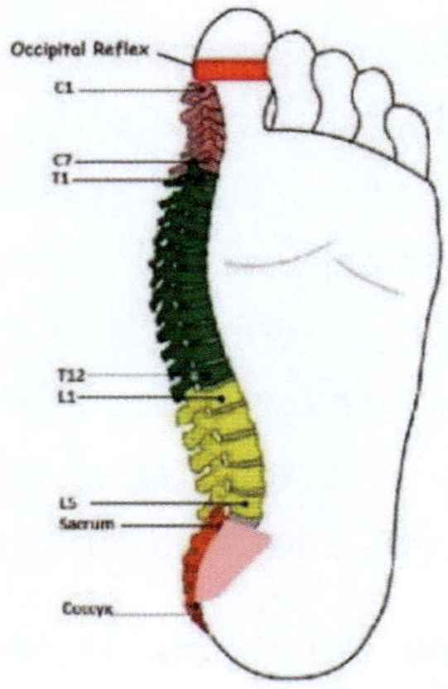

Associations and Reflections of the Occiput

Emotional and Personality Link

The Occiput is associated with 'Movement, Family, Security and Finance' in the overall and detailed pictures. This means that any type of insecurity in one's life can lead to occipital lesions. People who cannot earth or ground themselves will also tend to have occipital lesions. Long standing financial worries can also affect the cranial base. Because of its link with the Crown chakra, the cranial base region is associated with our 'spirituality'. I have seen at first hand where folk who are denied what they consider to be their calling (such as entering the church as a profession) will get occipital lesions with all the associated physical and emotional symptoms that are linked with these.

The Sphenoid

The Sphenoid bone is in the base of the skull in front of the occiput and temporal bones. It is often described as resembling a bat with its wings expanded and its feet below. It is a complicated structure consisting of the greater wings, lesser wings and a central part (sellae tursica) that houses and protects the pituitary gland. As it can be felt on the outside of the skull at the spheno-basilar synchondrosis and spans the whole length of the floor of the skull, it is of great significance to bodyworks, especially craniosacral therapists and cranial osteopaths.

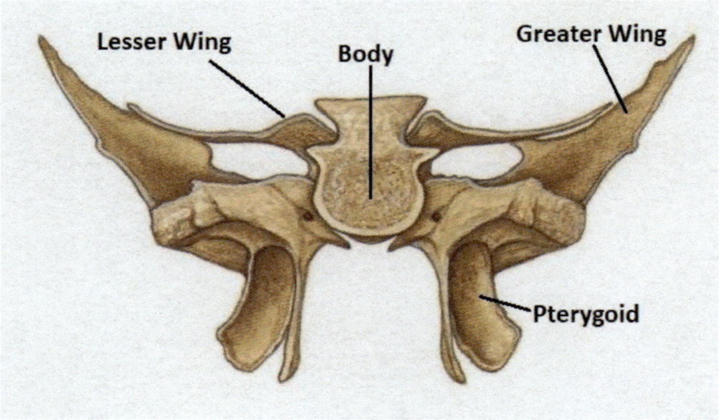

Figure 5.2 Posterior aspect of the Sphenoid

Effects of Misalignment

Severe trauma inflicted by road traffic accidents, for example, would be life threatening as fractures and gross misalignment will affect the blood flow to the brain and upper spinal cord. Less severe problems of misalignment may stem from imbalance with the coccyx and pelvis or to the cranial base and occiput, as there is a fixed link between the two cranial bones. Symptoms would include migraine, sinus inflammation, endocrine disorders, allergies, TMJ dysfunction, learning disabilities, reading problems and emotional imbalance such as depression and OCD. I am a strong believer in each baby who has been born with the aid of forceps should be checked out by a professional craniosacral therapist or similar. All the above symptoms, and more, may stem from pressure by forceps on the sphenobasilar synchondrosis.

Spinal Couple and Harmonics

The main spinal harmony is the coccyx with further harmonics at T2 and T10

Energetic Influence

The part of the sphenoid that can be accessed on the skull may be influenced by the Stomach, Triple Energizer and Gall Bladder meridians. Specific local acupoints are GB1, GB2, TE22, TE23, ST 7, ST 8 and Taiyang. Taiyang is the non-meridian acupoint that is specifically situated on the sphenobasilar synchondrosis (SBS) used so much in subtle bodywork

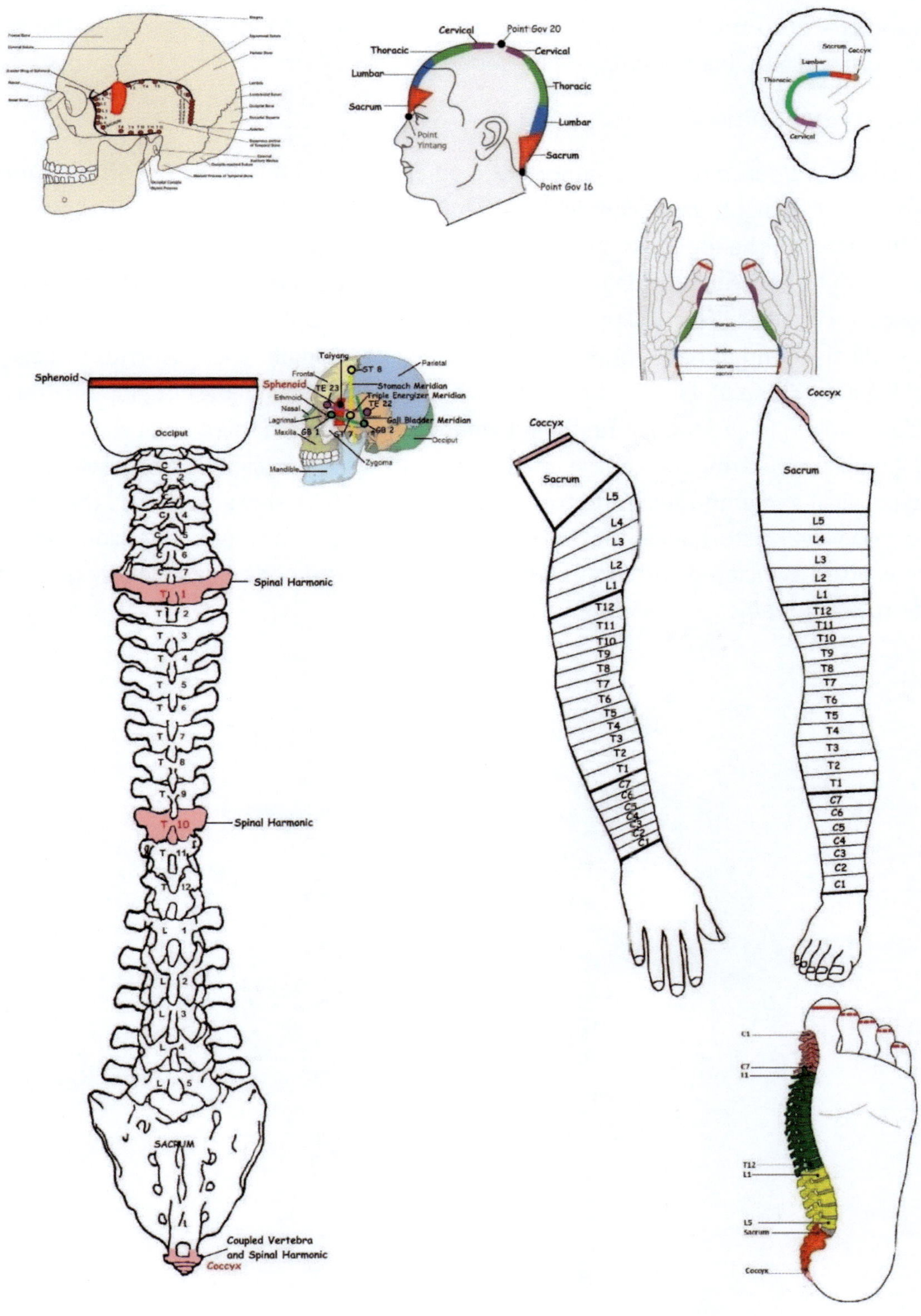

Associations and Reflections of the Sphenoid

Major Chakra Influence

The sphenoid is influenced by both anterior and posterior Brow chakras plus a high degree of influence from the Crown chakra.

Reflections

Foot and Hand – The reflected sphenoid is to be found on the upper aspect of the lateral side (inside) of the great toe and thumb, but the influence traverses around these digits. The sphenoid is not reflected on the arm, leg or skull.

Emotional and Personality Links

The Sphenoid is considered the most important cranial bone and the one most often found to be out of alignment. It is highly significant in 'left-right' cerebral imbalance and anomalies may produce dizziness, light headedness, and postural conditions. Like the Occiput, it is associated with 'Movement, Family, Security and Finance' in the overall and detailed pictures. This means that any type of insecurity in one's life may lead to sphenoid lesions. People who cannot earth or ground themselves will also tend to have sphenoid lesions. Long standing financial worries can also affect the cranial base. Because of its link with the Crown chakra, the cranial base region is associated with our 'spirituality'. I have seen at first hand where folk who are denied what they consider to be their calling (such as entering the church as a profession) will get occipital lesions with all the associated physical and emotional symptoms that are linked with these. Whereas the Occiput is associated with visual disturbance, the Sphenoid is associated with sinus congestion. Sinus congestion is often associated with one's life being in a 'rut' and not being able to expand one's horizons or to break free.

PART TWO

Treatment of Acute and Chronic Spinal Conditions

CHAPTER SIX – Assessment and Analysis

It goes without saying that before any treatment can take place, the condition needs to be assessed. Assessment and diagnosis of a condition depends on the type of therapist you are. If you are a physical therapist or osteopath, your professional training demands that you observe, palpate and take a case history before embarking on treatment. If you are experienced it takes less time than if you are new to the profession, but at each stage strict notation must be observed. A traditional acupuncturist may assess in a different way, by using the patient's own 'signalling' via the tongue, pulses, abdomen – although with a mechanical condition it isn't always an advantage to be able to have these extra skills. The naturopathic skills are an advantage to ascertain if the seemingly mechanical/physical condition is being caused by some type of internal organic, chemical or emotional imbalance. A reflexologist generally assesses whilst the first treatment is taking place as the client reacts with various tender and 'ouch' points and areas that usually indicate areas that are out of balance. I do not intend, in this book to teach the many and varied ways of ascertaining what type of spinal condition you are dealing with, such as case history, spasm and postural awareness – this is a book about the practicalities of treating acute and chronic conditions with acupressure and reflexology, so it is assumed that you have a clear idea of what is being presented. Does an accurate diagnosis or analysis really matter? If I answered 'no' to this question, my physiotherapy colleagues would be up in arms and if I answered 'yes' then my subtle energy colleagues would equally be offended at the absurdity. As I intimated in the opening chapter in Book One, these books represents a half- way house between the orthodox and 'alternative' approaches to looking at spinal conditions, so I shall simply say that it is essential that you understand the anatomy and physiology of the spine et al and have an educated working knowledge of the many and varied types of spinal anomalies that one encounters, and if is not the case, then you should consider referring to a more experienced and competent practitioner. Analysis is possible by two types of touch and feel – one by ascertaining an appropriate tender, focal or 'ouch' point on the many and various reflected spinal areas and the other by what I call 'hold and listen'

The reflected spine and the focal or 'ouch' point

We all have wise bodies, and we possess several spinal reflected areas by which you should be able to ascertain the degree of severity of the spinal condition. I wrote in 'Light Touch Reflextherapy' "You already know, through the initial consultation, where the main thrust of the imbalance lies, and it is now that you ascertain the cause of this imbalance. You simply *ask the body*". The main reflected areas (see Book One for details) are the Foot, Hand, Arm, Leg and Temporo-Sphenoidal Line (TSL). Once the general region of the spinal anomaly is known e.g. cervical, lumbar etc. you then *gently* palpate in that area of one or more of the reflected regions. You have previously indicated to your patient that they inform you when a point is tender. If the patient recoils or tells you in no uncertain terms that you have 'hit the right point', this generally indicates an acute condition with a specific vertebra. If the tissues in the region feel sluggish or you don't elicit a tender or 'ouch' point, it usually indicates a chronic situation in that specific spinal region. To ratify your suspicions of a chronic disorder you must proceed from gentle palpation to a more robust and deeper form of touch. It goes without saying that you must inform your patient before this is done. If you palpate the TMS line, be careful that your touch isn't too severe. Below are three illustrations showing where the reflected regions are. I have chosen C5, T5 and L5 as representatives of the whole. Please note that although the reflexes are predominantly on the medial aspects of the hand and foot, the reflex exists the *whole way around the limb* and the 'ouch' or focal point may be somewhere on this line. Also, please note that the L5 reflected line on the foot goes all the way around the heel region and is difficult to show in the illustration (Figure 15.1).

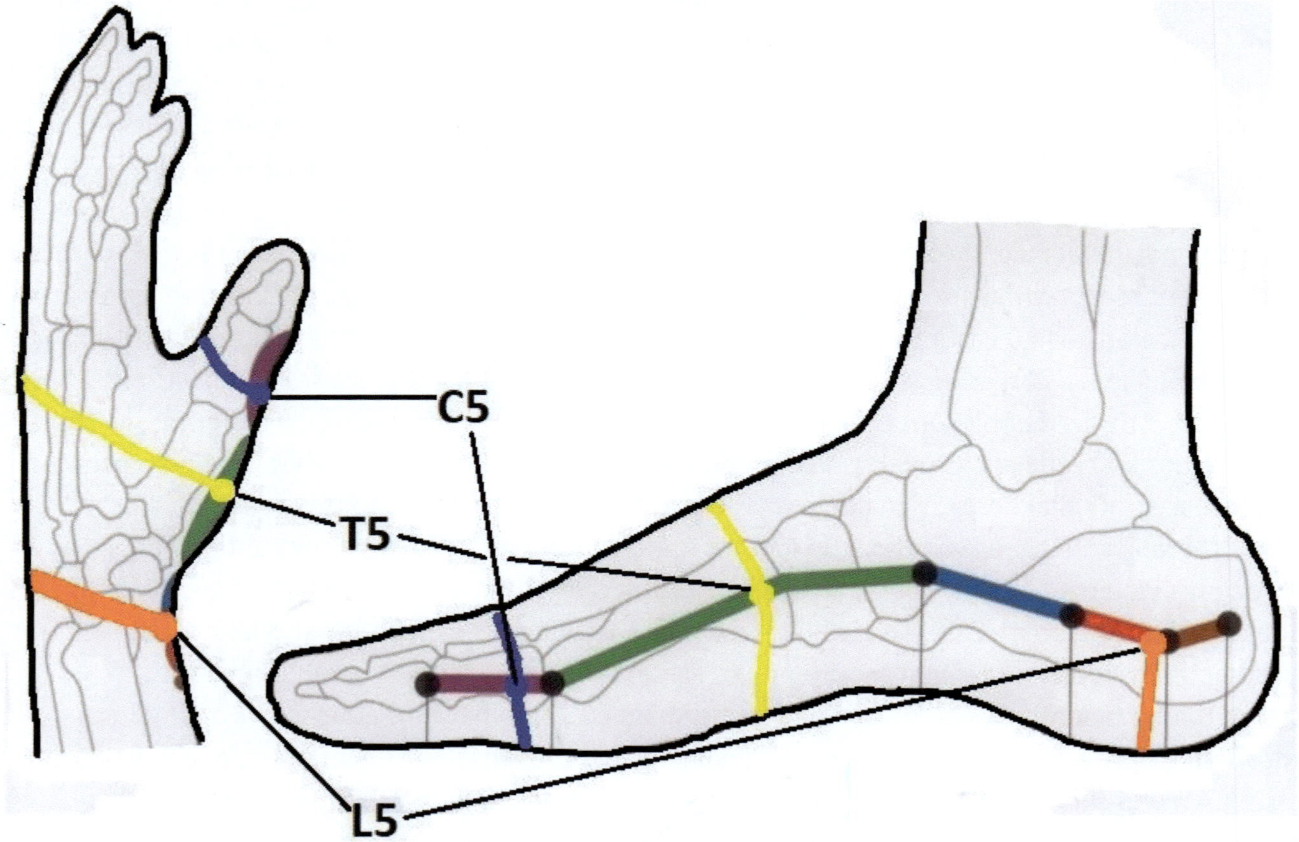

Figure 6.1 The reflected areas of C5, T5 and L5 on the Hand and Foot

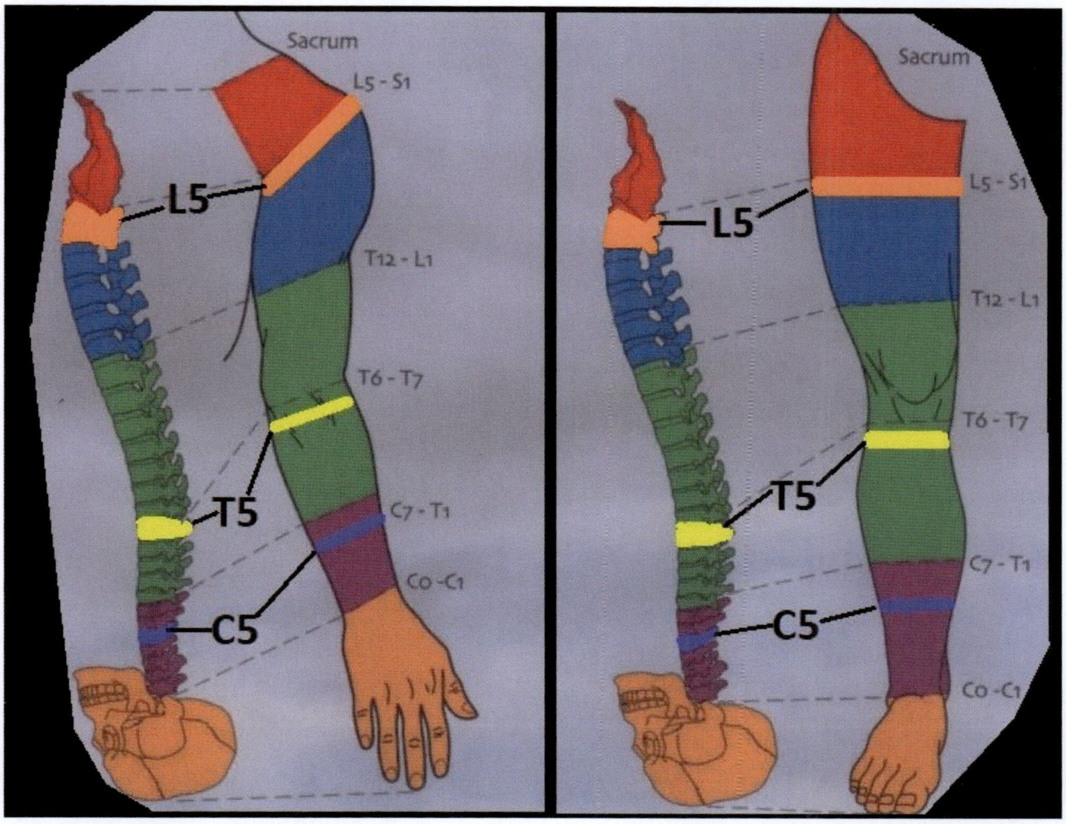

Figure 6.2 The reflected areas of C5, T5 and L5 on the Arm and Leg

Similarly, the reflected region on the arm and leg circumvent the limb and the 'ouch' or focal point may not be on the medial aspect. Please forgive the differing colours in Figure 6.2, it was scanned from my poster The Holistic Spine (with embellishments!)

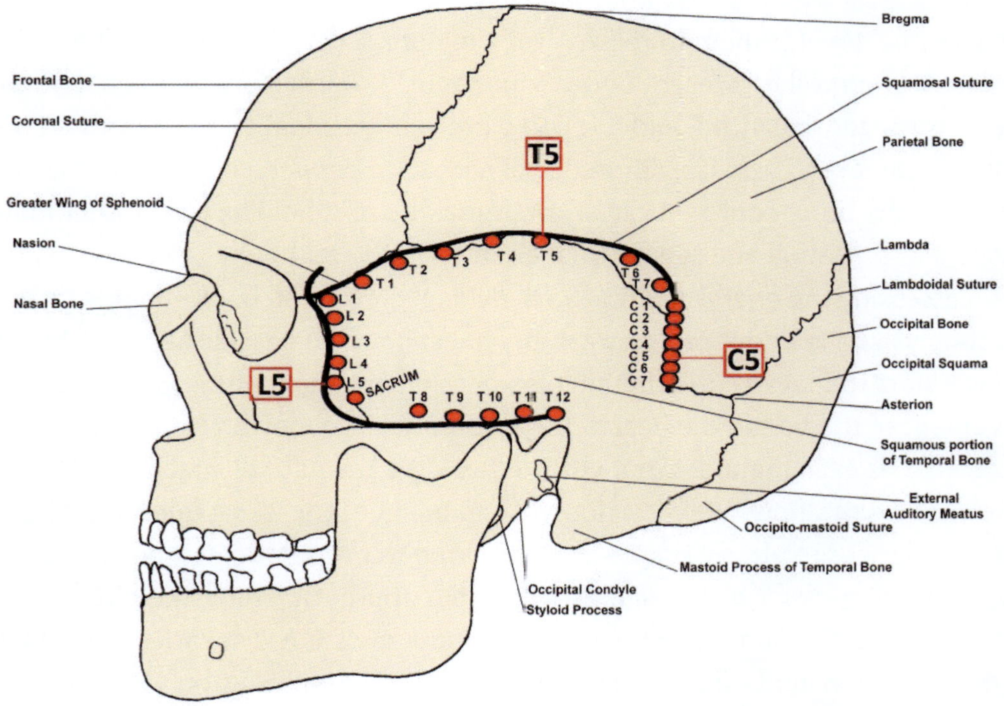

Figure 6.3 The reflected areas of C5, T5 and L5 on the TS Line

The reflected spinal vertebrae on the temporo-sphenoidal line come under the general heading of 'listening posts' that were discussed in my book 'Acupressure and Reflextherapy in Medical Conditions'. As well as being tender to the touch if the vertebra has an acute condition the TMS points may also be used in the second type of analysis – hold and listen.

'Hold and Listen'

The two main regions of the body where you can 'hold and listen' are the occiput and heels. The occiput, as previously mentioned, is used as the 'vault' hold in craniosacral therapy. There are also several specific listening posts around the head and feet that may be used to ascertain the energetic quality of a specific internal organ. For the spine per se, the main 'listening' area is the heels, but acupoint BL 62 is also excellent. There are several aspects to 'hold and listen', and it is such an important and fundamental part of acupressure/reflexology that they are discussed below.

- Hold and Listen is the way that you 'listen' with your hands/fingers to what the patient's energetic system is attempting to tell you.
- The comfort of you and your patient is essential as the hold may be for several minutes.
- Palpate and hold the acupoint or heels gently – do not approach quickly and do not grab.
- Initially you will feel nothing, do not *will* anything to occur but adopt an open and clear mind with total focus on what you are doing
- As well as focus you must have intention. An easy way to remember this is to think of the pneumonic 'IF' and turn it round. Therefore, Focus and Intention are of paramount importance. The intention is to go through in your mind what you are attempting to do – e.g. if you are holding the heels to ascertain the condition of the lumbar spine, this must be held in your thoughts. Total concentration is essential.
- Initially it is a good idea to assess the general energy of your patient. The heels need to be held for at least a minute. Try not to move your hands, even slightly, within this time as it will take this time for them to relax. After a minute, a certain amount of heat, tingling or other sensation will be present under your hands. A warm glow suggests that their energetic system is roughly balanced, and it is OK to proceed to spinal assessment. With most patients, however, there is a difference of sensation between each heel. One heel may be warm and the other cool or sticky. If this remains whilst holding for another minute just accept that sensation and see if it changes after your treatment.
- When assessing the energy state of an individual part of the body – in this case, the spine – you simply ask the body! You may ask any question if the answer has a 'yes' or 'no' reply. You will start to feel a gentle rhythm of expansion and contraction like the ebb and flow movement of the tide at the beach. The rate varies from person to person at between six to sixteen cycles each minute. What you are feeling is the natural vital force flow of your patient. Once this flow is felt (do not *will* it to happen) try asking questions about the spine. This technique is relatively simple but takes time to master. Remember you are dealing with subtle energy so don't be too aggressive in your approach. Start asking general questions and proceed to the minutia. If the answer to your question is negative, the vital force rhythm stays constant - if the reply is positive, the rhythm will stop. When this occurs, wait for a few seconds and the rhythm will recommence and you may ask the next question. Examples of typical questions you may ask would be: -

1. “Is there a lesion within the cervical spine that is treatable with subtle bodywork?” If “yes”, proceed to
2. “Is the lesion at C0-C1? At C1-C2 etc. etc.” until you reach C7-T1 if the previous answers have been negative
3. When the vertebral level is known you may ask specific questions concerning pain, inflammation, mechanical lesions i.e. disc, facet joint, subluxation, fixation etc.

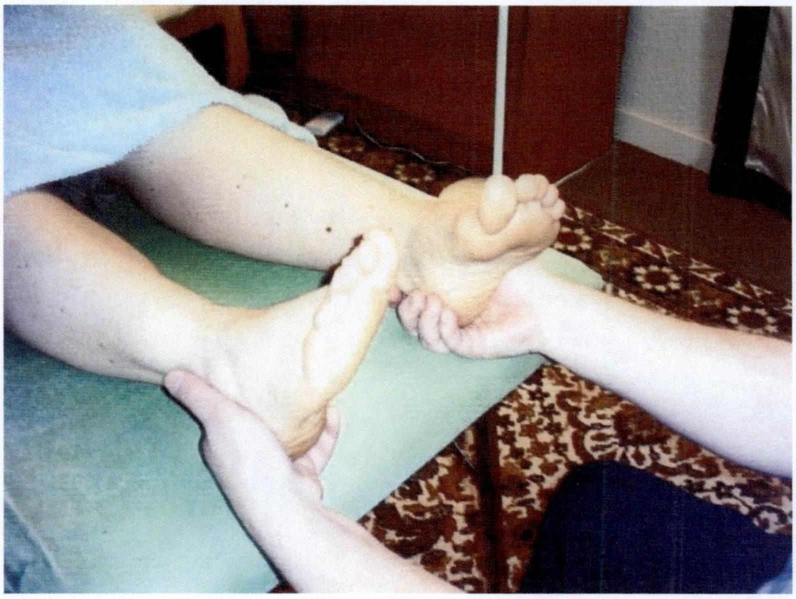

Photograph 6.1 Holding the Heels

You can see that the exact condition can be ascertained by this method. This may also be achieved by holding single acupoints but is slightly more difficult and takes more practice.

CHAPTER SEVEN – Acupressure and Reflexology in Acute Pain

I devised the method discussed in this chapter several years ago and have taught it to grateful practitioners on hundreds of occasions. The great beauty of this method is that it is quick, and it seems to work! It does not matter what your patient or client is suffering from on an ongoing basis, if they have acute pain, it must be treated immediately – they wouldn’t expect anything else.

Theory

Two points are chosen – a reflex point (usually but not exclusively on the foot) and an acupoint anywhere on the body. It therefore utilises a reflex point and an acupoint in tandem, hence giving us the best of both worlds – reflexology and acupressure – at the same time. It is important that the same fingers are used – either both index fingers or both middle fingers. This is because the ‘magnetism’ of the fingers (described later)

Method

Place one middle finger pad on the reflected area (reflex) on the foot, either left or right foot as the spine is represented on the very medial aspect of either foot. Gently feel for the 'ouch' point and ask the patient to guide you as to which point is the most tender – once found, leave one finger in situ or mark it with a pen. Then place the middle finger pad of the other hand on the associated acupoint (see diagrams) on the leg, having felt around until the focal or 'ouch' point is located. Now gently massage both fingers on their respective points for a few seconds before just holding them quite still – making sure you are comfortable, and your forearms are supported. Do not give any stimulating massage as their discomfort could become worse. Even if you keep your fingers still, the patient's pain may become slightly worse for a few seconds as you experience some kind of subtle 'barrier'. You will need total focus and intention whilst doing this technique and don't let the mind wander. Your focus is on the two points being held and your intention is the reduction of your patient's discomfort. After a couple of minutes or so you should find the tissues under your fingers appear warmer and have a different sensation to before (I call it warm putty). It is usually at this stage when you and your patient are entering theta brainwave mode that the pain will start to subside, and they will feel more relaxed. The following illustrations show the two points for five levels of spinal pain.

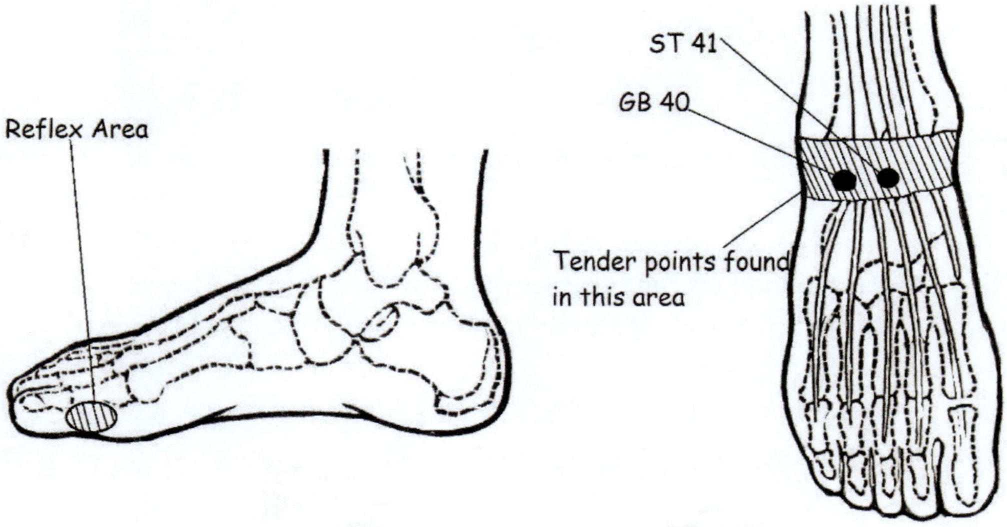

Figure 7.1 Treatment of Upper Cervical Pain

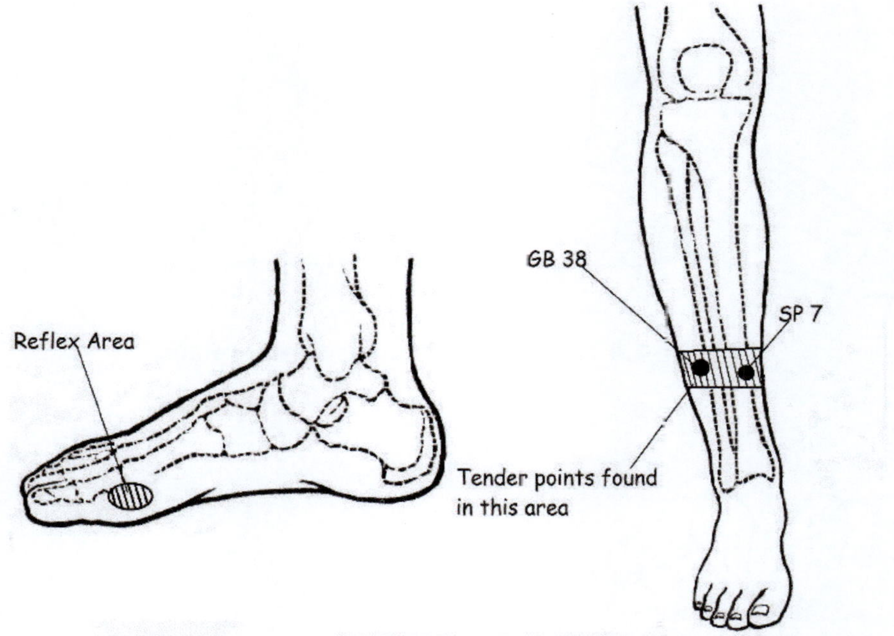

Figure 7.2 Treatment of Cervico-Thoracic pain

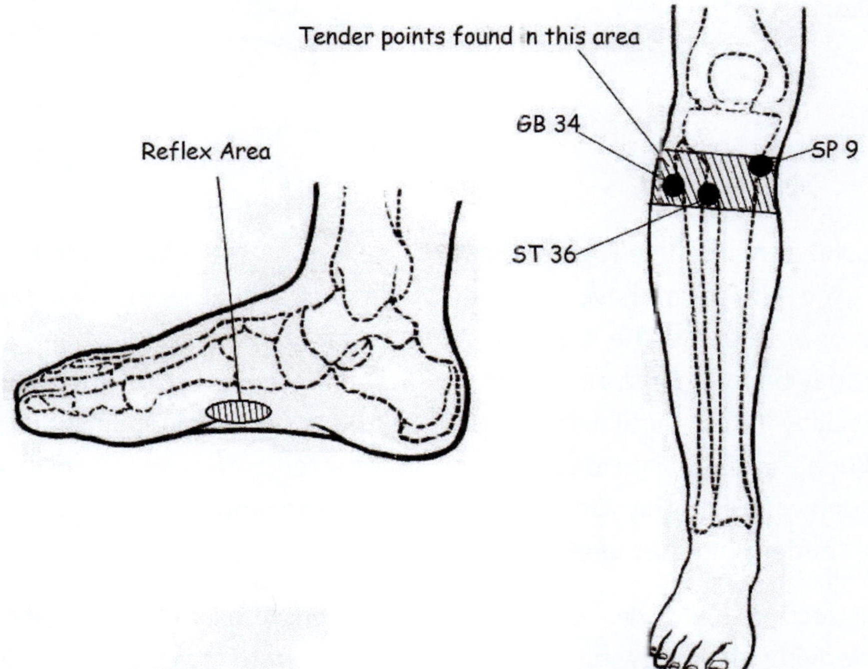

Figure 7.3 Treatment of Mid Thoracic Pain

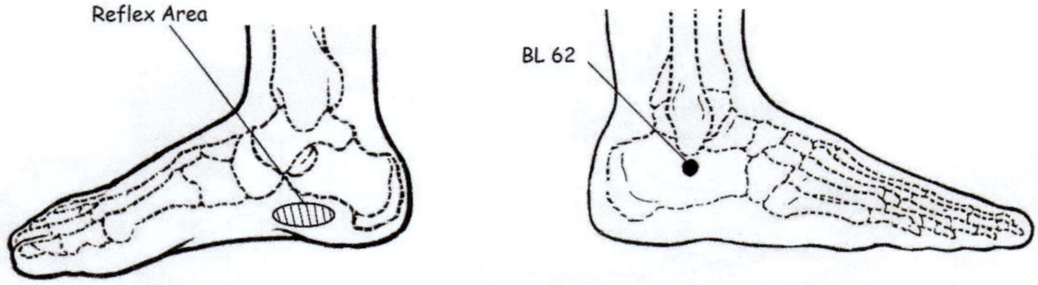

Figure 7.4 Treatment of Lower Lumbar Pain

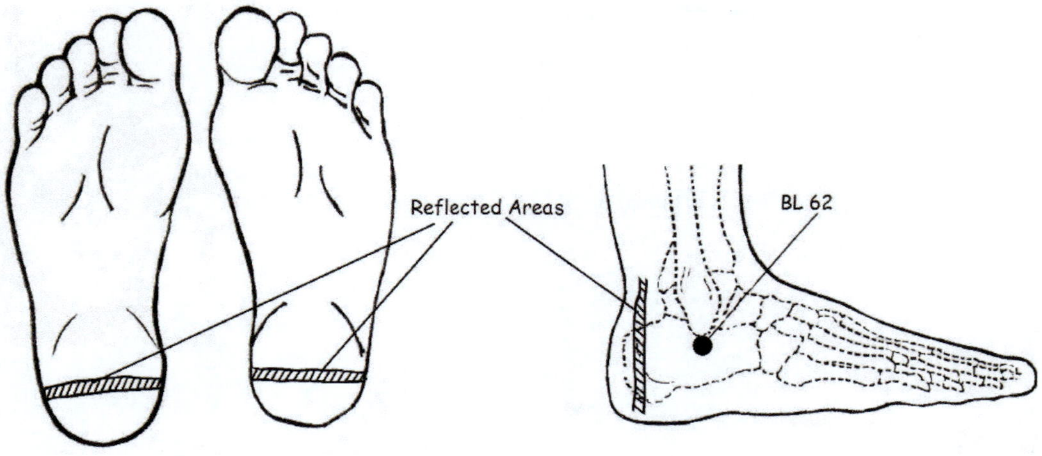

Figure 7.5 Treatment of Sciatica

The first three sites show the reflected spinal areas on the leg and the main acupoints within the 'band' that may be used – it doesn't have to be any of the ones that are indicated, just gently feel around for the focal or ouch point. The latter two of lower lumbar and sciatica pain both include acupoint BL 62 that may be found just inferior to the lateral malleolus. BL 62 is a major player in spinal pain, but especially lumbosacral discomfort. This is because the bladder meridian flows either side of the spine. When treating sciatic pain, the sciatic reflected area is quite extensive. The 'ouch' point may be found anywhere on the sciatic line. Don't forget to work alongside your patient to constantly ask if the tender point has been located.

Please note that this section deal with acute pain with little regard for the actual condition, either symptomatic or underlying, the following chapter deals with how to treat spinal conditions with subtle touch and massage.

CHAPTER EIGHT – Treatment of Spinal Conditions

Examples of spinal conditions include:

- **Muscle tears** to varying degrees of the deep intravertebral muscles. These produce pain, localized inflammation and swelling, but rarely deformity.
- **Ligamentous tears** to varying degrees of the intervertebral ligaments, these produce pain, spasm, inflammation and localized deformity, resulting in the facet joints becoming subluxed or hyper-stretched.
- **Nerve root inflammation**. This is caused by a sudden overstretch or lateral disc protrusion and produces very acute pain – local and radiating – localized muscle spasm and inflammation. This can result in in neuritis of the whole length of the inflamed nerve e.g. sciatica.
- **Centralized disc protrusions**. These can cause excruciating localized and referred pain, spasm and inflammation. Requires initial complete rest and anti-inflammatory medication for 48 hours. Acupressure may commence after this time.

It is often the case that a spinal lesion occurs because of a chronic (long lasting) spinal weakness that may have been caused from a fall or other accident as a child. The damage is done in infancy and the person spends many years compensating for their underlying weakness. Eventually, during some activity (not always needs to be strenuous) the original weakness will rear its ugly head and exhibit acute symptoms.

Before discussing the order of treatment, it is important to mention two aspects of the procedure – energy balancing and magnetism of the fingers.

Energy Balancing

Energy balancing (chi) is performed between two acupoints or an acupoint and reflex point, either using the finger pads or whole hand. Place the SAME finger of each hand on the two points to be balanced and after an initial massage of the points (five seconds), keep the two fingers quite still – with your focus and intention. Energy balancing occurs when the sensation under the two fingers is the same. This may take some time and sometimes not happen at all. It is important that you do not *will* or encourage the energy balancing – just let it happen. There are two aspects to energy balancing – firstly a simple energy balance that occurs usually within one minute, before you proceed to the next stage of the treatment. Another aspect of energy balancing involves continually holding the points after the initial similar sensation, through a *change of emphasis*, the point of oneness between you and your patient when genuine contact healing may take place. Some folk get a little 'hot under the collar', dismissive or even abusive when the word 'healing' is used. I always explain that a dictionary definition of the word is 'to make whole'. There are, of course, very many aspects to healing (and I given my fair share of lectures on this topic). The type used here is simple 'conductive' healing that may occur with any form of touch and the correct mind set. The 'oneness' between you and the patient is often called the A/T state when both adopt the passage from alpha to theta brain wave activity – in other words the patient is as relaxed as possible, without falling asleep (delta).

Magnetism of the Fingers

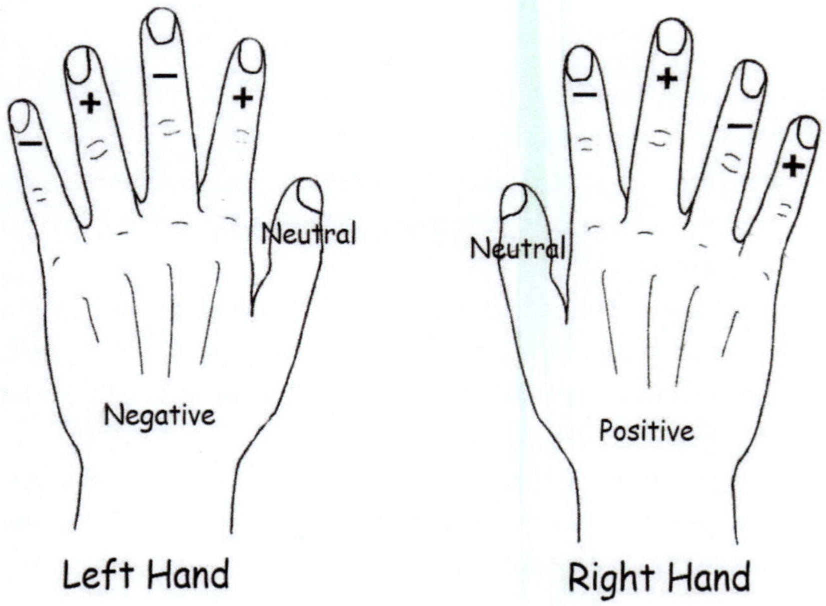

Figure 8.1 Magnetism of the Fingers

In touch therapy, as discussed in this book, it is important to use both middle finger pads (or both index if it is more comfortable) – why is this? It is said that each finger possesses either a negative or positive magnetic influence so that they may be utilised in simple conductive healing. The thumbs are said to be neutral and should not be used in energy balancing. Electricity and magnetism flows from the negative towards the positive pole and this appears to be replicated in the human body. The left hand is said to be negative and the right hand positive. The left middle finger is negative, and the right middle finger is positive – thus it follows that in order to create an energy balance between two points, it is best to hold the two points that have an opposite 'charge' so that the energy link is stronger. Please note that this is only pertinent in this type of contact healing and may not apply in other forms, of which there are many. When treating spinal conditions there is a logical 'batting order'. This is not 'set in stone' and could vary according to individual circumstances, but this is a good template to follow.

General Order of Treatment

1. Palpate the painful area gently to ascertain the exact lesion – so that you also know where the various reflected points on the limbs, feet and hand should be. This is often known as the *focal* or *ouch* point. Make sure your patient is comfortable.
2. Locate acupoint **SI 3** on the ulnar aspect of the little finger (see illustration). This point is the 'key' point of the Governor/ Du Mai meridian, so is used to 'open up' this important energy channel. The technique is to locate SI 3 on the side of the lesion and give some gentle circular massage for approximately twenty seconds.
3. Locate a suitable 'distal' point – this is an acupoint on the spine that is massaged with some degree of stimulation for about 20 seconds to 'create a reservoir of energy'. This acupoint is

often one of the posterior major chakra points but could be on the leg/foot for sacral and coccyx lesions.

4. Locate a suitable 'proximal' acupoint, always on the Governor meridian but not necessarily on the spine and create an 'energy balance' between the two, thus allowing energy flow through the lesion – this is the most difficult aspect and may not occur quickly.
5. Balance the lesion with suitable reflected and local powerful acupoints – these could be the reflected point on the limbs, hand, foot, nearest major chakra point, same vertical or horizontal point. With acute spinal lesions, there is often a facet subluxation, however minor, that will need rectifying. If you have been trained in such procedures, this is the time to do this *gentle* manoeuvre. You will find the tissues are more pliable to allow this to be carried out.
6. The final procedure is to 'unwind' the lesion. This is to correct the tensions in the soft tissue around the lesion that have undergone torsion strain during and after the initial spinal lesion. There are three ways of unwinding, and with each type (you don't have to do them all), you merely place the fingers or hands on the sides of the lesion, adopt some focus and intention with your mindset and allow the tissues to gently unwind under your hands. Do not *will* anything to happen and do not oppose any unwinding that occurs – go with the flow!

Ways of Unwinding the Tissues

1. The most used and possibly most effective way to unwind the tissues is to place both hands gently either side of the lesion, firstly on the spine just proximal and distal and secondly either side. Each unwinding may take a couple of minutes – even longer with a long-standing condition.
2. Place one hand over the lesion and the other hand on the spinal harmonic vertebra. This represents a terrific way of unwinding that works well.
3. Place two or three fingers bilateral to the spine with one set of fingers on the lesion (muscle spasm) and the other fingers on the opposite side of the spinous process. Patient is supine with cervical lesions and prone further down the spine. The fingers on the spasm side will soon become warm and start to free up the lesion whilst the other fingers will be drawn towards the lesion. Go with the movement and don't oppose it. After a couple of minutes, a 'still point' will be produced when no movement occurs for quite several seconds. There will then follow a sudden movement away from the lesion site as the localized ligaments unwind.

Treatment of specific spinal regions

For purposes of simplicity, the spine has been divided into 5 sections – upper cervical, lower cervical, thoracic, lower lumbar and sacro-coccyx. All other regions of the spine will adopt the same treatment routine. The symptomatology of each level is available for you in Part One.

Upper Cervical Spine – C1, C2, C3

1. Locate the focal or ouch point of the lesion and possibly mark it with a pen (if there is no hair).
2. Locate and massage SI 3 for a few seconds.
3. The distal point is Gov 14, on the mid line between C7 and T1. This point should be stimulated for about thirty seconds or until an appreciable amount of heat is felt under the fingers. This part is essential especially in long standing conditions where vital force in the region is low.
4. The proximal point is Gov 20 on top of the head. Gently stimulate this point before energy balancing it with Gov 14. This may not be achievable in long standing lesions. When this is the case it is important that it is repeated after the unwinding stage, to test that there is now free energy flow through the lesion.
5. Now place the pad of the dominant middle finger on the focal point (often over the transverse process) and energy balance with the following: -
    - Distal Point Gov 14
    - Posterior Brow chakra point at Gov 16 (if not too adjacent to the lesion)
    - Anterior Brow chakra point at Yintang
    - Acupoint LI 4 on the same side as the lesion (this is particularly useful if there is much discomfort in the area)
    - The hand reflex of the upper cervical region
    - It won't be possible to balance with the foot reflex, but this reflex may be gently massaged as a separate part of the treatment
    - The arm reflex positioned just above the wrist (see illustration). You need to feel round for a focal point (there will be one)

All the above may be carried out with you seated comfortably behind the patient's head. Now you may position yourself at their feet and massage the foot reflex and the leg reflex just above the ankle.

6. The final part is to unwind the lesion. The best ways for the upper cervical is to: -

- Sit yourself at the side of the patient. Place one hand underneath the upper cervical region and the other hand under the lower lumbar to affect the spinal harmonic area of L3-L5. The sensations under your hands initially will be quite different to each other (one warm, one cool), but as time goes by they appear to be more in harmony and the tissues more relaxed. There may be a gentle movement under your hand (even though you keep them still) but this will not be excessive as with other areas of unwinding. This procedure should take a couple of minutes.
- Position yourself at the patient's head and place one middle finger, superimposed with the adjacent fingers under the lesion and the fingers of the other hand on the other side of the spinous process. The lesion area should unwind within a couple of minutes if acute and slightly more if chronic. Finally, if you were unable to energy balance between the proximal and distal points before, then do this again and feels the difference.

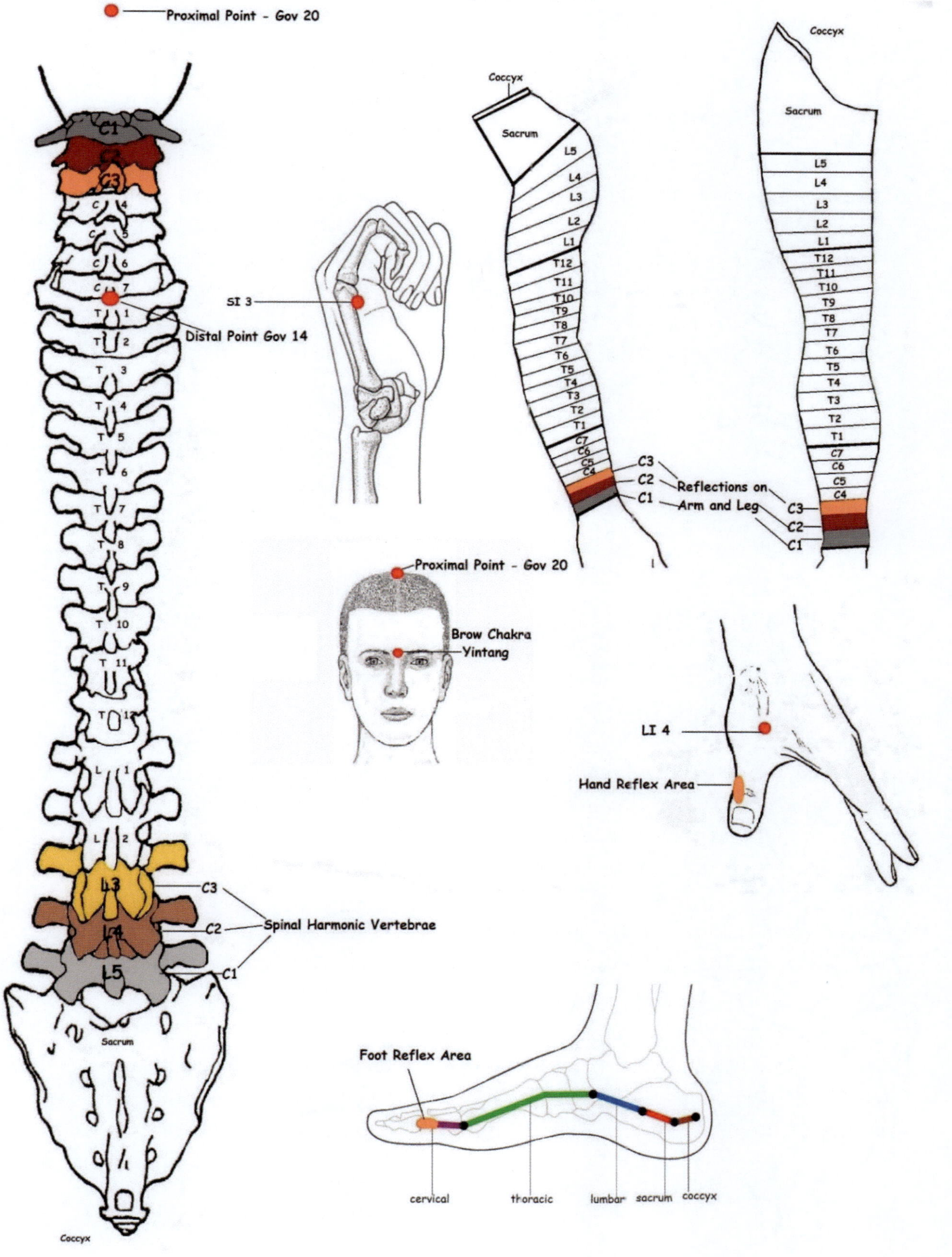

Figures 8.2 Treatment of Upper Cervical Conditions

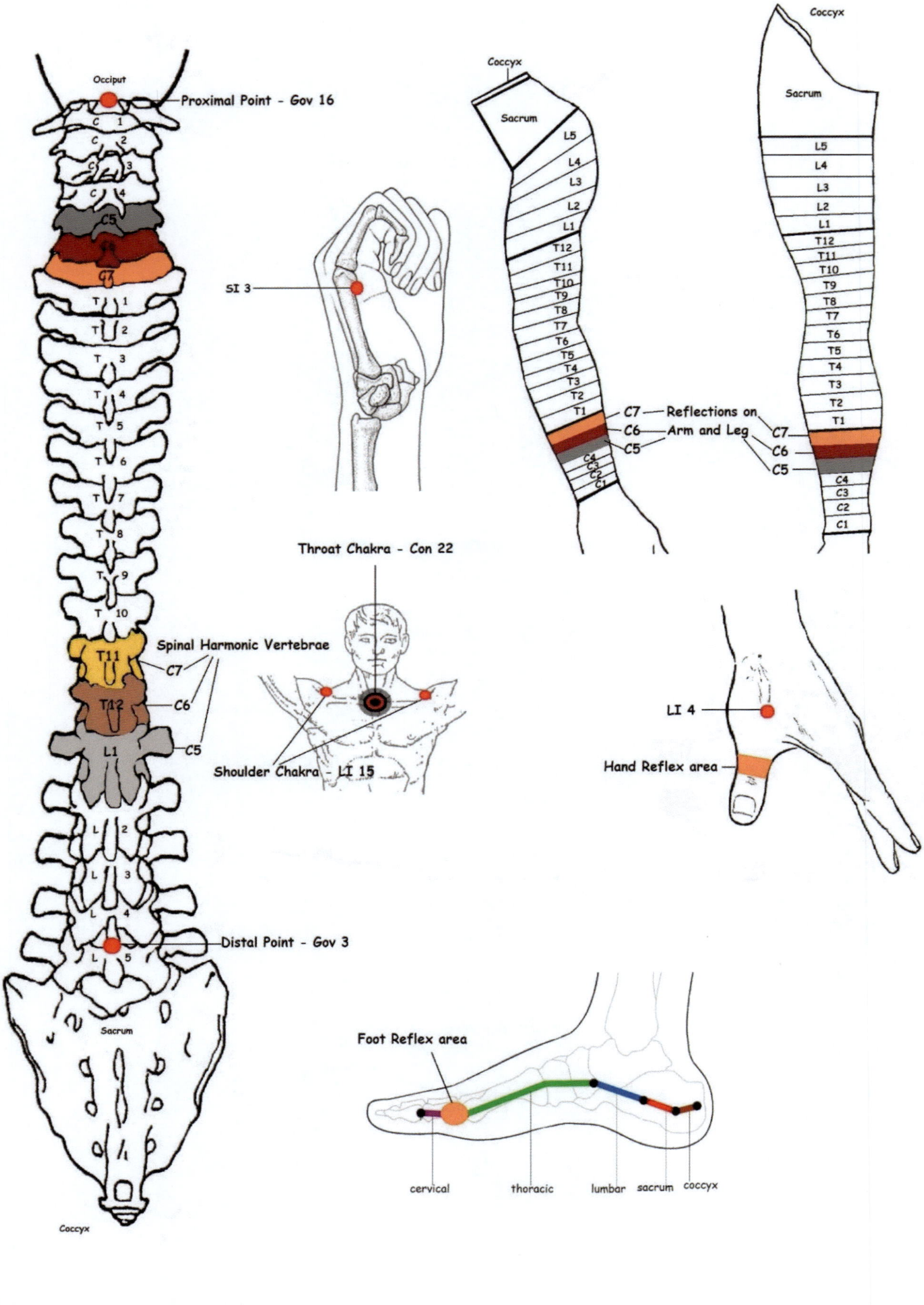

Figures 8.3 Lower Cervical Treatment

Lower Cervical Spine C5, C6, C7

1. Locate the focal point of the lesion and mark with a pen
2. Locate and massage SI3 for a few seconds
3. The distal point is Gov 3 – mid line between the spinous processes of L4 -L5. This may appear to be low in the spine, but experience has shown that higher ones aren't as beneficial. Massage this point in a stimulatory mode for about thirty seconds or until heat is felt under your fingers.
4. Locate proximal point Gov 16. Gently massage this point for a few seconds before energy balancing it with Gov 3. In chronic conditions this balance may not be successful.
5. Place the pad of your dominant middle finger under the lesion (either with your patient in prone or supine) and energy balance with the following: -
    - Distal Point Gov 3
    - Posterior Throat chakra point Gov 14 (if not too adjacent to the lesion)
    - Anterior Throat chakra Con 22
    - Bilateral Shoulder chakra points LI 15
    - Special point LI 4 (especially in pain relief)
    - The Hand reflex on the thumb
    - The Foot reflex on the great toe
    - Reposition yourself to sitting side on to the patient and energy balance between the lesion and the arm and leg reflexes as shown on the illustration.
6. The next part is to unwind the lesion. The best and easiest way for the lower cervical region is to place the hand either side of the lower neck – often the shoulders are the best and most comforting. This is followed by placing the hand inferior and superior to the lesion i.e. one hand on the upper cervical and the other hand on the upper thoracic. Take your time and never *will* anything to happen. The next best way is to place one hand underneath the lower cervical region and the hand underneath the spinal harmonic couples at T11, T12 and L1. This one usually takes a little longer, but well worth the effort.
7. The final part is to do another energy balance between the proximal and distal points of Gov 3 and Gov 16 to test what you have done has been successful.

Thoracic Spine T1-T12

The thoracic spine is subject to tension and stress that may lead to scoliotic and kyphotic curvatures. Acute forms of these and other thoracic imbalance answers superbly to this kind of approach. It represents a much larger area and treatment must be tempered to the specific area of the lesion

1. Locate the focal or ouch point and mark with a pen.
2. Locate and massage SI 3 for a few seconds
3. The distal point is Gov 4 between L2 and L3 OR Gov 3 between L4 and L5 I find that Gov 4 works best as it more of an 'energy' point to the kidneys and 'bone related' conditions. Massage this point for a few seconds until an appreciable amount of heat is built up under the fingers.

4. The proximal point is Gov 14 between C7 and T1. Gently massage this point before energy balancing it with Gov 4. This is the most important aspect of the treatment and may not be successful, but time must be taken to attempt a balance.
5. Place the middle finger pad of your dominant hand on the lesion and energy balance with the following: -

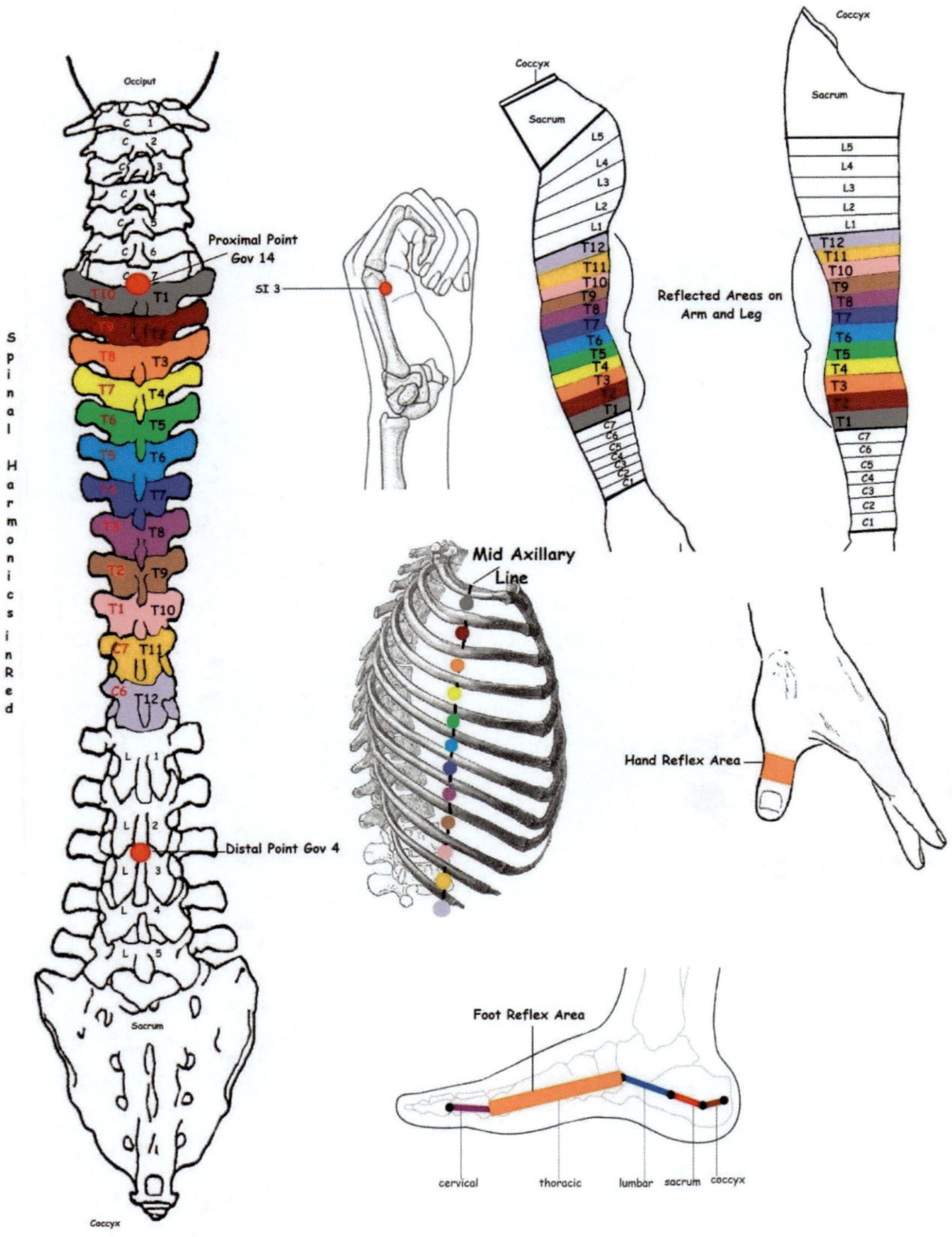

Figures 8.4 Treatment of the Thoracic Spine

- Distal Point Gov 4 or 3
- Focal point of the Hand reflex on the thumb
- Focal point of the Foot reflex on the great toe
- Focal point of the Arm reflex
- Focal point of the Leg reflex
- Special points for the thoracic spine, especially in pain to be found on the mid axillary line of the thoracic spine. Follow the line of the rib that articulates with the specific vertebra and the trigger point is found on the very lateral aspect of the rib cage. The technique is to place middle finger pad on the focal point of the spinal lesion and the other middle finger pad on the mid axillary point. Hold until an energy balance occurs. This technique is excellent in pain relief. (see illustration for colour coded vertebrae and points)
- The next procedure is to unwind the lesion. This is particularly effective in the thoracic spine, especially so for mild scoliosis. Place one hand over the lesion and the other hand over the spinal harmonic – see illustration for details. Surface anatomy knowledge is important here and it is just a question of counting down from C7/T1 to find the correct level. Unwinding with hands either side of the spine at the level of the lesion is also effective
- Finally, energy balance between the proximal and distal points.

Lower Lumbar Spine L3, L4, L5

This region of the spine is the one that takes most of our bodyweight and is therefore subject to a great deal of strain.

1. Locate the focal point and mark it with a pen
2. Locate and massage SI 3 for a few seconds to 'open up' the Governor meridian
3. Locate the distal point – Gov 2 between the coccyx and sacrum in the mid line. Please be aware that this extremely useful acupoint has anatomical sensitivities in that permission must be sought to place your finger there and that, ideally, you have a chaperone in the room. Give some stimulating massage to Gov 2 – a few seconds in an acute or sub-acute condition but around half a minute in long-standing and chronic ones.
4. Locate the proximal point of Gov 6 between the spinous processes of T12-L1. Give a few seconds massage to this point and attempt an energy balance between it and Gov 2. This will not be possible in long-standing conditions.
5. Place the middle finger pad of the dominant hand on the lesion and energy balance with: -
    - Distal point at Gov 2
    - Focal point of the Hand reflex
    - Focal point of the Foot reflex
    - Focal point of the Arm reflex
    - Focal point of the Leg reflex
    - Special point for pain is BL 62, located just inferior to the lateral malleolus. Try for an energy balance here. Another useful distal point is BL 40 in the middle of the popliteal fossa.
    - Now unwind the lesion. This region lends itself for unwinding as you can place the whole of the hands both either side and proximal and distal to the lesion. If done

well, this should afford much relief of spasm and pain in the area. The other way to unwind is to use the spinal harmonic, previously described.

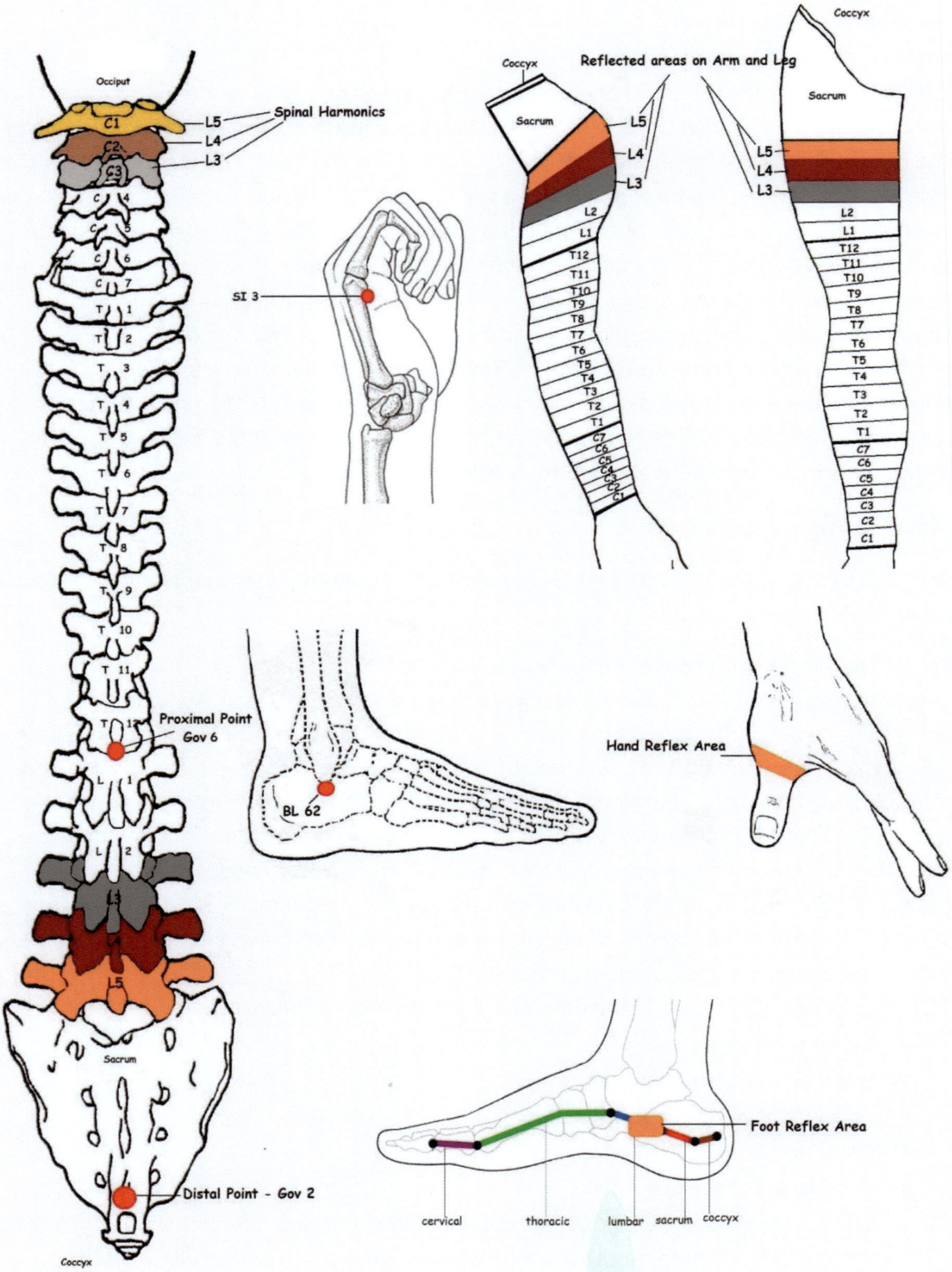

Figures 8.5 Treatment of the Lower Lumbar Spine

Sacrum

The sacrum, that has been stated many times, represents the foundations of the structure that is the spinal column. It is therefore imperative to have a stable foundation, otherwise the other storeys may become out of alignment with ensuing mechanical lesions.

1. Locate the focal pain point and mark with a pen
2. Locate and massage SI 3 for a few seconds
3. Locate the distal point of Gov 2 (same as the lower lumbar) and massage for about thirty seconds or so in chronic conditions
4. Locate the proximal point of Gov 3 between the spinous processes of L4-L5. Massage this point for a few seconds and try an energy balance between it and Gov 2
5. Place the middle finger pad of the dominant hand on the lesion and the other middle finger on the following: -
    - Distal point at Gov 2
    - Focal point of the Hand reflex
    - Focal point of the Foot reflex
    - Focal point of the Arm reflex
    - Focal point of the Leg reflex
    - Special point of BL 62 especially in pain. In sciatic pain, also try BL 40 in the middle of the popliteal fossa.
    - Next unwind the lesion. The sacrum answers well to this although it may take several minutes to achieve due to the strength of the sacral ligaments and solidity of the sacrum itself. Craniosacral therapists will know all about sacral unwinding as it is a core procedure. Although you can do this procedure with the patient in prone, it is easier to do it with them in supine lying on a soft couch or foam placed on the couch. The reason for the foam is that your hand will be placed underneath the sacrum (fingers pointed towards to head) and your patient must be asked to totally relax with, seemingly, their whole weight on your poor hand – hence the foam. With your hand 'cuddling' the sacrum, place the top hand over the symphysis pubis. As stated before, permission must be sought before the hand is placed there and best to have a chaperone in the room. This unwinding procedure may take up to five minutes, but it is well worth the effort. The other procedure is to place your hand on the lesion of the sacrum and the other hand on the occiput (the spinal harmonic). This may be carried out with the patient in prone. This procedure is one of several ways to perform sacro-occipital manoeuvres.
    - The final part of the treatment is to energy balance between the proximal and distal points if an energy balance wasn't achieved initially.

Coccyx

Please note the coccyx and sacrum treatment share the same illustration – Figure 8.6. The coccyx, as stated before, is prone to accidental misalignment such as when some 'person' removes a chair that was just about to be sat on! Coccyx pain is one of the most severe for the poor sufferers. There is limited 'space' for inflammation and congestion. Specialized training must be taken if there is any type of mobilizing or manipulation.

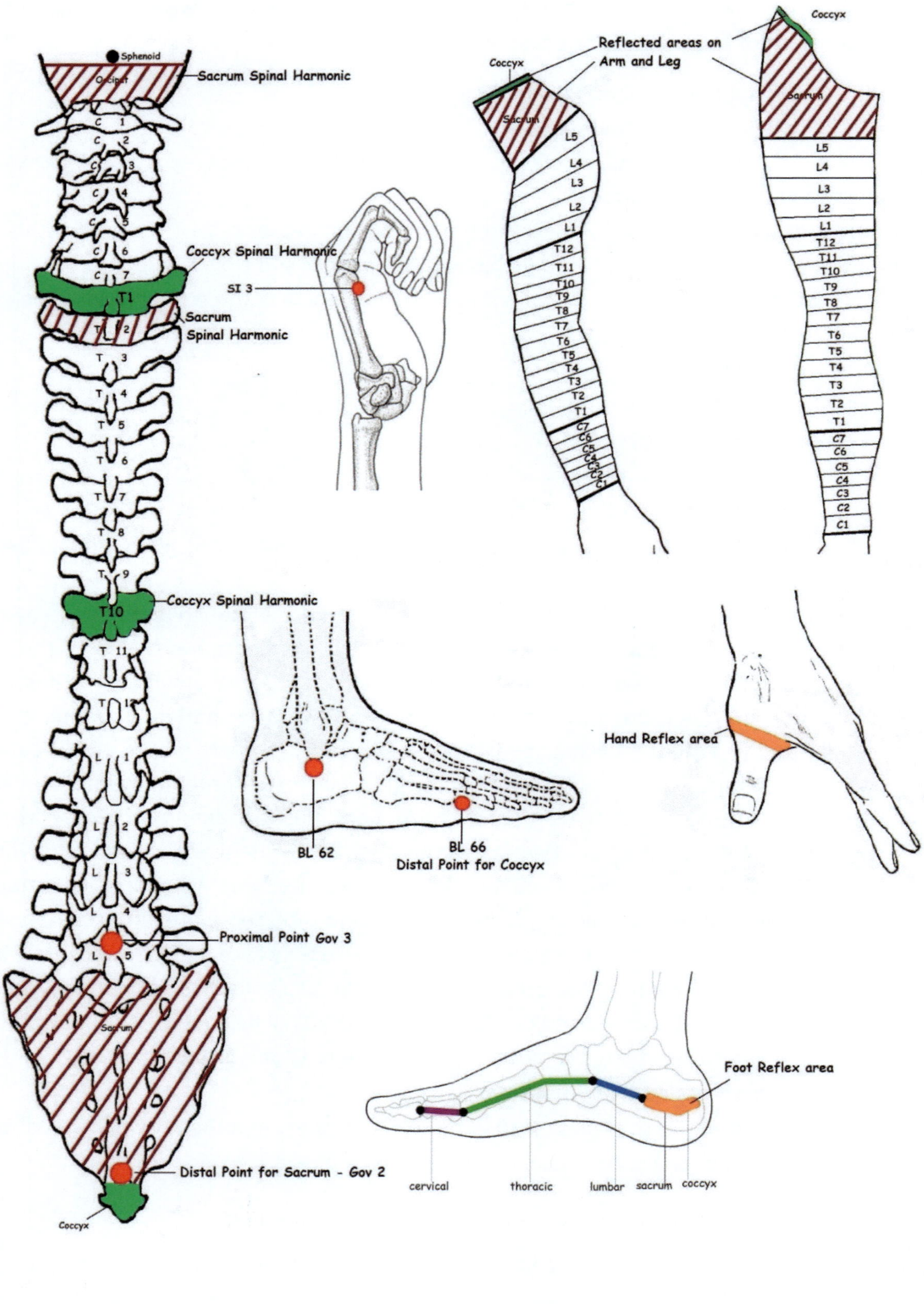

Figure 8.6 Treatment of the Sacrum and Coccyx

1. There is no need to locate the lesion as the area is so small.
2. Locate SI 3 and massage for a few seconds
3. Locate the distal point and massage it for up to half a minute, this is BL 66 at the lateral aspect of the little toe. There are two alternative distal points BL 62, just inferior to the lateral malleolus, and LR 8, on the medial side of the knee joint.
4. Locate the proximal point of Gov 3 (between the spinous processes of L4 and L5) and massage for a few seconds before trying and energy balance between it and BL 62 (or BL 62 or LR 8)
5. Place the middle finger pad of the dominant hand on the lesion and energy balance with the its various reflected points. Only touch the inflamed coccyx when you feel that it won't give more discomfort and with the express permission of the patient. I always prefer to treat the coccyx at a distance and not touch it at all. Try the following: -
    - Distal point of BL 66, BL 62 or LR 8
    - Focal point of the Foot reflex (this is particularly effective)
    - Focal point of the Hand reflex (this may be taught the patient to do at home)
    - Focal point of the Arm reflex
    - Focal point of the Leg reflex (not always possible due to it adjacency)
    - Special point for the coccyx is Gov 20 (located at the top of the head)
    - The only way to unwind the lesion (and only when it is possible to touch it) is to place two adjacent fingers of the dominant hand on the lesion and the other hand on the spinal harmonics of T1 and T10, one at a time.
    - Finally, energy balance between the proximal and distal points if this wasn't possible before.

Further considerations when treating chronic conditions

Most of your patients will have chronic and long-lasting symptoms. All the previous information is valid and will work in chronic conditions. There are, however, four extra techniques that should help in the grand scheme of things. They are **Leg Length Differentials**, **Chapman's Reflexes**, **Feet Alignment** and **Sacro-Occipital Therapies**. The last one is being discussed fully in the next chapter

Leg Length Differentials

Every patient with long standing spinal conditions need to have their leg length checked prior to any other treatment and it is important that each leg be as close in length as possible. Even without a spinal condition, most of us have some degree of leg length differential of up to two centimetres due to pelvic hitching.

The leg length differential is measured with the patient in prone and supine as there is often a difference. When measuring the leg length take hold of both legs with the patient relaxed and straight on the couch, then compare the levels of the two ankle bones (medial malleolus). Do not compare the heels! There are a possibility of six different possible imbalances – Types 1-3 are comparatively common with the others less so. I learnt this technique over thirty years ago when the acupressure points used were the key points of the eight extra meridians and, although they were relatively easy to learn, it was still a problem in remembering which ones to use - and when. I refined this procedure by only needing to remember two points – PC 8 (the Hand chakra) and KID 1 (the Foot chakra) – Figure 17.7 shows their position. Hold the points with the pads of the middle fingers with gentle pressure until an energetic balance (a oneness of sensation) occurs under your fingers. It may take anything from a few seconds to a minute. The results are instant and sometimes remarkable.

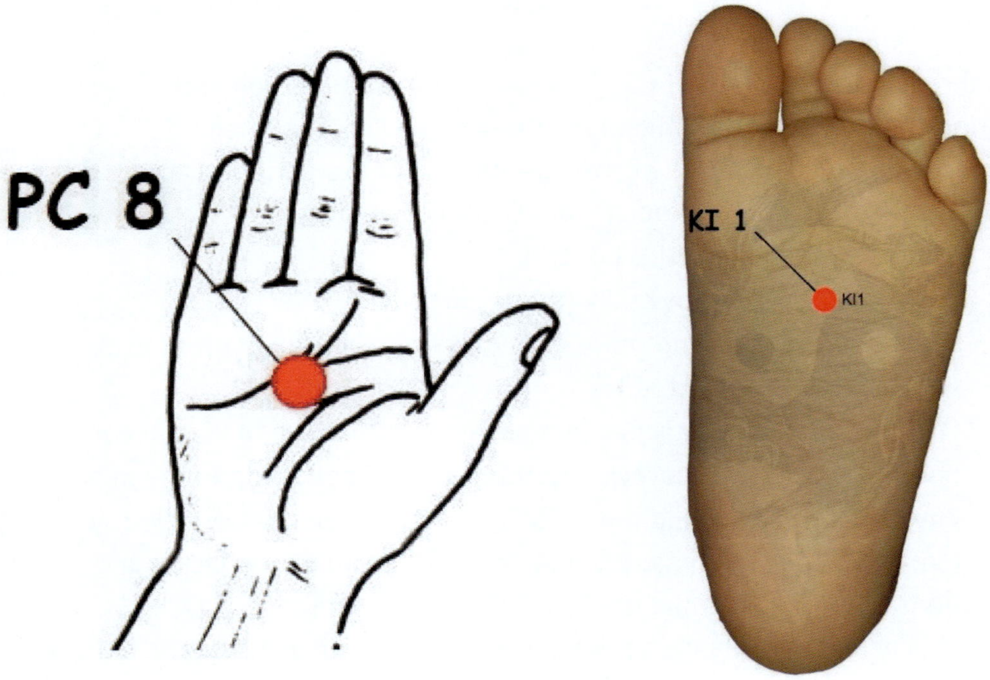

Figure 8.7 Anatomical positions of PC 8 and KID 1

Type 1 – Sacral Condition

The patient is PRONE. Examination reveals a long leg and low buttock on the same side. When the knees are flexed, this does not change.

Treatment – Energy balance PC 8 and KID 1 on the SHORT LEG side.

Type 2 – Sacral Condition with Atlas involvement

The patient is PRONE. Examination reveals a long leg and low buttock on the same side. When the knees are flexed, the long leg appears to become short.

Treatment – Energy balance PC 8 and KID 1 on the LONG LEG side.

Type 3 – General Spinal Condition

The patient is PRONE. Examination reveals a long leg and a high buttock on the same side.

Treatment – Energy balance KID 1 on the LONG LEG side with PC 8 on the SHORT LEG side. If this doesn't do the trick, this usually indicates a cervical or upper thoracic condition is causing the differential. Simply energy balance both PC 8 points to rectify it.

Type 4 – Lower Back Pain

The patient is SUPINE. Examination reveals a short leg and high iliac crest on the same side.

Treatment – Energy balance KID 1 and PC 8 on the SHORT LEG side.

Type 5 – Lower Back Pain, with Sciatica

The patient is SUPINE. Examination reveals a short leg and high iliac crest on the same side, with the patient complaining of sciatica along some or all the nerve.

Treatment – Energy balance KID 1 and PC 8 on the SHORT LEG side (as per Type 4), but then energy balance BL 40 (middle of the popliteal fossa) with KID 1 on the PAINFUL side.

Type 6 – Differentials that cannot be adjusted

These may be due to long standing spinal conditions such as ankylosing spondylitis, osteoarthritis or even a severe pelvic misalignment such as a fractured pelvis, femur or tibia.

Chapman's Reflexes

This topic was mentioned in Book One (page 17). The salient text is repeated here: - Frank Chapman was a doctor of osteopathy in the early part of the 20th century. He found over two hundred regions of the body that felt sore when an internal organ was 'congested'. When these points and areas were massaged, the organic congestion seemed to ease, as if the tension had been removed. His pioneering work was based upon the idea that each of these sore regions was engorged lymphoid tissue within the body's fascia. The areas that are massaged can ease congestion at some considerable distance from the target organ. This is based upon the complexities of the sympathetic nervous system. I consider Frank Chapman to be a true bodywork pioneer and the profession owes him a debt of gratitude. Chapman's Reflexes are sometimes extremely tender to the touch, so they may be used in analysis as well as treatment.

The early days of Applied Kinesiology (AK) in the late 1950's and early 1960's resurrected Chapman's work. The Chapman's Reflexes were coined by the name **Neurolymphatic Reflexes (NL)**, and they are still taught as one of the pillars of AK, alongside muscle testing and other forms of work such as acupressure and neurovascular points. The early AK pioneers instead of using them for organic congestion, dedicated each point to a specific muscle. Most of the body's muscles has a dedicated NL point or area and it is beneficial to give all of them some massage to maintain health. However, if it is apparent that an individual muscle is in a state of imbalance and requires treatment, massage to its NL point will be beneficial in helping the whole muscle. It is still possible to use strong massage on these points and this will be of benefit. However, in the early 1980's I worked out a system that uses both the NL point and a point on the spine that cuts out painful massage when worked together. The various NL points and areas that are linked to various muscles have been converted to being linked to meridians/internal organs. My research into these points and areas have taken out the need to muscle test to ascertain which muscles are in a state of imbalance. Figure 17.8 shows the meridian/organic organs areas of massage and a few of them indicate the spinal levels to which they refer. They are based, mostly but with a few exceptions, on the autonomic nervous system.

Techniques

1. One simple method would be to massage all the paravertebral NL points, very similar to massaging down the inner Bladder line as described in Book One. The technique is to massage with the index and middle finger of your dominant hand, preferably with some oil. Pressure should be quite firm. With one hand on either side of the spine it should improve your joint range and dexterity. This is, obviously, a 'catch all' approach. To be more specific the following should be adopted.
2. This is a useful procedure in all chronic spinal conditions and should be carried out at the end of the usual treatment session. When you know what vertebral level is in a state of imbalance, massage (again with some degree of firmness) the associated areas, both anterior and posterior. An area that is particularly effective is the lateral aspect of the ileo-tibial tract that is linked with L5/S1. Please note that this is a very sensitive region and patients should be warned before you start.

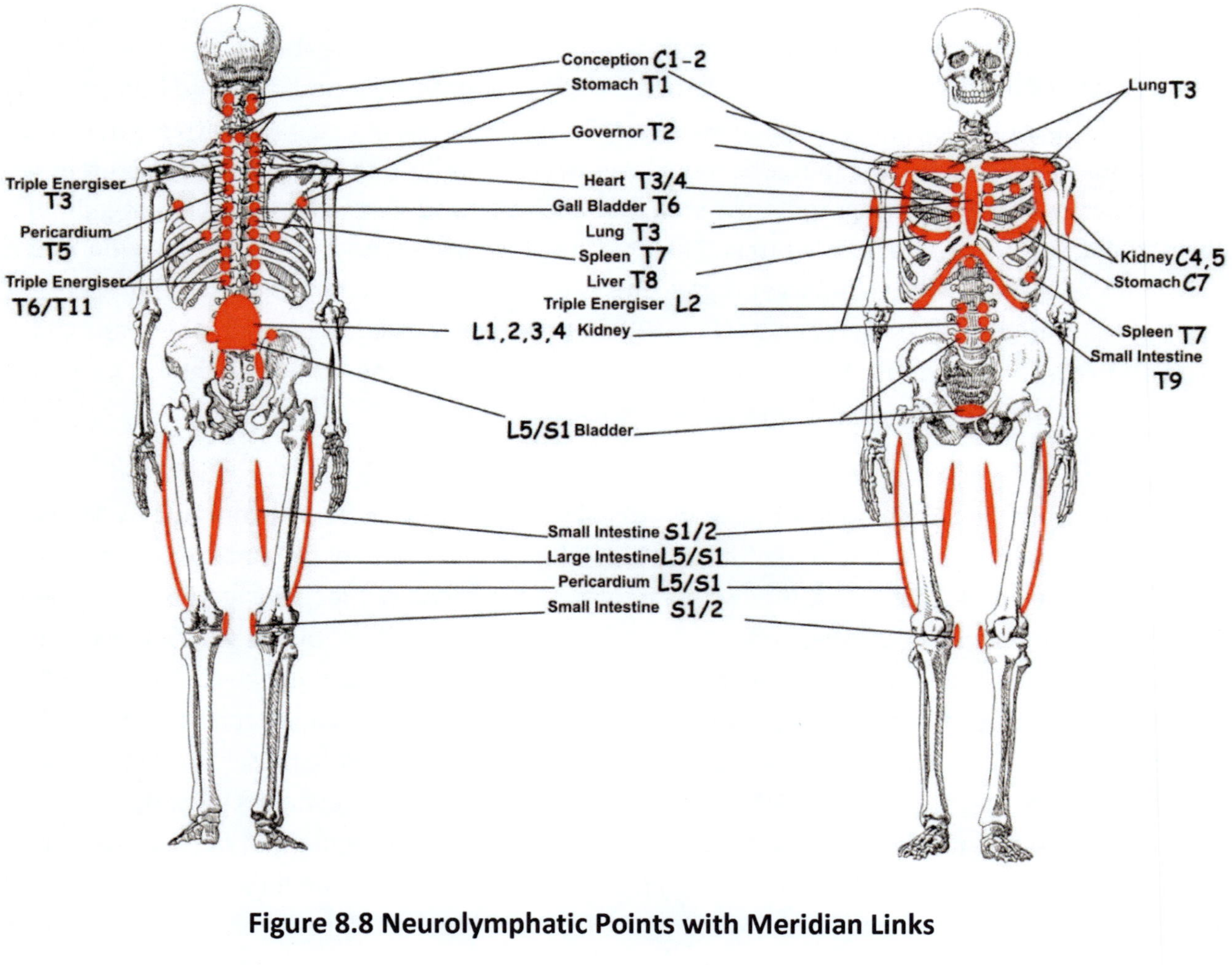

Figure 8.8 Neurolymphatic Points with Meridian Links

Feet Alignment

This is a combined assessment and treatment technique. If our feet are 'out of kilter' this will affect the rest of the body. It is true that feet are the most important part of the body and it is imperative that we take care of them and have regular check with our favourite podiatrist to keep them in good order. There is a huge amount of information that we can glean from the feet, and this is merely one small aspect of a huge topic

To test feet alignment, your patient should lie supine with arms by their side. Take one of their feet and hold the little toe metatarsals in one hand and the great toe metatarsals in the other and invert and evert the foot, noticing the mid line of axis as their foot is turned in and out. You may have to bend down almost to the foot to gauge it properly. The ideal line of axis should go through the middle of the second toe. If this is the case, that foot is aligned correctly. Repeat with the other foot.

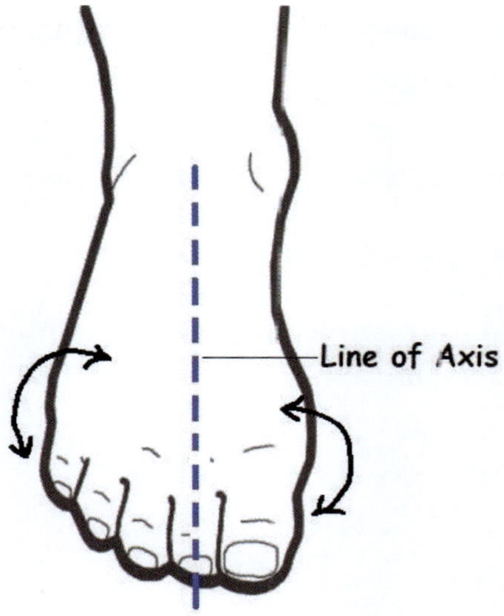

Figure 8.9 Foot Alignment

Feet being out of alignment may indicate several things: -

- A problem with one of the intrinsic foot bones e.g. the talus being too tight on the calcaneus
- A problem with the knee joint, often putting too much strain through either the medial or lateral aspect.
- A problem with the superior tibio-fibular joint, either a subluxation, congestion or blocked.
- A problem with the sacro-iliac joint, usually being blocked
- A problem with the lower lumbar spine putting strain on the supporting ligaments or the discs
- A mid thoracic scoliosis – this is a simple way for the spine to compensate for misalignments elsewhere.

- The most long-standing of feet misalignment would produce an atlas condition, either at the transverse process or the C0-C1 level.

If the Line of Axis is slightly out i.e. through the great toe or middle toe, this usually indicates an intrinsic foot problem that can be corrected if the talus is freed (this requires specialist training). The further out the Line of Axis is i.e. through the little toe or to the medial side of the great toe, the further up the body will be the cause. Apologies if the reader isn't a physical therapist or bodyworker as correction needs this specialist training. Acupressure/Reflexology alone cannot do it. However, the technique is so important that it needed to be mentioned.

CHAPTER NINE – Sacro-Occipital Reflextherapy

Please note that this chapter does not deal with Sacro-Occipital Therapy - a chiropractic offshoot founded in 1925 by Dr. De Jarnette. He appreciated the fact that the sacrum and occiput are mechanically and energetically linked, and on that fact, there is a link with my work. The two bones have a similar shape – one being the inverse of the other. The sacrum is the basement of the spine and the occiput the roof. Previous chapters have also indicated that they are linked via the Lovett Brother, Spinal Harmonic, plus energetically linked by the Governor and Bladder meridians. I pioneered this treatment over thirty years ago and created a new version about ten years ago. The first section deals with the way I evolved the theory, followed by how to use it as a therapy.

Sacro-Occipital Reflextherapy – Original Therapy

We start with the well-known naturopathic reflexology theory of Zone Therapy – Figure 9.1 refers

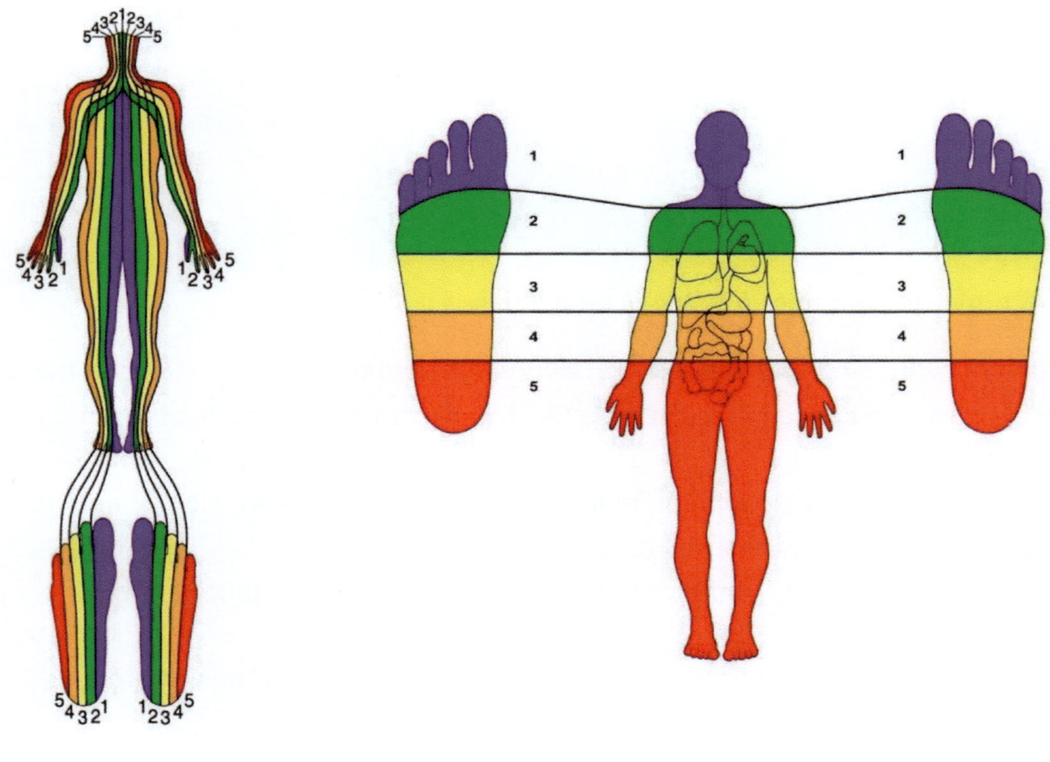

Figure 9.1 Vertical and Horizontal Zones

The diagram shows the vertical and horizontal zones of the body, Zone 1 being the very medial or inner zone and Zone 5 the outermost. The horizontal zones show that Zone 3 is in the centre of the body. Zone therapy works extremely well, and I have used it as part of my practice for over 40 years. The next stage of development was to take the sacrum, spine and occiput and create five vertical zones from these. In the many and various reflected areas of the body, each 'zone' may be sub divided into other 'mini' zones. This is like using the foot to represent the head, but another theory has the great toe alone representing the head. Reflexes and reflected areas should be viewed as overlapping – there are as many theories as the cultures and individuals that have pioneered them. View them as being holographic interpretations. The vertical zones around the spinal column were easy to depict as the Inner and Outer Bladder meridian lines of force already span between the sacrum and occiput whilst the Governor meridian covers the mid line. In Ayurvedic medicine, the Governor meridian is represented as the Sushumna nadis and the left and right Bladder meridians are the Pingala and Ida nadi. Figures 9.2 and 9.3 show these. The diagram of the inner and outer bladder lines shows these meridians not being parallel to the Governor channel, thus indicating the natural curves of the body and that nothing in the body is in a straight line. The Pingala and Ida nadis are, though, shown as straight lines as well as the posterior major chakras.

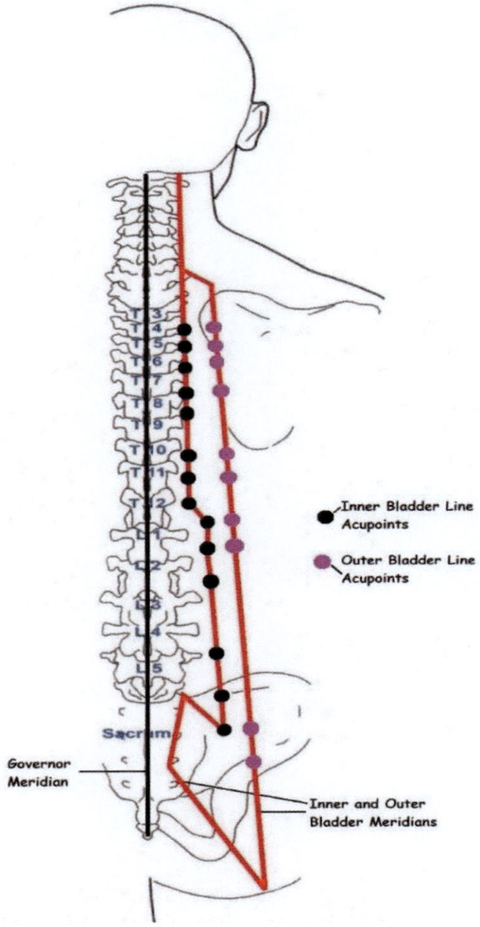

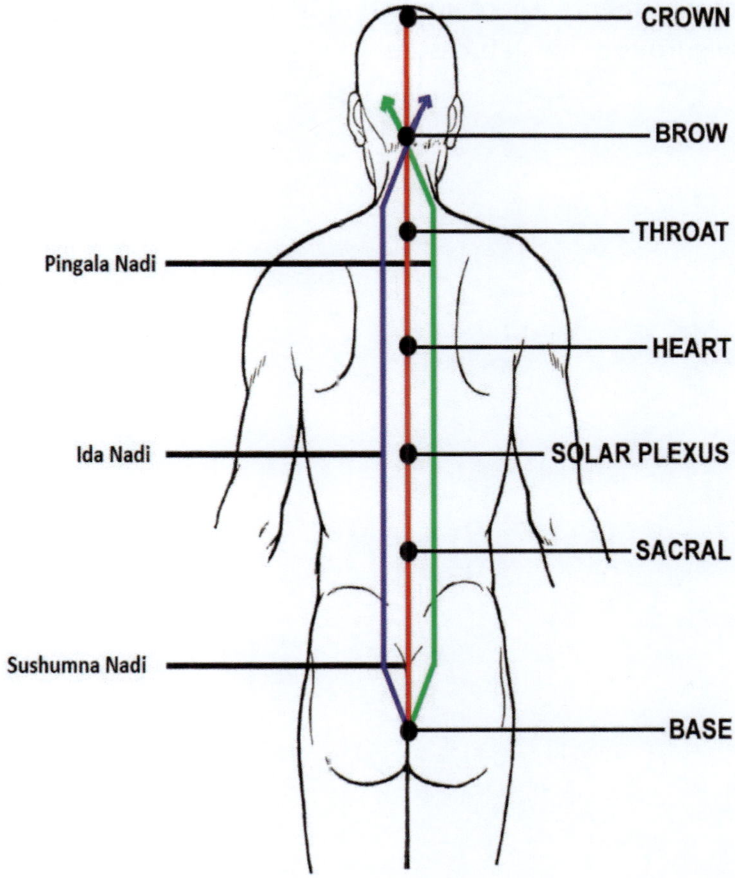

Figure 9.2 Inner and Outer Bladder Meridians

Figure 9.3 Pingala and Ida Nadi

The horizontal zones of the spine, shown in Figure 9.4, are again numbered 1-5, with Zone One being the middle of the spinal column and Zone Five the two extremities of upper cervical lower lumbar. Zones 2,3 and 4 are between these two. The sacrum is also subdivided into five horizontal zones with Zone One at the lower end adjacent to the upper end of the coccyx and Zone Five being at the upper end adjacent to the lower end of the fifth lumbar. The occiput cannot easily be divided into five horizontal zones due to its size, but it may be divided into 3 zones between the superior and inferior nuchal lines. Figure 9.4 shows the horizontal zones of the spine and sacrum and Figure 9.5 shows a composite of the vertical and horizontal zones, that you will recognise from the front cover of the 2 books. The black 'dots' shown on the inferior aspect of the occiput, the superior and lateral aspects of the sacrum don't necessarily show recognised acupoints, although some of them are – they are points on the inferior nuchal line of the occiput and upper aspect of the sacrum where the five imaginary vertical zones reach these bony aspects. The ones on the lateral aspect of the sacrum i.e. sacro-iliac joint are to be found where the imaginary five horizontal zones of the sacrum reach their extremities. Please note that most, not all, the acupoints on the sacrum and nuchal line are naturally tender to the touch. This needs to be taken into consideration when using this system. Sacro-Occipital Reflextherapy (or Reflexology) is mostly used in pain syndromes of the spine and should be tried at the onset of other approaches. It can sometimes seem to be miraculous, especially when there is a long-standing painful condition that hasn't answered to other treatments. There are different approaches you may try, they are all subtle and do not rely on any vigorous or harsh pressure.

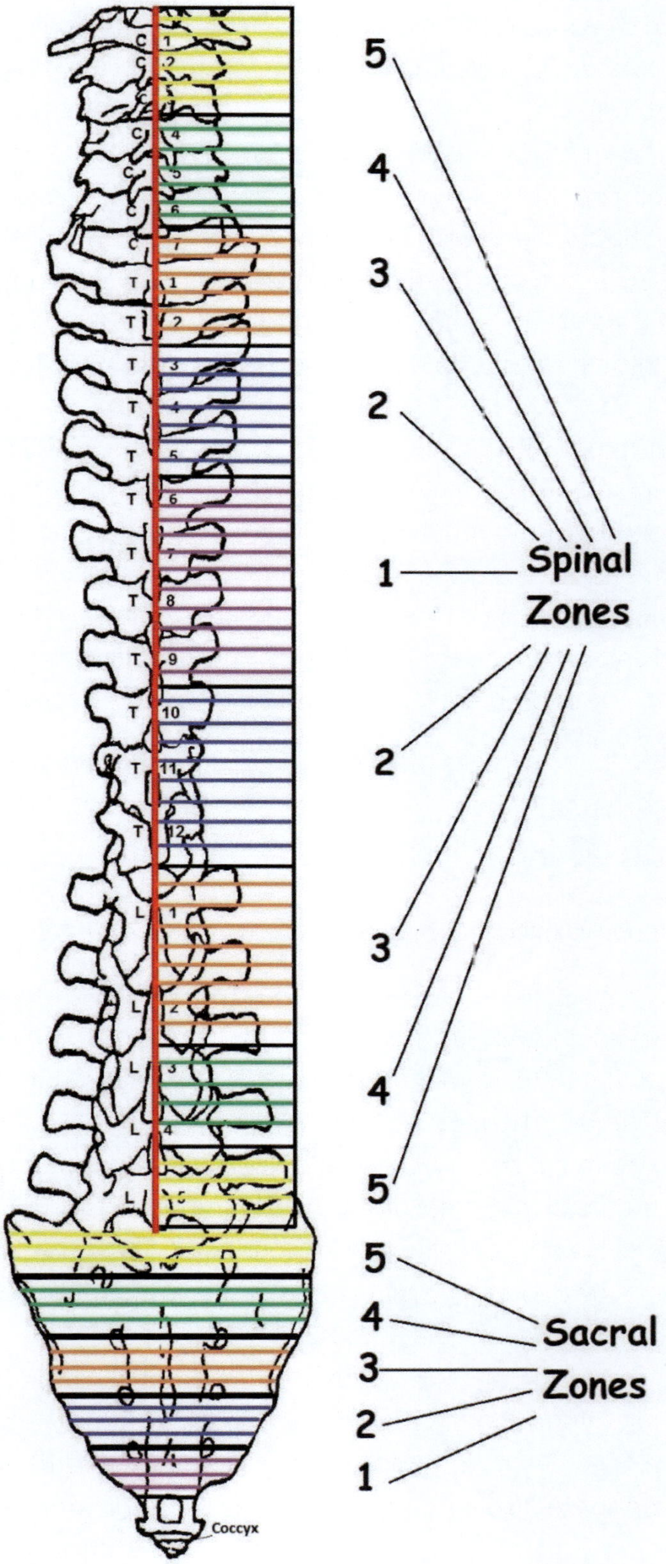

Figure 9.4 Horizontal Zones of the Spine and Sacrum

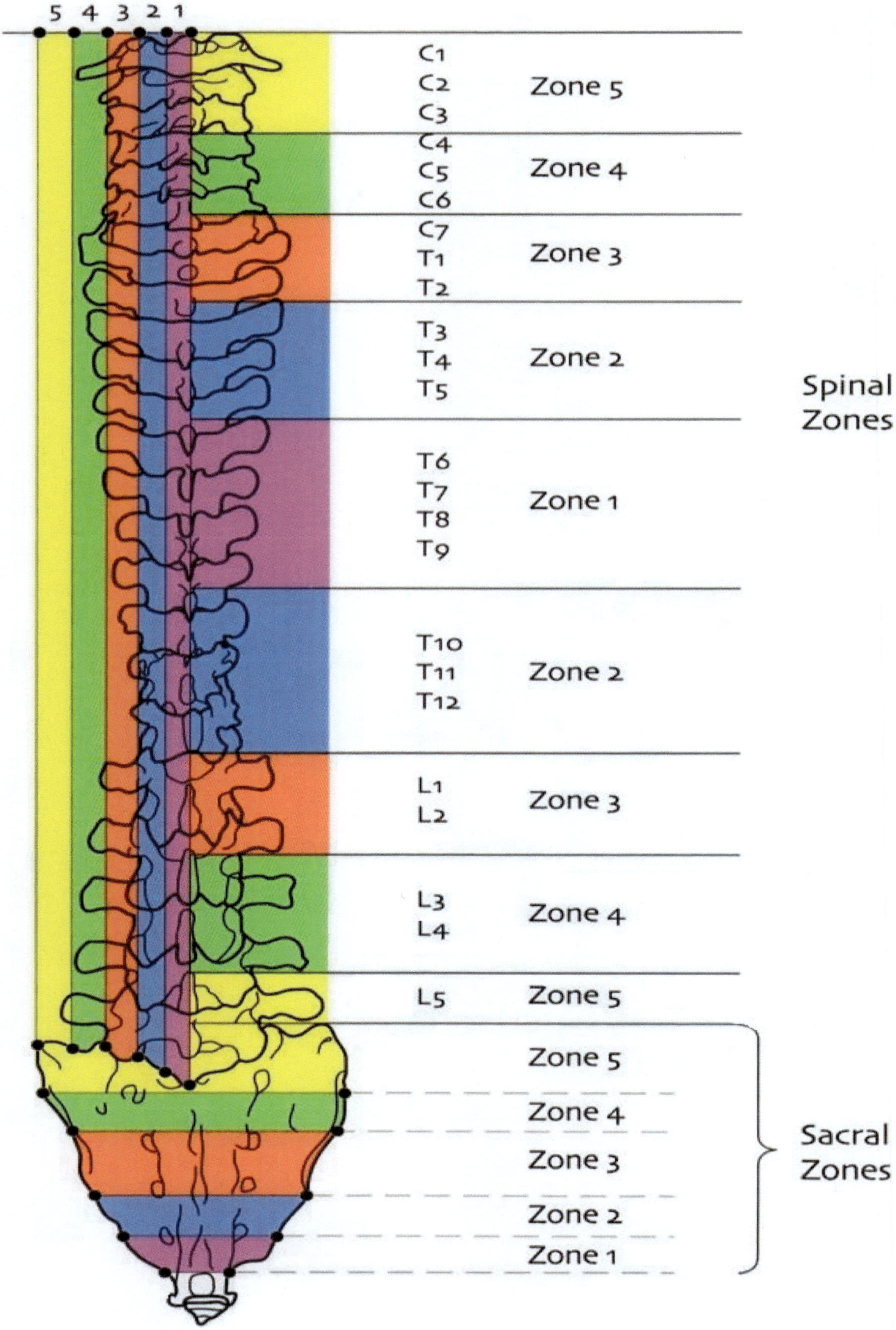

Figure 9.5 Horizontal and Vertical Zones of the Spine

Treatment Methods - Original Therapy

Method 1

1. Palpate each of the acupoints on the superior aspect of the sacrum in turn commencing with the most medial on Zone 1 and ask the patient if it is painful. As stated previously, most of the points will be tender, but experience will tell you which points are extra sore. Ask the patient to tell you the relative 'soreness' of each point. The most painful point usually indicates an imbalance within the Zone – anywhere. With one middle finger pad on the point, place the other middle finger pad on the vertical zone equivalent on the inferior aspect of the occiput. Hold these two points until you have an energy balance – often this will occur within a few seconds. Take the occiput finger away, re-palpate the sacral point and ask the patient if the pain has eased. Do this procedure on each point that exhibits tenderness.
2. Palpate each of the acupoints on the lateral aspect of the sacrum (sacro-iliac joint) and ascertain from the patient which ones are tender. Keeping the middle finger pad of one hand on the point place middle finger pad of the other hand on the other side of the sacrum on the same horizontal level and try for an energy balance between them. This may not be achievable, especially with chronic conditions. Follow this by energy balancing one of the sacral points with the zone equivalent on the occiput. This one stretches the brain a little further as it is a combination of vertical and horizontal zone theory.

A combination of these two approaches should ease quite a bit of spinal discomfort and is ideal if the pain originates from the spine and there is no pain referral from the spine.

Method 2

The following is applicable for most other spinal discomfort and pain that originates from the spine e.g. sciatica.

1. Palpate each of the acupoints on the superior aspect of the sacrum, as per Method 1 and ascertain which points are tender. With the middle finger pad of one hand on the sacral point, place the middle finger pad of the other hand on the corresponding horizontal zone of the spine. If the Zone 1 superior sacral point is tender, place the middle finger pad of the other hand somewhere up to 10 centimetres (four inches) away from the spinous process between T6-T9 (horizontal Zone 1). You must 'feel around' for the exact point that is always tender. Once this point is found, proceed with an energy balance between the two points. The remaining four superior sacral points correspond with two spinal horizontal zones and each will need to be palpated to find the 'focal' point.
2. As with Method 1, palpate the sacro-iliac points to find a tender point and energy balance with its parallel point on the opposite side of the sacrum. Then with the middle finger pad placed on one of these points place the middle finger pad of the other hand on the spinal horizontal zone as previously described.

If you are new to these techniques, it all seems a little innocuous that you can achieve pain relief by this relatively simple technique – but it really works!

Sacro-Occipital Reflextherapy – New Version

Although I have taught this new therapy on a few occasions, this is the first time that details have been in print. Approximately ten years ago I did some research into how to improve the techniques in sacro-occipital reflextherapy as my delegates often found it difficult to ascertain where the occipital and sacral points were located. To make it simpler, I reduced the number of these points from five to three. I had also realised that there was total emphasis on physical discomfort and mechanical conditions and it did not take account of conditions where the aetiology was from either the autonomic nervous system or the emotions. These would include internal organic conditions that are caused by sympathetic nervous system irritation and emotional conditions caused by spinal anomalies. Regarding the spinal vertical zones, the outer bladder meridian line is associated with emotional conditions and the inner bladder meridian line is associated with autonomic nervous system conditions as it is strongly linked with the paravertebral autonomic chain. The physical condition symptoms are therefore treated by the area no wider than a finger's width from the central line. The spinal horizontal zones are divided into a central region (T6-T9) that deals with emotional symptoms, two regions (C7-T5 and T10 – L1) that deal with autonomic symptoms and two regions (C1-C6 and L2-L5) that deal solely with physical conditions. Figure 9.6 shows the way I divided the spine into the horizontal and vertical zones.

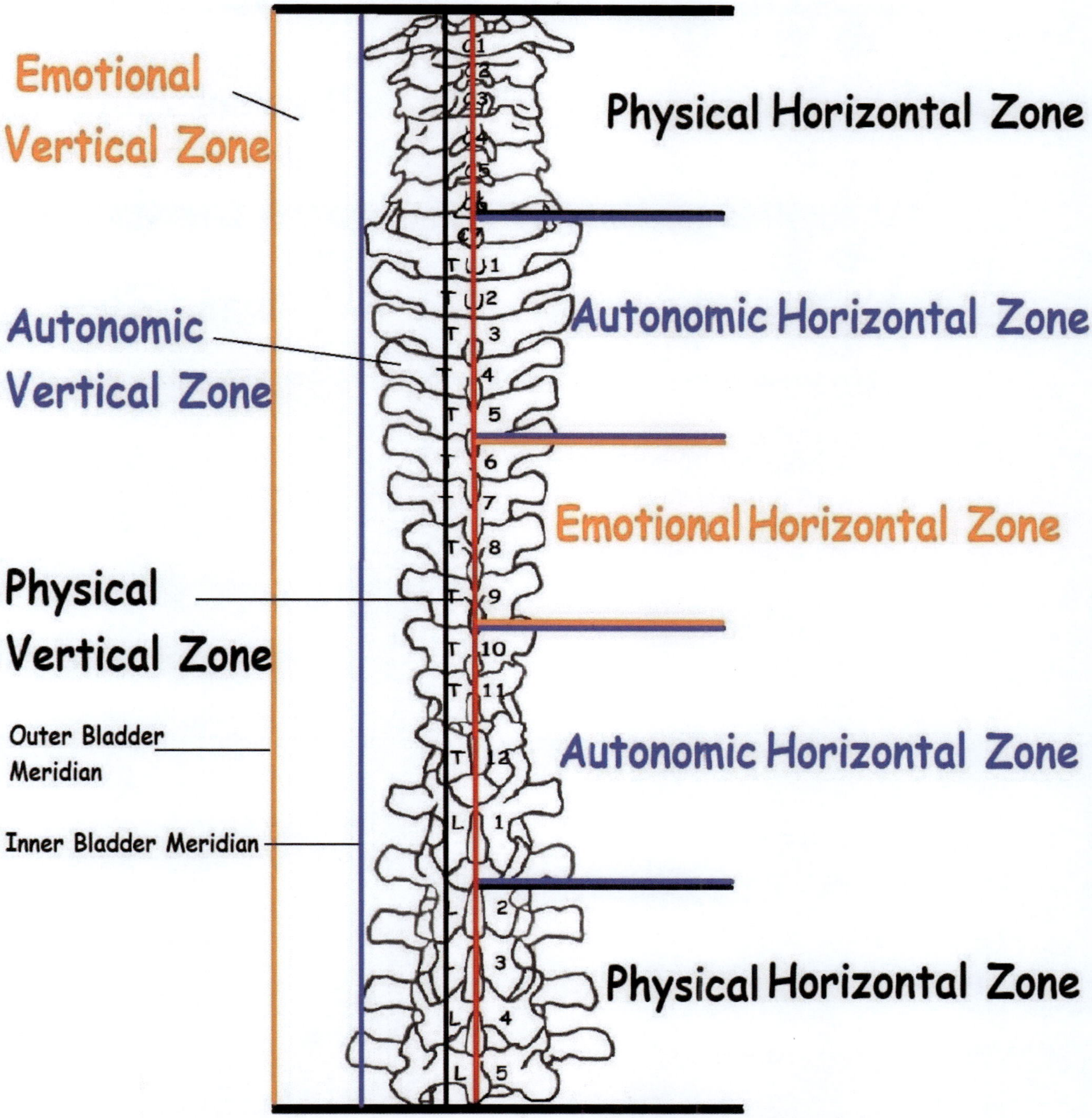

Figure 9.6 The Spine showing Vertical and Horizontal Zones

The Sacral and Occipital acupoints and zones were then worked out by much trial and error. The Physical horizontal zone is the nearest to lumbar 5, the autonomic zone in the centre and the emotional zone by the upper level of the coccyx. On the occiput, the top line of the emotional zone is on the superior nuchal line and the lower end of the physical zone is on the inferior nuchal line. The area of the occiput that is palpable is obviously less than the sacrum. The exact positioning of the acupoints used are not that important, it is the *zone* that is important. Figure 9.7 shows the sacral horizontal zones and acupoints and Figure 18.8 the occipital ones. Figure 9.9 shows the composite picture of occiput, spine and sacrum.

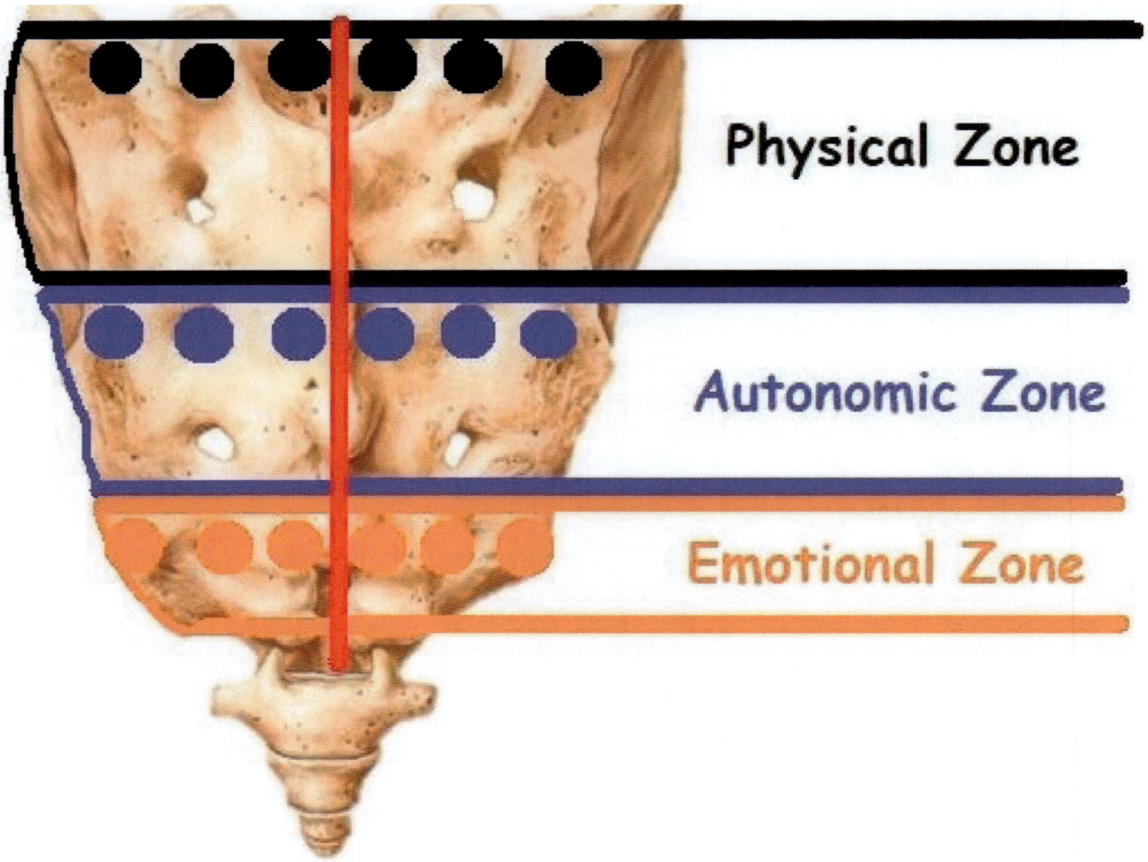

Figure 9.7 The Sacrum with the three Zones and the Acupoints

Figure 9.8 The Occiput with the three Zones and Acupoints

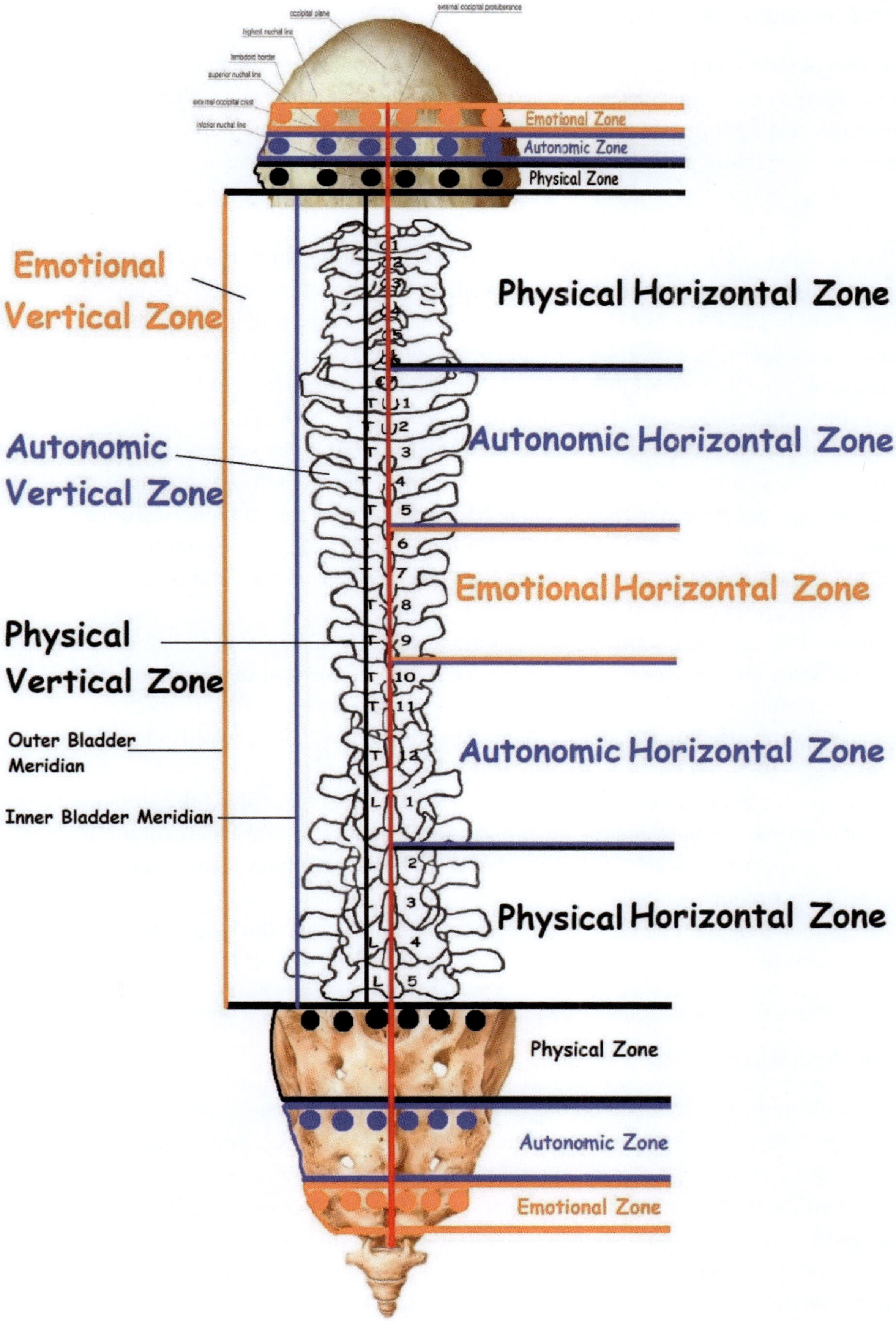

Figure 9.9 The New Version of Sacro-Occipital Reflextherapy

Treatment Methods – New Version

The new version of sacro-occipital reflextherapy (SOR) is designed to treat spinal conditions that are caused by mechanical, autonomic and emotional conditions, also it helps where these symptoms may be caused by spinal anomalies. This system may also be used for assessment, in case the remainder of the assessment procedure hasn't given a firm analysis or diagnosis.

Analysis

1. With the patient prone, palpate firmly around the upper aspect (physical) of the sacrum and enquire where points are tender. When the answer is in the affirmative, this indicates that either there is a localised imbalance or there is a mechanical condition of the spine on the side of the tenderness. Now take the hand to half way down the sacrum (where the fused S3 would be) and palpate around that area (autonomic). Where there is tenderness within the points of this zone it would indicate that the spinal condition that your patient complains of has its aetiology in some form of irritation within the autonomic nervous system, either sympathetic or parasympathetic – at this moment of the analysis procedure it could be anything. Now take the dominant hand to the lower aspect of the sacrum and repeat the process. It is possible that all three zones have tender points, but this is unlikely. One would always commence with the physical and proceed via the autonomic to the emotional. Mark all ouch points with a pen.
2. If a physical tender point is elicited and you are unsure which area of the spine is involved, slowly take the middle finger pad of the other hand up the vertical zone adjacent to the spinous processes (the TCM ah-shi points). The lesion is where you elicit tenderness – of course it may be more than one level. Remember this as it will be required in treatment mode.
3. If an autonomic tender point is elicited, then take your other hand along the autonomic vertical zone that lies between the inner bladder line and the lateral aspects of the spinous processes – approximately 3 cms. Remember where you find a tender point as this may be needed in treatment.
4. If the emotional tender point is elicited, take your other hand up the emotional vertical zone that lies between the inner and out bladder meridians.

Remember where the tender points are or mark them with a pen.

Treatment of Physical/Mechanical Conditions

When you have elicited an 'ouch' point on the 'physical' surface of the sacrum and marked it, keep your middle finger pad on it. Then take the middle finger pad of the other hand to the physical acupoint on the same vertical line. For instance, if the medial aspect of the sacrum is tender then place the finger on the medial aspect of the inferior nuchal line of the occiput. Initially give some gentle massage to each point and then energy balance them. This may take up to a minute. This is followed by placing the middle finger pad that was on the occiput to feel around for another tender point within the physical horizontal zones that are to be found at the extremities of the spine – see diagram. You must stay within the vertical physical line i.e. within one thumb width of the spinous process. You will probably find the tender point in the part of the spine that is painful and requires treatment – but this is not always the case. Once a focal point is found, this needs to be energy balanced with the sacral point, followed by energy balancing the spinal point with the occipital point. It is therefore a three-way energy balance. This is all done on the same side of the spine as the sacral tender point.

Treatment of Autonomic Nervous System Conditions

Firstly, you need to find a tender point within the sacral horizontal zone area as you did in the analysis. It is usually a good idea to mark this with a pen if you take your finger away. This is generally more difficult to do than on the superior crest. When a tender point has been found, keep the middle finger pad on it and take the other middle finger point to the parallel point on the occiput on the same vertical line– between the lower and upper nuchal lines. Give some massage to both points for a few seconds and then energy balance the two. Follow this by energy balancing the sacral point with a tender point that you will find on one of the two horizontal autonomic regions. The point should be located between the 'physical' region and the inner bladder line. This is followed by energy balancing the occipital point with this one. When the three points have been energy balanced, the cause of the spinal condition will have been addressed. The discomfort will not ease immediately, as it does with a physical condition, but will feel easier the next day.

Treatment of Emotional Conditions

Commence by finding a tender point on the lower aspect of the sacrum and energy balancing with the parallel point on the upper nuchal line of the occiput. The ongoing procedure is the same as for the previous two, with the exception that there is only one horizontal emotional region between T6 -T9 and the ouch point is to be found at this horizontal level between the inner and outer bladder lines. This may seem an innocuous procedure, but it is very powerful. Be ready with the tissues!

Other Aspects of Sacro-Occipital Reflextherapy – Self Treatment and Reflexology

Self-Treatment

The following may be performed by the patient to augment your treatment. I have personally performed this procedure every day for as many years as I can remember as I was born with a mid-thoracic scoliosis that has caused many other problems. I find that by doing this simple procedure each day for about five minutes it helps with discomfort and energy levels.

Technique

This may be performed in the seated position but ideally it should be done lying supine – so first thing in the morning or last thing at night in bed is ideal. Place the right hand under the sacrum and the left hand under the occiput. This becomes an acquired art as initially it can feel a little disconcerting because it is the dorsum of the lower hand in contact with the sacrum. Your focus is on the sacrum and occiput, so you should not be so concerned about the weight on the hands. Your intention should be to visualise movement of cerebro-spinal fluid or energy from one hand to the other. After about half a minute you should find that tension eases in the abdomen, followed by tension and discomfort easing in the spine. Five minutes duration is about the maximum time before the hands/arms tell you that they don't want to be in that position any longer. Correct breathing whilst performing this is essential, with hara breathing being the best. This is such a simple exercise, but it is well worth doing.

Reflexology

I appreciate that both types of Sacro-Occipital Therapy are best performed by bodyworkers such as physical therapists or osteopaths who are used to working directly on the spine. Therefore, for reflexologists, it is possible to perform it by using the reflected points and areas on the feet. Figure 9.10 shows how to use the new version, but it is possible to use it with the original version as well. The diagram shows the physical, autonomic and emotional points on the sacrum and occiput along with the sacral and occipital zones, the spinal vertical and horizontal zones. The zones and reflected points are drawn approximately as they will vary and, of course, the horizontal and vertical zones of the spine exist on both feet but only drawn on one.

Technique for Physical, Autonomic and Emotional Symptoms

Locate the physical, autonomic or emotional reflected points of the occiput and sacrum on either foot with the middle finger pads of each hand and energy balance the two. Although I have placed the reflected points on the medial aspect of the foot, the tender point may exist anywhere on the horizontal zone.

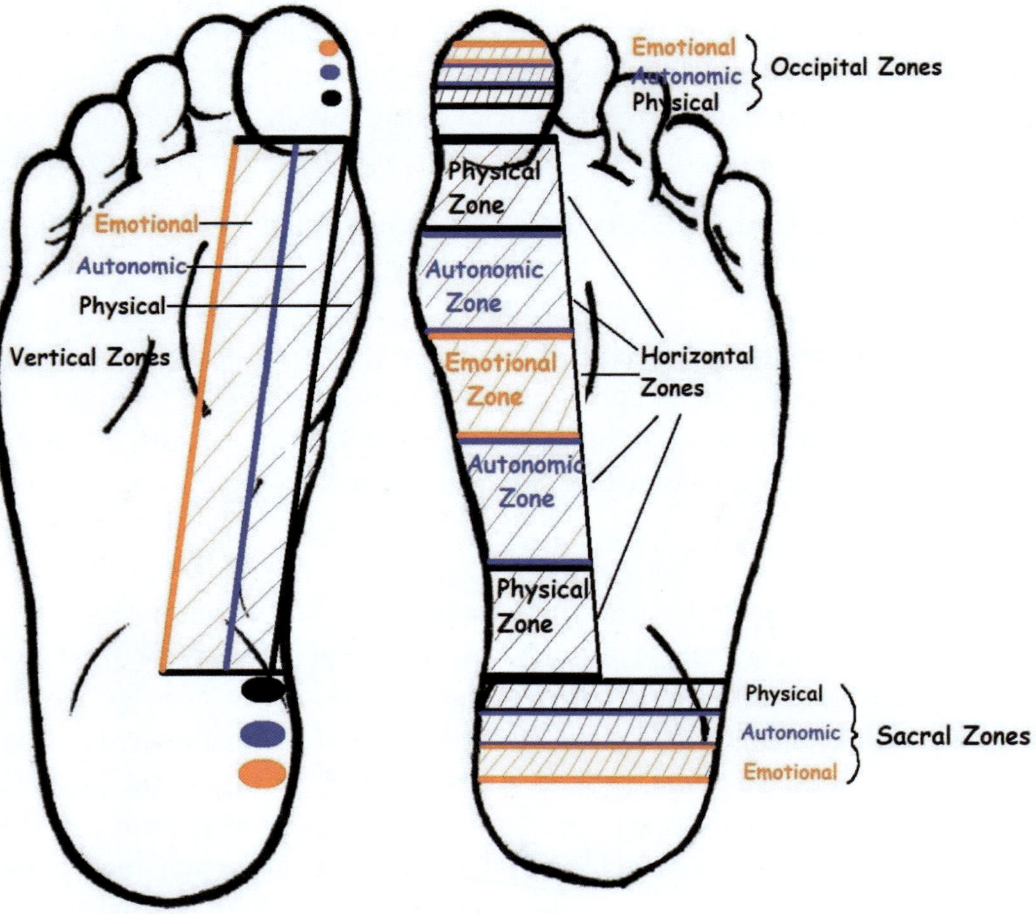

Figure 9.10 Reflexology with the New Version of SOT

Locate a tender point within the physical aspect of the sacral zone (not always on the medial line) and place the middle finger pad on its equivalent on the occiput (great toe). Energy balance these two, that shouldn't take too long. Keep the finger on the occipital point and place the other finger on a tender point within the associated horizontal zone – there is a choice of two for physical and autonomic and one for physical. Energy balance between this point and the occipital point and finally between the sacral point and horizontal zone point. Repeat the procedure with the autonomic and emotional zones. This represents a terrific treatment for relaxation and stress release as well as pain relief.

I hope you enjoyed reading these two books. If you have, please tell your friends! Please don't hesitate in sending me feedback via email and I am always willing to answer any queries you may have. Above all – ENJOY!

John Cross FCSP, Dr.Ac.
12 Upper Milovaig
Glendale
Isle of Skye
Highland
United Kingdom
IV55 8WY
Email - **jrcacupressure@hotmail.com** or **johnc1112@yahoo.co.uk**
Web site – www.johncrosspublications.com

References

Academy of Traditional Chinese Medicine. *An Outline of Chinese Acupuncture*. Beijing: Foreign Language Press, 1975

Brand, B. and Yancey P. *Fearfully and Wonderfully Made*. New York, USA: Zondervan Publishing, 1993

Cross, J.R. *Healing with the Chakra Energy System- Acupressure, Bodywork and Reflexology for Total Health*. Berkeley, California USA: North Atlantic Books, 2006

Cross, J.R. *Acupuncture and the Chakra Energy System – Treating the Cause of Disease*. Berkeley, California USA: North Atlantic Books, 2008

Cross, J.R. *The Concise Book of Acupoints*. Chichester UK: Lotus Publishing, 2010

Cross, J.R. *Reflected Energy Pathways – A Practical Workbook for Physical Therapists*. Chichester UK: Lotus Publishing, 2008

Gifford, Louis Ed. *Topical Issues in Pain 3 – Sympathetic Nervous System and Pain*. Physiotherapy Pain Association Bloomington, USA: Author House, 2013

Key, Sarah. *Sarah Key's Back Sufferers' Bible – You Can Treat Your Own Back*! London, UK: Random House, 2000

Lignon, Alain. *Schematisation Neuro-Vegetative En Osteopathie*. France: Editions de Verlaque, 2014 (In French)

Myers, T. *Anatomy Trains – Myofascial Meridians for Manual and Movement Therapists.* London and New York: Elsevier, 2014

Oliver, J and Middleditch, A. *Functional Anatomy of the Spine*. Oxford, UK: Butterworth-Heinemann, 1991

Sarno, J.E. *The Mind Body Prescription – Healing the Body, Healing the Pain*. New York, USA: Grand Central Lifestyle, 1998

Shapiro, D. *Your Body Speaks Your Mind – Understand How Your Thoughts and Emotions Affect Your Health*. London, UK. Piatkus, 1996

Stormer, C. *Language of the Feet – What Feet Can Tell You*. London, UK. Hodder and Stoughton, 1995

Williams, T. *Complete Chinese Medicine – A Comprehensive System for Health and Fitness*. Shaftesbury, Dorset UK. Element Books, 1996

I am indebted to the internet for several of the illustrations used in this book. With gratitude to Pinterest.

Printed in Great Britain
by Amazon

58483632R00073